The Faces of Depression in Literature

This book is part of the Peter Lang Humanities list.
Every volume is peer reviewed and meets the highest
quality standards for content and production.

PETER LANG
New York • Bern • Berlin
Brussels • Vienna • Oxford • Warsaw

The Faces of Depression in Literature

Edited by
Josefa Ros Velasco

PETER LANG
New York • Bern • Berlin
Brussels • Vienna • Oxford • Warsaw

Library of Congress Cataloging-in-Publication Data

Names: Ros Velasco, Josefa, editor, author.
Title: The faces of depression in literature/edited by Josefa Ros Velasco.
Description: New York: Peter Lang, 2020.
Includes bibliographical references and index.
Identifiers: LCCN 2019033841 | 978-1-4331-6597-9 (hardback: alk. paper)
ISBN 978-1-4331-6598-6 (ebook pdf)
ISBN 978-1-4331-6599-3 (epub) | ISBN 978-1-4331-6600-6 (mobi)
Subjects: LCSH: Depression, Mental, in literature. | Melancholy in literature. | Depression, Mental—History. | Depression, Mental—Religious aspects. | Depression, Mental—Social aspects. | Psychology and literature.
Classification: LCC PN56.D474 F33 | DDC 809/.9335274—dc2 3
LC record available at https://lccn.loc.gov/2019033841
DOI 10.3726/b15213

Bibliographic information published by **Die Deutsche Nationalbibliothek**.
Die Deutsche Nationalbibliothek lists this publication in the "Deutsche Nationalbibliografie"; detailed bibliographic data are available on the Internet at http://dnb.d-nb.de/.

The paper in this book meets the guidelines for permanence and durability of the Committee on Production Guidelines for Book Longevity of the Council of Library Resources.

29 Broadway, 18th floor, New York, NY 10006
www.peterlang.com

Printed in the United States of America

Table of Contents

List of Contributors

Josefa Ros Velasco (Harvard University, Cambridge)

Derek McAllister (Baylor University, Texas)

Nancy Ciccone (University of Colorado)

Miriam Muccione (University of Chicago)

Pawel Zagozdzon (Medical University of Gdansk, Poland)

Søren Harnow Klausen (University of Southern Denmark)

Shannon Hayes (Tennessee State University)

Gail Shanley Corso (Neumann University, Pennsylvania)

Nora Augustine (The University of North Carolina at Chapel Hill)

Hannah Ming Yit Ho (University of Brunei Darussalam)

Josie Billington (University of Liverpool)

Lucia Gagliese (York University, Ontario)

Angelika Potempa (The University of Texas Rio Grande Valley)

Ioana Unk (Independent Scholar, California)

Preface: From Boredom to Depression (From Philosophy to Psychology)

Josefa Ros Velasco
Harvard University, Cambridge

"You get depressed because you know that you're not what you should be."
Brian Hugh Warner (Marilyn Manson)

The Long Hard Road Out of Hell (1998)

I had never been interested in depression *academically* speaking, or so I thought. Depression was, for me, a state of anguished sadness—whose roots or reasons were sometimes explicable and sometimes *nonconceptualizable*[1]—generally experienced as a constant whisper and, from time to time, more intensely and painfully. I know it because I suffered from such a state throughout my entire life: a permanent restlessness. I am convinced that this was what prompted me to study philosophy at the age of 17 to better understand myself. I never considered the option of enrolling in psychology and much less in psychiatry or something like that. I did not appreciate any connection between that state and the mental health sciences, even though I had seen a therapist, on two or three occasions—when the intensity curve reached unbearable peaks—who gave me tablets for combating depression that, I have to say, made me feel much better—I do not remember the name of that drug, it sounded like … *I-don't-know*-nine. Philosophy did not help me at all. On the contrary, it increased my malaise to astronomical levels. When I hit rock bottom—I knew it because melancholy turned into paranoia and, in a short run, I developed an exaggerated arachnophobia—one of my last visits to a mental health professional—this time a psychiatrist—at the age of 22 concluded with the diagnosis of an Obsessive-Compulsive Disorder (OCD) with depressive symptoms. I went straight to the pharmacy—as I would have to do every month for the next few years and, as I later realized, for the rest of my life—to buy my *Aremis*;[2] this time I remember the name. Except when I had the brilliant idea, a couple of years ago, of stopping the treatment—coinciding with a professional promotion that took me to Harvard University, in Massachusetts, to work on my subject of research: boredom—I have not experienced such a time of collapse or crisis again. In those days, I had such a wrong time, and it took me so long to rediscover a zest for life after resuming my treatment—which, by the way, took more than a month to arrive in the United States—that I have never cast doubt again on the fact that my proneness to depression had *at least* something to do with the mental health sciences—or maybe I had become addicted to pills. However, at that moment, I did it, and I argued that the melancholy that had made Kierkegaard or Sartre so special had to be released. In an attempt to accept and self-affirm myself with my multiple defects, I was convinced that the state I called—and also other people called—*depressive* was part of me. I remember myself that summer deciding to open the Pandora's Box that my *Aremis* so carefully guarded. My doctoral work on boredom was the culprit.

My doctoral dissertation was devoted to deepening and relating the positions of the German philosopher Hans Blumenberg and Professor of Classical Studies Peter Toohey (University of Calgary, Alberta) on the adaptive function of boredom and its role in human evolution as a counterweight to current mental health professionals who claim the existence of a problem of *chronic boredom* fundamentally physiological. Then I came into contact for the first time with the question of depression from an objective point of view: researchers often linked boredom and depression as two mutually influencing states, often dependent on each other, as part of the same phenomenon that feeds back incessantly—a snake biting its own tail. My refusal to accept boredom as a state-related to mental health, even if we call it *chronic*, also led me to distrust what I believe that were other states or other personality traits assimilated: depression, anxiety, stress … It was my interest in boredom that made me come into contact, by chance, with the world of mental illness, with personality and behavior disorders, with the DSM and, of course, with the critics of the latter and its excesses. That is how I came to think, when I concluded my doctoral dissertation, that whatever was happening to me was outside of the sanitary domain and that everyone was wrong. That time, like many others, the wrong one, and who was exceeding the competences was me.

After recognizing my mistake and regaining the strength to continue working on my research on boredom—down-to-earth—I decided to adopt another approach to boredom: I began delving into the philosophical, theological, and literary narratives throughout the history of the West in which boredom had been understood as a phenomenon related to health to clarify the path by which it had come to become a matter of psychological and psychiatric interest in the 20th and 21st centuries. To that task, I dedicated my time in the Department of Romance Languages and Literatures at Harvard University. Moreover, once again, I came across the couple boredom-depression. However, this time, it was not just a promising partner for contemporary researchers but one of those lifelong marriages in which one of the spouses does not go anywhere without the other, and only death separates.

Boredom and depression went hand in hand from the texts of antiquity to those of the most immediate present. Suffice to mention the biographies of Gaius Marius and Pyrrhus of Epirus, in Plutarch's *De viris illustribus* (see optionally Toohey 1987, 1988, 2004—especially the first one, "Plutarch, Pyrrh. 13: ἄλυς ναυτιώδης"—and also Ros Velasco 2017, 2021). Notably, this union began becoming more evident from the late Middle Ages and early Renaissance, when *acedia* started to merge in melancholy (see, at the beginning, Ponticus, according to Hernán Vázquez 2015; Cassian, from the point of view of Peretó Rivas 2010, 2011, 2013 [in this last work we can see also the association of boredom and depression in Hugues of Miramar], 2014, 2017; Saint Thomas, as Echavarría stated in 2005 [see also, again, Peretó Rivas 2011, 2014]; or, more generally, Márquez 2001 and Piovano 2016, to name a few—by the way, many disagree with this thesis [see Aguirre Baztán 1994; Rovaletti and Pallares 2014; and especially Forthomme 2000, 2003, among many others]. With regard to its secularization into melancholy, see Bunge 1999; Bäumer and Carm 2011; Eisenberg 2013; the list of works is endless)[3] and later during Romanticism and the birth of Existentialism, with the *ennui* and the *mal de vivre* (see, to choose some cases among millions, the novels by Goethe, Flaubert, Dostoevsky or Tolstoy—these are my favorite examples). In this sense, the Greek terms aegritude (*θλίψη*, *aegritudo*) and black bile (*μέλαινα χολή*, *melaina chole*), the Latins *acedia* and *taedium vitae*, Renaissance *tristitia* and *melancholia*, the modern ones *spleen*, *nausée*, *noia*, *Weltschmerz* ... were all of them one and the same thing or did they refer to different phenomena?

Since the second phase of my postdoctoral time began, I realized that if I wanted to track the history of boredom as psychopathology through philosophical, theological, and literary sources, I would have to venture into the history of depression. Now I see that they are two inseparable tasks and, in the same way, two tough challenges. That is because boredom and depression are intertwined, mistaken one for the other, coated on the same and different clothes at the same time over the centuries. I figured I would find lots and lots of books and papers on the history of depression, and that was the case. However, most of them were part of a purely medical framework. What I did not find was any title to explore the presence of depression in its different variables through different narratives that go beyond mental health disciplines such as philosophy or literature, which are precisely the ones I work with. Apart from those authors who cover the topic of depression from the most orthodox mental health field, some others have devoted their efforts to analyze mental diseases in literature but go through depression superficially. Just a few focus on the antecedents of depression by taking into account literary, philosophical, and theological narratives (e.g. Clark Lawlor *From Melancholia to Prozac: A History of Depression*, 2012). To sum up, I realized that many titles, including both books and papers, were addressing the topic of depression nowadays. However, almost none of them were focused on such a multidisciplinary approach to depression. Then, I was clear that it was time to get in touch with those who were interested in this approach worldwide to get to know each other, share our concerns, and contribute something valuable to the scientific community.

This book project was conceived during the last summer (2018) as part of my own postdoctoral research abovementioned, at Harvard University, under the guidance of Prof. Dr. Mariano Siskind, through which I attempt now to analyze the antecedents of some contemporary mental disorders, such as boredom and depression, from the wide variety of narratives at our hands beyond medical treatises. As I have already introduced, I particularly focus on those literary, philosophical, and theological narratives of the past, in which such conditions were understood not as mental disorders themselves, in the contemporary sense, but as existential, and even moral conditions, to track the evolution of their understanding until the present time. When dealing with depression, I am always surprised by how famous this disorder is today and how little is known about its antecedents in human cultural manifestations over history.

We all know that the NIMH (National Institute of Mental Health) has meticulously defined depression as a common but serious mood disorder that causes severe symptoms (asthenia, anhedonia, abulia, among many others) that affect how people feel, think, and handle daily activities such as sleeping, eating, or working. The NIMH has also established the cause of depression is a combination of genetic, environmental, and psychological factors that affect approximately 216 million people (3% of the world's population), mostly ranged from 20 to 30 years old. Nowadays, depression is also known for its many synonyms: clinical depression, MDD (Major Depressive Disorder), unipolar depression, unipolar disorder, depressive episode, and recurrent depressive disorder, to name a few. However, do we agree concerning the historical antecedents of depression? Are we working hard enough to clarify them and to reach an agreement? Are we taking into account the multiple narratives through which depression has been described over history from a multidisciplinary approach?

The impulse of delving into those antecedents, and keeping on going with my own research, motivated me the most to be in touch with colleagues who were working on this topic and with whom I shared these concerns. After launching a call during the last summer, I received a response from about twenty people with whom I keep in touch—at least with most of them—until now. We then decided to contribute our works to a collective book to move forward the research on the antecedents of depression, which we considered we should clearly understand not only to improve diagnosis and treatments at present but also to know more about some other related phenomena such as boredom. Under the title *The Faces of Depression in Literature*, this collective book attempts to bring together specialists and scholars in the topic from a multidisciplinary approach to explore the narratives of depression over time and discuss about their approximations to current, clinical understanding of MDD, that is, their similarities and differences, taking into account the environmental and psychological factors on which such a mental disorder depends in each historical period. Our goal is to clarify the background of depression by paying attention to its representation through these narratives and revaluate them as means of acquiring knowledge in an interdisciplinary way. While psychology and psychiatry may have the correct terminology and definitions, these narratives have the unique power of exemplification and clarification. Ultimately, we attempt to facilitate the understanding of MDD, the task of diagnosing, and the application of therapies related to narrations of depression.

The Faces of Depression in Literature comes to rethink depression by collecting in one place the most innovative approaches to the many names and shapes of depression we can find in literary, theological, and philosophical texts over time. This is, to my very knowledge, the first time that a well-experienced, diverse, and multidisciplinary group of specialists focused on the study of the antecedents of depression gather to promote a cross-border dialogue in order to overcome the recognized limitations of the current understanding of this topic. We want to publish the book to which researchers and academics, from one end to the other, have to come to be updated and clarify their ideas concerning the antecedents of depression according to a wide variety of narratives. We want to give a voice to underestimated manifestations of depression we can find in literature, philosophy, theology, and even early medical works. In this sense, this book will take a fresh look at an old phenomenon by considering it from rather unusual angles, trying to widen our understanding of depression and related phenomena.

This book meets the interests of graduate students and researchers in humanities, including philosophers, historians, cultural theorists, literature and art experts and enthusiasts, and even artists and writers themselves and, even, specialists in mental health and cognitive psychology because the study of depression involves mental processes such as attention, memory, perception, creativity or language use, to name a few. Moreover, our approach is not exclusively directed towards a specialized audience but wants to also reach out to the non-specialists. Considering how many people, friends, families, and colleagues are impacted in one or another form by depression, our project meets a broader need, too: that of educating ourselves about how to live and cope with depression.

The following break-down of our efforts attests to the multi and interdisciplinary approaches to depression. Part one, entitled "Spirituality and Depression from the Middle Ages to Modernity," will consist of four chapters explaining how predecessors of depression and depression understood as we do today can be found in medieval, Renaissance, and modern narratives through different names such as *acedia*, *tristitia*, *melancholie*. The authors will discuss to what extent modern depression can be seen as the natural evolution of those *old* concepts grounded in the phenomenon of spirituality.

Chapter one, "*Acedia* and Its Relation to Depression," by philosophy Ph.D. candidate Derek McAllister (Baylor University, Texas), goes through the relationship between *acedia* and depression after claiming that the results of the recent work done in this regard are a mixed bag. In this first chapter in which he engages the recent scholarship comparing *acedia* with depression, McAllister endeavors to clarify the concept of *acedia* used by Medieval authors such as Evagrius, Cassian, Gregory, and Thomas Aquinas, to name a few, using literature from other disciplines, including specialists such as Wenzel, Bloomfield, Newhauser, and others. His key two theses are: first, the concept of *acedia* is not identical to the concept of depression. *Acedia* is not merely a primitive psychological predecessor to depression, but it marks off significantly different ways of being, not least because of one's spiritual relation to God. Second, however, it is still possible that an instance of *acedia* can coincide with an instance of depression, if one's condition, or state of affairs, is such that each term can be correctly and truthfully applied.

Dr. Nancy Ciccone (University of Colorado, Denver) is in charge of the second chapter of this volume, "Depression in Ricardian Dream Visions." The specialist in medieval literature showed that whereas Chaucer provides salient examples of depressive symptoms in Middle English dream visions, beginning with his narrator's inability to either eat or sleep, the anonymous *Pearl*-poet presents a father unable to recover from the death of his daughter. According to her approach, Chaucer's narrators find relief in reading, sleeping, dreaming, and presumably the activity of writing the dream narrative. Whether or not the *Pearl*'s narrator finds relief from his dream, however, is questionable, despite his ghost-daughter's Christian teachings. As Dr. Ciccone admits, some scholars accuse the narrator of *acedia*. However, her presentation argues that his *acedia* is a symptom, not a sin fostering his continued grief. To support this point, she focuses on the definitions and cures for depression recommended by Avicenna and embedded in images throughout the narrative in terms of flora, jewels, and exercise. These images suggest somatic healing available to the poem's audience, still reeling from their losses in the Black Death, on the one hand, and the political upheaval caused by the Richard II and the Lords Appellant, on the other hand. Whereas Christianity provides spiritual and intellectual comfort for late 14th-century England, the *Pearl* narrative reveals the gap between religious ideology and emotional recovery.

Chapter three, "Giambattista Vico and the Melancholy of History," by Ph.D. candidate at the Department of Romance Languages and Literatures in the University of Chicago, Miriam Muccione, is about the Neapolitan philosopher who said that all human civilizations develop through a cycle of birth, growth, maturity, and decadence, bracketed between two forms of barbarism; a *barbarism of the senses*, belonging to the infancy of human mind and societies, and a conclusive corruption of human rationality and civic cohesion, which Vico calls *barbarism of reflection* or *second barbarism*. By comparing Vico's main work, *The New Science*, with Vico's autobiographical account in his *Life of Giambattista Vico Written by Himself*, Muccione's chapter has the twofold purpose of examining Vico's barbarism of reflection both at the individual and collective level, and to attempt a reading of the role that such a malady of human reason may still have in a Vichian conception of social advancement, though a melancholic one. A reflection on the limits that Vico assigns to human rationality will be of current interest in the perspective of a critique of the material progress of humankind in present times.

Chapter four was contributed by the academic teacher at the Medical University of Gdansk, Poland (Department of Hygiene and Epidemiology), and psychiatrist Dr. Pawel Zagozdzon. "Depression in the Literature of the Health Reform and Mental Hygiene Movement: An Example of Ellen G. White Writings" recovers the health principles from the writings of the most translated female non-fiction author in the history of literature, Ellen G. White, which contributed to making the Seventh-day Adventists—one of the most extended living groups of people in the world. Zagozdzon's chapter explores how White used the concept of depression. Moreover, he analyzes how she understood the causes of a depressed mood and how to preserve one's mental health.

Part two, "Secularization of Depression in Modern and Contemporary Literature," will show the manifestations of modern and contemporary depression in five chapters that revolve around the 18th, 19th, and 20th centuries to the present narratives to analyze how depression was secularized from the spiritual framework. From philosophical to purely literary approaches, authors will deal with the concepts and issues surrounding depression in modern and post-modern approaches such as nihilism, identity, or feminism.

Søren Harnow Klausen, Professor of Philosophy at the University of Southern Denmark, proposes a chapter entitled "Nihilism, Depression, and Wholeheartedness. Metacognitive Strategies in 19th-Century Literature," in which he explains how in 19th-century literature and philosophy, depression-like states of mind were associated with nihilism, which was depicted more like a condition that befalls individuals than a deliberately adopted attitude. Professor Harnow Klausen looks at two insightful and literarily engaging treatments of depression and nihilism from the mid-19th century, one by Kierkegaard, the other by Tolstoy. In Kierkegaard's "Crop Rotation," the principal challenge to a meaningful life is diagnosed as boredom. It provides indirect evidence for the pathological condition of its pseudonymous author and the limitations of the otherwise ingenious techniques he devises for overcoming boredom (some of which resemble what is now referred to as metacognitive strategies). The author will further illustrate this view of depression with Tolstoy's description in *War and Peace* of the main character, Pierre Besuchov, as suffering from a lack of orientation and self-acceptance, which at times takes on pathological forms.

Chapter six, "Can Melancholy Be Heroic? Walter Benjamin and the Vicissitudes of Melancholy," by Assistant Professor of Philosophy, Dr. Shannon Hayes (Tennessee State University), establishes, despite the long-standing association of melancholy with creative, poetic activity, that melancholic depression remains chastized as an unpolitical mode of existence associated with stagnancy, paralysis, and a willful alienation. If one accepts Marx's claims that under capitalism, we are already dismembered and distanced in our strategic relations, then melancholy has a political aspect and can be understood as a mood. As Benjamin recognized, the fatigue and weariness of the melancholic body grant us an insight into the decay and fragmentation that characterizes social existence. For Hayes, melancholy does not produce one's alienation; it reveals it and exacerbates it in its unveiling. In her chapter, she explores the vicissitudes of melancholy in the poetic figures of Charles Baudelaire and Erich Kästner, the latter a poet of the Weimar Republic. Although both are melancholic and share an insight into the social, these figures differ in how they put their melancholic insights to work: according to Benjamin, Baudelaire enacts a heroic, emancipatory melancholy, while Kästner enacts a dangerous, nihilistic melancholy, coined by Benjamin as left-wing melancholia. It is precisely the difference between heroic and nihilistic melancholy that this chapter will illuminate.

Professor of English, Dr. Gail Shanley Corso (Neumann University, Pennsylvania), contributed chapter seven "Anhedonia, Dysthymia, and Tristasia: Depressed Characters in Alice McDermott's Novels" in which she delves particularly into Alice McDermott's contemporary fiction, whose characters exhibit a range of response to love and loss—sorrow, pretense and lies, delusions, loss of interest in pleasure, and even, attempts at suicide. She demonstrates that these characters often exhibit depression in many forms. While some might experience memory loss concerning trauma, others experience a heightened sense of specific incidents in their life.

Chapter eight "Broken Promise: Depression as Ex-Gifted Girl Identity in Elizabeth Wurtzel's *Prozac Nation*," by English and Comparative Literature Ph.D. candidate Nora Augustine (The University of North Carolina at Chapel Hill), addresses Elizabeth Wurtzel's bestselling 1994 memoir, *Prozac Nation: Young and Depressed in America*—a creative non-fiction account of the author's lifelong depression and eventual recovery with the aid of medication. Augustine reads Wurtzel's depressed persona through the lens of longstanding cultural discourses that link depression to thwarted childhood giftedness. In particular, *Prozac Nation* is seen to illustrate a range of so-called Gifted Girl dilemmas as described in feminist psychology research of the 1960s and 1970s. Exploring how Wurtzel's contexts (slightly) value her extraordinary achievements and yet harmfully contrast them with "normal" femininity, Augustine revisits the often-devalued *Prozac Nation* as a valuable case study in the troubled relationship between giftedness, depression, and gender in a post-feminist United States context.

Chapter nine, "Unclean Subject(s) of Depression within the Singaporean State," by Dr. Hannah Ming Yit Ho (University of Brunei Darussalam), closes this third part. Here, this expert in melancholy within contemporary fiction addresses Amanda Lee Koe's *Ministry of Moral Panic* by discussing the gendering of a diseased mind and body within Singaporean experiences of self-injury, suicide, sickness, and homosexual tendencies. Focusing on the *depressed subject*, she argues that the literary expressions of the unclean citizen-subject are wrought with (non-)dysphoria, which, in turn, reveals the intricate complexities of the depressive affective disorder to expose the individual's anxiety with the body politic and attendant distress with social stigmatization. Psychosomatic depression is thus explored and illuminated within intersecting cultural and political contexts. By interrogating the cultural burden, identity politics, and human fallibility associated with such an affliction, this chapter challenges gendered instances of distress that taint the wholesome image of the self, which is promoted within Singapore's national interests in the *clean city.*

Finally, part three, "Narrations and Metaphors on Depression from and for the Clinical Practice," will consist of four chapters in which authors will explain how narratives and metaphors themselves, contemporary or not, can help fight against depression and understand our symptoms of depression nowadays. In this case, the contributors will introduce innovative and well-known methodologies to fight against depression through literature from fiction and non-fiction writings, clinical experiences, and critical theory.

First of all, Prof. Josie Billington, from the University of Liverpool, opens the last section with chapter ten, "Inner Voices: Literary Realism and Psychoanalysis." In this contribution, Prof. Billington argues that the realist novel and psychoanalytic theory and practice might be regarded as analogous projects, connected mainly via the realist novel's virtuoso employment of free indirect mode, against those who claim the realist novel and the development of psychoanalysis are usually regarded as two historically distinct and consecutive responses to the loss of religious explanations for mental suffering, rather than intrinsically connected. Following this proposal, Prof. Billington states that as a means to capture and give back to the subject thoughts or emotions which the subject hardly dares or bears to own—especially what Wilfred Bion calls 0, the moment of reality, or the powerful no thing of experience and thought—FID probes the hidden and inner as psychoanalysis seeks to do, "piercing the obscurity of those minute processes which prepare human misery and joy, those invisible thoroughfares which are the first lurking-places of anguish or unhappy consciousness." (George Eliot) The explication of this prior connection is particularly pertinent at a time when literary reading (of fiction and novels in particular) is increasingly used as an adjunct or alternative to establish psychological therapies for mental health issues (see Billington 2016).

Chapter eleven "Rewriting Mecca: Teaching about Late-Life Depression Using John Metcalf's 'The Years in Exile'," by Clinical Health Psychologist and Associate Professor of Kinesiology and Health Science at York University, Toronto, Dr. Lucia Gagliese, reminds us that late-life depression is highly prevalent and is associated with physical, cognitive, and social dysfunction as well as increased mortality, including suicidality. She is worried that despite this, clinical understanding and treatment of late-life depression remains inadequate; many healthcare professionals are poorly trained in its recognition. In this chapter, the depiction of late-life depression in a Canadian short story,

"The Years in Exile" by John Metcalf, will be considered from psychological and gerontological perspectives. The protagonist of the story will be presented as a case study employing current and historical approaches to the assessment and diagnosis of depression, including DSM criteria. The risks and buffers of late-life depression, as depicted in the story, will be considered, with attention paid to gender, marital status, independent vs. dependent living, physical function, trauma, and social isolation. Concordances and discrepancies with cognitive-behavioral and lifespan-developmental theories of late-life depression and meaning-making through life review/reminiscence are considered too. Dr. Gagliese's chapter argues that analysis of short fiction through a health narrative lens may be an effective interdisciplinary educational strategy.

Chapter twelve, "This Aisle Has More Than Two Sides: Insights into Depression, Provided by Medical Doctors," by Angelika Potempa, Assistant Professor of Philosophy at The University of Texas Rio Grande Valley, is on whether and how the difficult topic of depression is talked about in the memoirs of medical doctors in the United States. As she affirms, depression enters the life of the medical professional not only in the pursuit of diagnosing, treating of and caring for patients but also in the form of their suffering and/or that of colleagues, friends, and family members. Of special interest for this chapter are the particular framework of background values and the understanding of medicine and illness that shines off in the professional healers' memoirs and that are tied to their characterizations of depression and the depressed. The times remembered reach mainly from the 1950s to the present. Her approach is interdisciplinary but grounded in philosophy, especially, epistemology and ethics.

Finally, from California, the independent scholar Ioana Unk wrote chapter thirteen, "Metaphors of Depression in American Short Fiction." As a member of the American Psychological Association, Unk aims to illustrate depression as a disintegration of the psychological mechanisms that hold the frail human life together and make it look meaningful, in the American short fiction of the recent years. She recognizes that psychologists and psychiatrists have a particular arsenal of tools (diagnostic manuals, depression scales, elaborate descriptions of symptoms) that help them define depression in its many forms. People suffering from depression, on the other hand, may experience this mood disorder differently, as a collapse of their hopes and illusions about life and its purpose. When this illusion is replaced by a brutal and constant awareness of the human limitations, and of the only sure thing about life, namely its ending, depression happens. She will go through the many metaphors of depression in the literature that can help us clarify the understanding of depression.

The Faces of Depression in Literature is not only a book consisting of isolated proposals on the relationship between literature, philosophy, theology, and depression. Contributors have read in-depth others' chapters to ensure the composition was coherent enough and that the progression presented represents a strong achievement in the understanding of depression through the introduced narratives. We all are engaged with this topic to the point that we wanted to meet each other to share our approaches face-to-face, so I organized a homonymous Seminar as part of the ACLA Annual Meeting in March 2019 (Washington D.C.) from which some of the final ideas for this book emerged. We also met each other again in May 2019, as part of the workshop *Depression as a Creative and Destructive Force in Contemporary Literature* I organized at Harvard University.

I would like to thanks the contributors to this volume—especially Dr. Potempa for her double-check of this preface—as well as Peter Lang and my first contact the editor Meagan Simpson—thank you always for your interest in this book, your trust, and patience. As editor of *The Faces of Depression in Literature*, I cannot but be grateful with the Department of Romance Languages and Literatures (RLL) at Harvard University and the Real Colegio Complutense (RCC) at Harvard for granting me with the postdoctoral fellowship that made possible for me to complete this work. Finally, my personal acknowledgments or dedications are for my favorite artist—whose words opened this introduction—the American singer, composer, actor, writer, painter, and director Brian Hugh Warner (Marilyn Manson): in your art I always found relief; when I listen to your songs, I know that I am what I should be.

Notes

1. This term was coined by the German philosopher Hans Blumenberg (1920–1996), to refer to those absolute realities or phenomena that cannot be described under rational premises. See his Theory of Nonconceptuality in "Ausblick auf eine Theorie der Unbegrifflichkeit." (1979 [1996])
2. *Aremis Sertraline* is an antidepressant in a group of drugs called selective serotonin reuptake inhibitors (SSRIs). Sertraline affects chemicals in the brain that may be unbalanced in people with depression, panic, anxiety, or obsessive-compulsive symptoms. Sertraline is used to treat depression, obsessive-compulsive disorder, anxiety disorders (including panic disorder and social anxiety disorder), post-traumatic stress disorder (PTSD), and premenstrual dysphoric disorder (PMDD) (Aremis Sertraline 100mg Tablets Patient Information Leaflet, 2019).

3. Apart from the above mentioned, some other titles I consider of enough importance in this regard are "Acedia: Its Evolution from Deadly Sin to Psychiatric Syndrome" (1965), by psychiatrist Mark Altschule; "Acedia: The Etiology of Work-Engendered Depression" (1990), by Steven Bartlett (Willamette University); *Mística y depresión: San Juan de la Cruz* (1997), by psychiatrist Francisco Javier Álvarez Rodríguez (CAULE); or "Before Depression: The Medieval Vice of Acedia" (2007), by Robert Daly (Medical Upstate University), among many, many others. I strongly recommend the reading of my forthcoming book *La enfermedad del aburrimiento*, to be published presumably along 2021, to delve into this topic.

References

Aguirre Baztán, Á. 1994. *Estudios de etnopsicología y etnopsiquiatría*. Barcelona: Marcombo.

Altschule, M. D. 1965. "Acedia: Its Evolution from Deadly Sin to Psychiatric Syndrome." *The British Journal of Psychiatry* 111 (475): 117–119. https://doi.org/10.1192/bjp.111.471.117.

Álvarez Rodríguez, F. J. 1997. *Mística y depresión: San Juan de la Cruz*. Madrid: Trotta.

Bartlett, S. J. 1990. "Acedia: The Etiology of Work-engendered Depression." *New Ideas in Psychology* 8 (3): 389–396. https://doi.org/10.1016/ 0732-118X(94)90026-4.

Bäumer, R., and M. Plattig Carm. 2011. *Noche oscura y depresión. Crisis espirituales y psicológicas: naturaleza y diferencias*. Bilbao: Desclée de Brouwer.

Billington, J. 2016. *Is Literature Healthy?* Oxford: Oxford University Press.

Blumenberg, H. 1996. *Shipwreck with Spectator*. Cambridge, MA: The MIT Press.

Bunge, G. 1999. *Akedia. Il male oscuro*. Magnano: Qiqajon.

Daly, R. 2007. "Before Depression: The Medieval Vice of Acedia." *Psychiatry* 70: 30–51.

Echavarría, M. 2005. *La praxis de la psicología y sus niveles epistemológicos según Santo Tomás de Aquino*. Girona: Documenta Universitaria.

Eisenberg, E. S. 2013. "El retorno de la acedia. Una variante de la depresión en la actualidad." *V Congreso Internacional de Investigación y Práctica Profesional en Psicología XX Jornadas de Investigación Noveno Encuentro de Investigadores en Psicología del MERCOSUR*. Buenos Aires: Universidad de Buenos Aires.

Forthomme, B. 2000. *De l'acédie monastique à l'anxio-dépression: Histoire philosophique de la transformation d'un vice en pathologie*. Paris: Institut d'édition Sanofi-Synthélabo.

Forthomme, B. 2003. *Phénoménologie des sentiments corporels*. Argenteuil: Le Cercle Herméneutique.

Hernán Vázquez, S. 2015. "Las implicancias psicopatológicas de la acedia en Evagrio Póntico." *Revista Latinoamericana de Psicopatología Fundamental* 18 (4): 679–703. http://dx.doi.org/10.1590/1415-4714.2015 v18n4p679.7.

Lawlor, C. 2012. *From Melancholia to Prozac: A History of Depression*. New York, NY: Oxford University Press.

Márquez, F. 2001. "Posibles estados depresivos en la vida monacal: una aproximación psicológica." *Revista de Psicopatología y Psicología Clínica* 6 (3): 213–216. https://doi.org/10.5944/rppc.vol.6.num.3.2001.

Peretó Rivas, R. 2010. "Acedia y depresión. Entre pecado capital y desorden psiquiátrico." *IV Jornadas Nacionales de Filosofía Medieval.* Buenos Aires: Universidad de Buenos Aires.

Peretó Rivas, R. 2011. "Acedia y depresión. Aportes para una reconstrucción histórica." *Eä Journal* 3 (1): 1–20.

Peretó Rivas, R. 2013. "'Moritur in solitudine': la acedia en la vida de Hugo de Miramar." *Stylos* 22: 174–186.

Peretó Rivas, R. 2014. "Acedia y depresión como cuidado por la sepultura en el mundo clásico y sus ecos contemporáneos." *Acta médico-histórica Adriática* 12 (2): 231–246.

Peretó Rivas, R. 2017. "Angustia y acedia como patología en el monacato medieval, manifestaciones y recursos curativos." *Anuario de Estudios Medievales* 47 (2): 769–794.

Piovano, A. 2016. *Acedia.* Bogota: San Pablo.

Ros Velasco, J. 2017. "El aburrimiento como presión selectiva en Hans Blumenberg." Ph.D. Diss., Complutense University of Madrid, Madrid.

Ros Velasco, J. forthcoming 2021. *La enfermedad del aburrimiento. El camino de la metáfora hacia la medicalización y sus alternativas.*

Rovaletti, M. L., and M. Pallares. 2014. "La acedia como forma de malestar en la sociedad actual." *Revista Latinoamericana de Psicopatología Fundamental* 17 (1): 51–68. http://dx.doi.org/10.1590/S1415-47142014000100005.

Toohey, P. 1987. "Plutarch, Pyrrh. 13: ἀλνς ναντιώδης." *Glotta* 64 (3/4): 199–202.

Toohey, P. 1988. "Some Ancient Notions of Boredom." *Illinois Classical Studies* 13 (1): 151–164.

Toohey, P. 2004. *Melancholy, Love, and Time: Boundaries of the Self in Ancient Literature.* Michigan, MI: University of Michigan Press.

Warner, B. H. (Marilyn Manson). 1998. *The Long Hard Road Out of Hell.* New York, NY: Regan Books/Harper Perennial.

Abbreviations

ACLA	American Comparative Literature Association
AFSP	American Foundation for Suicide Prevention
AIDS	Acquired Immunodeficiency Syndrome
AMA	American Medical Association
APA	American Psychiatric Association
AWARE	The Association of Women for Action and Research
CDC	Centers for Disease Control and Prevention
DSM	Diagnostic and Statistical Manual of Mental Disorders
ECT	Electroconvulsive or Electroshock Therapy
EGW	Ellen G. White Estate Writings Application
ER	Emergency Room
HEPC	Hepatitis C
ICD-10	International Classification of Diseases, Tenth Revision
IMH	Singapore's Institute of Mental Health
IQ	Intelligence Quotient
MCD	Ministry of Community Development
MDD	Major Depressive Disorder
NIMH	National Institute of Mental Health
OCD	Obsessive-Compulsive Disorder
PAPa	The People Action Party's leader PM (Prime Minister) Lee
PMDD	Premenstrual Dysphoric Disorder
PTSD	Post-Traumatic Stress Disorder
RCC	Real Colegio Complutense
RLL	Romance Languages and Literatures
SSRIs	Selective Serotonin Reuptake Inhibitors
TEAMS	Teaching Middle English Text Series

Part I Spirituality and Depression from the Middle Ages to Modernity

1 Acedia *and Its Relation to Depression*

Derek McAllister
Baylor University, Texas

Introduction

There are *prima facie* grounds for thinking *acedia* and depression are somehow related. *Acedia*, that old deadly sin of sloth, is marked characteristically by idleness, laziness, aversion to work, slackness, and even sorrow. Depression is marked characteristically by sadness, dullness, loss of pleasure, emptiness, and, sometimes, irritability—these are stereotypical characterizations, to be sure; nevertheless, it is instructive beginning with such familiar but crude generalizations, then proceed to analyze, clarify and correct them as needed. The *Diagnostic and Statistical Manual of Mental Disorders* (DSM-5) identifies at least one necessary condition for inclusion in the category of depressive disorders, i.e., a sad, empty, or irritable mood:

> The common feature of all [depressive] disorders is the presence of sad, empty, or irritable mood, accompanied by somatic and cognitive changes that significantly affect the individual's capacity to function. What differs among them are issues of duration, timing, or presumed etiology. (American Psychiatric Association 2013, 155)

The DSM has, since its third iteration (1980), overtly eschewed reference to etiology as a diagnostic criterion for depression in favor of identifying symptoms and behavior in descriptivist language as diagnostic criteria.[1] This intentional move leaves room for clinicians and practitioners to theorize, on a case-by-case basis, about the etiology of any particular person's depression,[2] rather than have the matter settled legislatively at the outset. In what follows, I shall be assuming this descriptivist understanding of depression.

As for the relation between *acedia* and depression, no one doubts that there is a clear similarity between them. The trouble develops when we attempt to specify the relation further: are *acedia* and depression identical? Is *acedia* a kind of depression? Is there any historical continuity between them?

I should say at this point: there is a crucial distinction to be made between (1) the concept of *acedia* and (2) an instance of *acedia*[3]—and likewise for depression. The trouble that arises from asking the above questions is often the product of our own conflating of this critical distinction. For when one asks, *Are they identical?*, it can only mean to ask whether an instance of *acedia* is numerically identical with an instance of depression—the two concepts themselves are so obviously qualitatively non-identical that that question is hardly worth asking; and numerical identity, if it is the sort of thing that requires extension, would not seem to be amiable to abstract objects like concepts or definitions.[4] Yet when one asks, *Is there any historical continuity between* acedia *and depression?*, she obviously means to inquire about the conceptual history of depression, and not whether one's particular occasion of depression has arisen out of an earlier episode of *acedia*—although, as we shall see, this is certainly a question worth asking. Keeping this distinction in mind will be important going forward, and I hope, where I did not state it, the reader will be keen to discern which sense I am indicating.

In recent discussions, there is no consensus regarding the relationship between *acedia* and depression. While most writers consider them not to be identical, many opt to interpret *acedia* using more up-to-date, contemporary psychiatric terms, thus essentially medicalizing an otherwise spiritual ailment (Altschule 1965; Jackson 1981; Jehl 2005; Azzone 2012). Others consider *acedia* to lie on a continuum with other maladies like *ennui* (Irvine 1999),[5] or *taedium vitae* (Jehl 2005).[6] Still, others dismiss tying depression too closely to *acedia*, given the differences they present either in agential freedom (Daly 2007) or in sinful culpability (Altschule 1965; Webb 2017). In my view, there is something right about the latter two of these suggestions. More precisely, I argue for the following two theses. First, the concept of *acedia* is not identical with the concept of depression; nor, for that matter, is *acedia* merely a primitive psychological conceptual predecessor to depression, but it marks off significantly different ways of being not least because of one's spiritual relation to God. As Lucrèce Luciani-Zidane (2009, 13) has said, "*acedia* is entangled in the heart (or life) of Christian dogma." My second thesis, however, is that an instance of *acedia* maybe sometimes coextensive with an instance of depression. That means a case of one might also be a case of the other. Alternatively, if they are not the same, we can understand why someone might mistakenly identify them, given that these two conditions are so similar in their symptomatology.

I have divided this chapter into three cohesive movements or parts. First, in order to establish a correct conceptual understanding of *acedia*, I cull the main features of *acedia* as understood from the early Christian capital vices tradition.[7] We shall see that, within this tradition itself, while there is some divergence in the ways *acedia* is understood, there is still enough cohesive unity to detect an unbreakable strain, a "continuous exfoliation" (Wenzel 1960b, 175), each strand "representing the true main line of the concept's development." (Wenzel 1960b, 179) Second, I critically examine some recent attempts to define the relationship between *acedia* and depression in the scholarship of psychiatry, philosophy, and theology. Third and finally, I turn to my main topic concerning the relation of *acedia* to depression.

What Is Acedia? *Its Main Features Culled from Principal Historical Texts and Thinkers*

To begin, we require a precise answer to the question *What is* acedia? Those who have some familiarity with the conceptual history of *acedia* will perhaps suggest there is a prior question: *Which* acedia *are we inquiring about?* Siegfried Wenzel, in his masterful opus *The Sin of Sloth*, explains that, "in looking over the whole medieval period," there are at least "three types of *acedia*: monastic, Scholastic, and popular, which can be localized with some accuracy in time and, even more so, in literary genres." (1960b, 179)[8] However, *pace* the well-placed concerns of those with prior familiarity, we should not mistake this divergence for there being fundamental disagreement about what *acedia* is. As Wenzel immediately clarifies: "But never did a later form completely replace an earlier one." (1960b, 179) In the later forms, for example, we can detect the still-present monastic elements that were once characteristic of the earlier forms. Moreover, as Wenzel maintains, despite their differences, the different types of *acedia* enjoy a cohesive unity centered on an "unbroken mainstream in its history," namely, the association of *acedia* with "idleness and negligence in spiritual deeds." (1960b, 179) *Acedia* gets different emphases, in different people's hands, with different audiences—something we can expect with the different times and places *acedia* appears in the medieval literature.[9]

From that cohesive unity, we can cull the following main features of *acedia*. First, *acedia* is irreducibly spiritual. Second, *acedia* has especially notable psychological manifestations. In what follows, I shall briefly explain what I mean by these features.

Acedia *Is Irreducibly Spiritual*

By claiming that *acedia* is irreducibly spiritual, I am not claiming that it is merely spiritual, nor that it is an entirely spiritual phenomenon. Instead, it has a spiritual component that is both essential to it and which is irreducible. It is essential in the sense that *acedia* cannot be understood apart from its spiritual import. Moreover, this spiritual *sine qua non* is irreducible in that any attempt to analytically reduce it in simpler terms (such as its affects, an individual's psychological states) will be hopelessly incomplete. Moreover, *acedia* also has a proximate spiritual etiology.

Acedia is a capital vice, one of the seven deadly sins. That does not mean *deadly* in the sense that it is the worst possible sin that one can commit, but in how it can surreptitiously take root and lead to further sins. Its origins are from among the 4th-century desert monastics as one of the *logismoi*, or evil thoughts, which tempts the monk away from prayer and devoted religious life. However, importantly, it can be resisted. For Evagrius, the demon of *ακηδία* was to be countered with fortitude and perseverance, and "after its struggle the soul is taken over by a peaceful condition and by unspeakable joy." (1990b, 12) Cassianic remedies for *acedia* divide into two: (1) keeping the cell via cultivating fortitude (1894b) and (2) manual work (1894a). This latter remedy, of course, accords well with how we understand sloth today. If the connection from spiritual to manual work is not clear, manual work here is included because it is the external work of the monk, which itself is tied deeply to his religious vocation.[10] Even the sweeping of floors can be a deeply religious activity.[11] As one author puts it:

> If we give credence to the monks, we are therefore dealing with more than bad moods, psychic fluctuations or moral defects. It is a question of the resolve that arises in the wake of a decisive choice for which the monk has risked his life and to which he must hold no matter what: to realize one's full potential in oneness with God. He has bet everything that he has and everything that he is on this. *Acedia* is therefore so dangerous for him since it causes him to throw away everything and thus to miss out on what matters most in the realization of his full potential, which is the primary purpose of the monastic life. (Bamberg 1991, 87, qtd. in Joest 2004, 144 n.100)

Acedia eventually makes its way out of the desert to the wider world, evidence that it is not merely a monk's vice.[12]

Pope Gregory the Great in the 6th century also characterizes sloth in spiritual terms. One antidote he recommends for *acedia* is a "longing after the Creator, which gives over the sloth of negligence [*cum torporem negligentiæ*],[13] and kindles the frost of former insensibility with the fire of holy love." (1844, I.4.23.42) Gregory implores us to turn our attention upon things—spiritual things—that dispel despair and invigorate hope. First, we are to look to the saints that we may "be refreshed with the examples of the righteous ... Let us see then how beautiful is the activity of those who pursue their course, and learn how disgraceful is the sloth of the sluggish [*hebetudo pigrorum*]." (1844, V.24.8.17) Second, we are to reflect upon the cross, our own salvation, and the glory to come. After beautifully narrating the whole story of redemption and salvation, that gospel foolishness "that so far from the guilt of [the penitent's] debt being binding on him, gifts are heaped upon him more abundantly even after his sin," Gregory immediately interjects, "Whose sloth [*torpor*] would not be startled at the elevation of so high a thought?" (1844, V.27.15.30) Thus, Gregory clearly has in mind the spiritual vice of *acedia*. When transmitted to English as early as the 10th century, Ælfric abbot of Eynsham cites Gregory as a main influence and uses the word *slæpð* (an early version of *sloth*), making no secret that the referent here is the vice of *acedia* (1966, XVI, XXI).[14]

Aquinas in the 13th century follows this tradition of *acedia* as a capital vice, adding that "*acedia*, as we understand it here, denotes sorrow for spiritual good [*acedia … nominat tristitiam spiritualis boni*]." (2010, II-II.35.1.*co*) Previously, Cassian had distinguished between *acedia* and *tristitia*, while Gregory had *acedia* subsumed under *tristitia*; here, Thomas considers *acedia* a species of *tristitia*.[15] *Acedia* becomes a mortal sin, and is most destructive, when it "reaches to the reason, which consents in the dislike, horror, and detestation of the Divine good [*quae consentit in fugam et horrorem et detestationem boni divini*], on account of the flesh utterly prevailing over the spirit." (2010, II-II.35.3.*co*) Here, just as in the desert, the problem is centrally a lack of love or disconcern for the things of God. From its sapling stage as a *logimos* to its fully grown stage as a mortal sin, *acedia* is an irreducibly spiritual phenomenon.

Acedia *Has Especially Notable Psychological Manifestations*

From Evagrius to Cassian, Gregory to Aquinas, *acedia* has maintained a characteristic twofold effect: listlessness and restlessness. On the one hand, *acedia* evokes certain affects and behavior like sorrow, torpor, laziness (idleness), languor, lethargy, tepidity, and inertia. On the other hand, *acedia* evokes a certain restlessness: diversions (idleness), unwillingness to work, roaming of the mind on vain or trivial things, procrastination, and boredom.[16]

This latter effect of restlessness, or busyness, should not be mistaken for productive busyness.[17] It is characterized by a deep, inarticulable aversion to the meaningful, spiritually-imbued work of the cloister, in favor of other tasks that either are not as urgent, are not as important, or are simply not the task given to this individual monk. Whereas the first effect produces sorrow, this latter effect of restlessness may result in activities that are *entertaining*, or, as we would say in English, *diversions*.[18] This entertainment, however, is not lasting. Instead of gaining consolation by visiting the brethren, as Evagrius (1990b, 12) writes, the monk is weakened all the more by this very supposed remedy.

No amount of rest or frivolity will ever deeply satisfy the person plagued by *acedia*, since, as we saw, *acedia* is irreducibly spiritual and its roots lie much deeper than where temporary distractions can penetrate. This must be kept in mind even as we acknowledge that *acedia* characteristically manifests psychologically as either listlessness or restlessness.

Sloth's Lost Familiarity in Recent Times, which Coincides Historically with the Advancement of Psychiatry

After the Scholastic period, i.e. from the 13th century onward, the vice of *acedia* would reemerge periodically as an object of practical devotional interest, or as an item of theological study within the larger framework of virtues and vices, and emphasis was—though not always—typically placed on *acedia*'s external effect of laziness and slothfulness (to the neglect of its other effect, restlessness). Wenzel explains,

> The shift from a state of mind [*taedium*] to external behavior [*ydelnesse in servitio Dei*] pervades and informs the entire popular image of *acedia*, which emphasizes, not the emotional disorientation of disgust for the divine good, but rather the numerous observable faults which derive from such a state. (1960b, 88)

So even at this early point in history, we start to see a diluting of the old capital Sin—from its twofold effect to a single effect, laziness, from a focus on internal character and emotional disposition to external acts.

Over time, the capital vice of *acedia*, *de dicto*, would be more or less forgotten. When sighted, *de re*, one might recognize what the thing is, yet we would have no name for it. It is perhaps easy to understand why, since *acedia* is, after all, very difficult to identify in a person. As a nameless vice, it creeps in slowly and unseen. Boudon (1683, 337–338) does not use the term *acedia*, but his description is vividly similar:

> The venom of this vice consists of numbness, which sinks into the senses, by which the soul is made to slumber and remain in an idle state … It is recognized quite late …[and] almost no one knows it, because it does not lead directly to evil. (see also Surin 1829, 102–103)

All the while, it seems a good number of us can recall having "had something of this vice, as all men have it, being a strong general malady." (Surin 1829, 103)

In the 19th century, Søren Kierkegaard's character Judge Wilhelm in *Either/Or* (1987, II, 185) was familiar with the old deadly Sin, as such, mentioning it in his diagnosis of *A* the aesthete:

> Nero's nature was depression [*Tungsind*]. In our day, it has become somewhat prestigious to be depressed [*tungsindig*]; as far as that goes, I can well understand that you find this word too lenient; I hold to an ancient doctrine of the Church that classifies depression [*Tungsind*] among the cardinal sins.[19]

Unfortunately, the Hongs' translation, though it is the standard translation today, renders the Danish *Tungsind* (literally, *heavy-mindedness*) as the more loaded and presuming term *depression*. Kierkegaard, of course, did not use the term *depression*, which would not have been in common usage at that time, but neither did he elect for the contemporary Danish word *Melancholi*,[20] opting instead to give a descriptive and general label of *heavy-mindedness*. So it is a mistake to identify Kierkegaard's usage of *Tungsind* with our notion of *depression*. This concern aside, it is clear that Kierkegaard has in mind—by having some obscure, inarticulable notion in the mouth of Judge Wilhelm—both the vice of *acedia* and Romanticism's melancholy, the latter of which is seen as "somewhat prestigious" to have, and the former of which is clearly undesirable. By the end of the 19th century, from a psychiatric perspective, *melancholy* had become virtually synonymous with *depression*.[21] While the complicated relation of likeness between *acedia* and a melancholic disposition was indeed not lost on the melancholy Dane, *acedia* has come to be misunderstood by more recent authors.

Attempts to Delineate the Relationship between Acedia *and Depression in Recent Scholarship: Psychiatry, Philosophy, Theology*

We turn now to some recent attempts to specify the relationship between *acedia* and depression; the results are, as one might expect, a mixed bag. I shall take these in order roughly from the most grievously mistaken to those that are more delicately honest. It will turn out that any honest, rigorous account of *acedia*, let alone any comparison of depression to *acedia*, must be undertaken with careful nuance and distinctions which preserve the integrity of *acedia*'s spiritual reality while respecting its psychosomatic reality.

In a short article Mark D. Altschule[22] (1965) traces what he considers the visible, linear development of *acedia* from a deadly sin to a psychiatric disorder, but in doing so, he seems to neglect the importance of *acedia* entirely as a sin. Altschule rejects the notion that *acedia* is a sin at all, stating laconically, without any sense that what he is saying is controversial, that "according to Cassian, feelings of anger, *acedia*, and depression were deadly sins; however, today they are regarded as psychiatric symptoms." (1965, 117) This "we now know" posture[23] in the spirit of Enlightenment progress, as old theories come to be replaced, and we come to know better is oftentimes proven right. However, sometimes the attitude is a subtle mask for the "uncritical acceptance of the intellectual climate common to our own age." (Lewis 1955, 207)[24] To be fair to Altschule, we shall look at the support he offers to determine whether this posturing is warranted.

As support, Altschule points to two other instances in which he claims that psychiatric understanding gradually replaced a sin paradigm for explaining human action:[25] witchcraft in the 16th century and insanity in the 19th century.[26] However, these are both highly dubious cases of theory replacement. First, Altschule points to "a few sixteenth-century writers" who recognized that "witchcraft was a manifestation not of sin but of mental illness." (1965, 117n) He does not mention these writers by name, but he gestures in a note towards Richard Hunter and Ida MacAlpine's *Three Hundred Years of Psychiatry* (1963). Of course, witchcraft hysteria and overreaction is well-known. What Altschule misjudges is what difference this makes to a sin paradigm for explaining human action. It is not a mark against a sin paradigm *in toto* to say that level-headed contemporaries were offering better alternative explanations for alleged witchcraft behavior. Take, for example, Reginald Scot's "Not Witchcraft But Melancholie" (1584),[27] in which Scot offers melancholic behavior—understood broadly—as a reasonable explanation for producing some of the behavior associated with accused witches.[28] Even while offering this alternative explanation—and others, such as "coosinage,[29] dotage,[30] and poisoning" (1584, 11)—Scot nevertheless maintains the reality of sin and the supernatural.[31] If one looks closer, one can see that Scot's work is not so much a denial of the reality of witches or witchcraft; it is a reasoned censure upon (1) the guessing "proofs" and presumptions (2) by disreputable folk (3) on bad evidentiary grounds.[32]

More importantly, it is clear that Scot also still assumes, on the whole, a sin paradigm for explaining human action. Those who visited witches to seek counsel were guilty of idolatry,[33] because it was a sure sign that such individuals believed witches to possess certain supernatural powers[34] reserved only for God.[35] Therefore, in fact, Altschule is wrong if he is intimating that Reginald Scot thought that "witchcraft was a manifestation not of sin but of mental illness." (1965, 117n) Scot thought we could explain witchcraft behavior by intentional and malicious cozenage, or deception, just as much as by the melancholic or strange behavior of "poore ... old women, which are themselves deceived." (1963, 33) Furthermore, Scot rightly thought this melancholic possibility was consistent with and did not undermine a sin paradigm for explaining human action.

As for his second point, Altschule (1965, 118n) points to yet another truly bad example of, allegedly, psychiatric understanding replacing a sin paradigm: 19th century psychiatrists who gradually began to realize that it was "mental disease [that] caused what at that time was often called sinful behavior (For example, Feuchtersleben, in his *Principles of Medical Psychology* (1847), stated that in insanity as in sleep '"the old Adam" appears')." However, Feuchtersleben is in no way suggesting that mental disease is the superior explanation for what was once thought a sinful behavior. Feuchtersleben's quote appears in the context of a broader discussion concerning the nature of dreams, not insanity, as Altschule claims. Moreover, *pace* Altschule, Feuchtersleben's concern is well-placed. Feuchtersleben first acknowledges that very often dreams are not reliable: "It is evident that the understanding, fettered in dreams, can give no instruction to the understanding when unfettered." (1847, 166) For example, it is foolish for a military "general to abandon a good position because he has had an ill-omened dream." (1847, 166) On the other hand, he continues, sometimes a man's dreams can supply him with information about himself.

> But that dreams may, nevertheless, become psychologically and even ethically of deep importance as respects an individual, follows from the above-mentioned power of obscured ideas. Through this power, dreams may give a man historical information respecting himself, and hence, according to a favorite expression, "he may divine like a prophet looking backwards." As when the sun has gone down, the countless stars, not visible in the daytime, appear on the dark ground of the firmament, so, at the call of fancy, the forgotten images of bygone days rise up and show the mind its former shape. This observation likewise points to the delicate affinity of dreams with pathological states of mind, where, too, as it were, 'the old Adam' appears, and is in every sense interesting to the psychological physician. (1847, 166)

Some of this self-insight is of immense psychological and ethical importance; Feuchtersleben uses 'the old Adam' to refer to original sin, or a human's (Postlapsarian) natural propensity to be seduced away from the good. Nowhere does Feuchtersleben suggest a biocentric model or disease paradigm should replace this former way of thinking. If anything, his response here indicates that he considers medical science to be consistent with a sin paradigm—or, at the very least, consistent with the denial of materialism, as he explicitly states earlier.[36]

Not only are Altschule's supporting examples of purported theory replacement bereft of any real substance, but Altschule, in the remainder of his paper, also gives us no other reason to think that *acedia*, once a deadly sin, is now merely a psychiatric symptom. He claims that "the condition [*acedia*] came to be considered merely a subdivision or a variety of depression," saying further that "Depression was, of course, another of the deadly sins" (1965, 118), but this is untrue. To conclude something this extraordinary, Altschule would either have to have committed eisegesis or to have read a bad translation. More specifically, he claims, "the writings of … Aquinas included this definition of *acedia*." (1965, 118) In fact, Thomas never uses any variant of the word *depression* to define *acedia*. He uses "*aggravatio animi*" (2010, I-II.37.2), the weighing down of the soul, and "*tristitia aggravans*" (2010, I-II.35.8.*arg*3), a sadness which weighs down. But Thomas himself says that he is using this kind of *depression* only metaphorically, as when he compares love to heat, or pleasure to being widened.[37] In any case, Thomas certainly could not have had the psychiatric concept of depression that Altschule had. While we can admire Altschule's pioneering spirit on this topic, we cannot ignore that much of his commentary on *acedia* is simply misguided. Ironically, what he (rightly) accuses Petrarch of, Altschule falls victim to himself: "solipsistic misinterpretation of the meaning of *acedia*." (1965, 119)

Marcia Webb[38] (2017) also recognizes some similarities between early conceptions of *acedia*, which associate the sin closely with *tristitia* [sorrow], and the contemporary psychological disorder of depression. However, Webb rejects those associations of *acedia* with sorrow, let alone any association of *acedia* with depression, because, she reasons, it causes harm and perpetuates the stigma associated with mood disorders. Webb is willing to grant that *acedia*'s other features—restlessness, spiritual apathy, boredom, sluggishness—may have legitimate application in contemporary culture, but she explicitly rejects *acedia*'s connection to sadness.

Webb offers at least two reasons for this rejection. First, she thinks that there is so much conceptual confusion about the nature of *acedia* that this makes its purported connection to sorrow tenuous; if it is tenuous and if we have countervailing reasons to reject it (e.g. its harmfulness), then, *ceteris paribus*, we should reject this connection. Second, Webb thinks there is little theological or biblical grounds for considering sorrow to be sinful. In response to the first concern, I must point out that, while there is variation in the way authors through the centuries have conceptualized *acedia*, this does not imply any great disunity or confusion about what *acedia* is. Moreover, to support this charge of conceptual confusion, Webb offers shoddy evidence, quoting at length a 14th-century confessional prayer of *acedia*, then remarking that it is a "haphazard" collection of minor offenses: neglect in prayer, failure to rebuke one's wife, and indulgence in checkers, among other things (2017, 76–77). She concludes that this is evidence for *acedia*'s "confused and convoluted history." (2017, 79) However, Webb fails to note that this genre of literature—penitential and confessional formulas (see Wenzel 1960b, 83–84)—rather than being a conceptual account of *acedia*, is intended to function as an inventory of specific acts of sin under kinds of sin. These petty offenses, trivial as they seem, do nothing to confuse the concept of *acedia*; instead, they are given as practical examples of *acedia*'s application. Furthermore, the excerpt she quotes unsurprisingly includes other attributes of *acedia*,[39] but she does not take issue with these or propose that we reject these as veritable attributes of *acedia*. By parity of reasoning, if we reject the one attribute, sorrow, we should reject the other attributes, such as slothfulness and restlessness, for the same reason. Alternatively, we should reject neither, which is the better option, given what we have said about the genre of confessional formulas.

For Webb's second concern, she notes that not only does Christian Scripture contain precepts to love and comfort those who mourn, who are weary, and so on; but also the term ἀκηδία is found nowhere in the Greek New Testament (2017, 76). Webb either does not notice or coyly withholds the fact that Wenzel (1960b, 6–7), whom she cites for this fact, also tells us, in the very preceding paragraph, that the term occurs nine times in the Septuagint, a standard Greek translation of the Old Testament. In any case, it seems that much of what is driving Webb's aversion to associate sorrow with *acedia* is a misunderstanding of what these authors mean by *sorrow*. Taking Aquinas, for example, he defines *tristitia* as a species of *dolor* (pain). *Dolor* manifests when two conditions meet: (1) the conjoining of something bad [to oneself] and (2) the perception of this conjoining (2010, I-II.35.1.*co*). *Tristitia* is a specific kind of *dolor* that is caused by an interior apprehension on the part of the intellect or the imagination (rather than by exterior sensory perception) (2010, I-II.35.2.*co*). So *tristitia* is, very generally, just the essential cognitive awareness that something bad has met with me. As for *acedia* (*qua* passion), it is a specific kind of *tristitia* where "the mind is weighed down so much, that even the limbs become motionless." (2010, I-II.35.8.*co*) This would indeed appear to describe a weariness or sluggishness of a kind, such as when, for instead, I become aware of all the great burden of work I have to do. This slothfulness does not seem like sorrow, but in Thomas's technical sense of *tristitia*, it is.

There are yet other authors who have handled the relation more delicately, although space prohibits discussing each one in much detail. Robert

Daly's[40] (2007) concern with the recent discussion on agential freedom in depression leads him to argue that *acedia* is not identical to depression. What Daly gets right is that, yes, *acedia* is a condition for which one is (usually) culpable, whereas depression, commonly understood, is not. While this is enough to say they are conceptually non-identical, we might question the received wisdom of depression's non-culpability. By this, folks usually have in mind *direct* culpability, and in this they are right, but it does seem plausible that one could, in some cases, be *indirectly* or partially responsible for his depressed condition.[41] Another author, Jennifer Radden[42] (2002), acknowledges that *acedia* is a "disorder not of the body but of the soul" (2002, 70), thus giving due import to its status as a spiritual affliction, yet she strangely situates "Cassian's discussion of melancholy" (2002, 69)—not *acedia*—alongside other historical authors in her history of melancholy.

Perhaps most accurate is Stanley Jackson[43] (1981), who recognizes the real complexity of *acedia* and the subtlety of its conceptual evolution from the monastics to the present day. Nevertheless, Jackson overlooks or omits some essential features of *acedia*. He seems to conflate Aquinas's important distinction of *acedia* as a passion and species of *tristitia*, on the one hand, with *acedia* as a cardinal Sin, on the other hand (1981, 178). Also, while Jackson notes *acedia*'s obvious connection to idleness in work (1981, 174), he does not explain *why* this is important, and this is a critical omission. No mere historical accidental association, at *acedia*'s center, is an aversion to vocation (calling, *vocatio*), whether this is the spiritually imbued, meaningful work of the anchorite's cell or it is the rightly relating to and being drawn to union with God as we see in Thomas's writings.

What Is the Relation of Acedia *to Depression?*

As I have noted from the outset, a satisfying answer to this question requires distinguishing between (1) the concept of *acedia* and (2) an instance of *acedia*—and likewise for depression. Recall my two theses, first, the concept of *acedia* is not identical with the concept of depression; and that, second, it is possible that an instance of *acedia* could be coextensive with an instance of depression, in whole or in part, such that one could easily be mistaken for the other. And recall, importantly, that I am assuming here a descriptivist understanding of depression as represented in the DSM.[44]

The first thesis is easy enough to see. The concept of *acedia* is not identical with the concept of depression since they do not contain the same descriptive information.[45] It is likely why most writers have not taken a strong position of strict identity on the matter. Indeed, Daly (2007, 45) writes, "Any thesis that simply identifies *acedia* with melancholia or depression is not credible." A hundred years prior, in 1908, the Rev. Charles Taylor writes, "To replace the complex acedy by sadness or sloth is to evade a difficulty." (I, 66) If we assume the APA's DSM descriptivist account of depression, which is largely silent on the matter of etiology, we end up with distinct (i.e., non-identical) concepts: because, after all, the Desert Fathers, Scholastics, and spiritual writers were far from silent about the etiology of *acedia*. Plus, however one comes to acquire or be in a state of *acedia*, it was never regarded as merely a set of psychological and somatic symptoms, as a descriptivist would write it up. No, an instance of someone afflicted by *acedia* was viewed through the theological lens of (monastic) Christianity. So the two concepts are not the same, and thus what they describe may be entirely different goings-on.

This, of course, does not rule out the possibility that the two concepts might operate as different terms that, at times, pick out the same token instance. That leads to my second thesis: that an instance of *acedia* can be, sometimes, coextensive with an instance of depression, where an instance of one might be an instance of the other. That is, despite using different descriptive information (i.e., diagnostic symptoms), each term may refer (roughly, i.e., in whole or part) to the same object. That is more or less the way synonyms work (*frightened*, *afraid*), how translations work (*water*, *l'eau*), and how the genus-species relation works (*colored*, *red*).

Since, however, the terms *depression* and *acedia* function more like definite descriptions than rigid designators,[46] the problem is a little more complicated. While a rigid designator will invariably refer to the same object, and while an object can have multiple names rigidly designating it (e.g. Hesperus and Phosphorus), definite descriptions may or may not always pick out the same object. Take, for example, these two definite descriptions: *the United States president* and *the leader of the free world*. While they may at times designate the same individual, it is certainly not necessary that they always do so, as the latter, while it has sometimes designated the former, it may also genuinely designate—at various times, past, present, or future—some other head of state (though presumably not two individuals at once). Moreover, these designations are not arbitrary, since both descriptions have determinate content that either applies to an object or does not. My contention is that sometimes both descriptions apply to the same object.

The matter is further complicated by the fact that we are dealing not with an object like a human person, which we can easily see and identify, but with an object that is a state of affairs, diachronically continuous yet seemingly ephemeral when it comes to identifying and naming. Let us call this state of affairs one's *condition*. I do not mean the having of a specific condition or other, as when one has bronchitis, for instance; I mean, rather, the condition of, or current state of, one's mental states, affects, neurochemistry, dispositions to interact with the world, and so on. Besides, the *having* of a *condition* of the former sort is inexact, although a common way of speaking about depression, since depression is not like a bacterium, virus, or infection. Of these we might say (only when using shorthand) that an individual has *E. coli*,[47] for instance; but if we wished to be more precise, we would say that he *has* in his possession or his body a *specific strain or instance* of E. coli, for example: an instance (e.g. ~50 CFU, or *colony forming units*) of *E. coli* O157:H7 (Lim et al. 2010, 3). That is because the former is a kind and the latter is an instance of that kind. We can usually get away with such verbal shorthand, but sometimes it goes awry.

This is all the more apparent when we are discussing mood disorders. When I say a person *has* depression, there remains a looming ambiguity. For this could mean that a person *possesses* either (1) the kind itself of depression, or (2) an instance of that kind,[48] or (3) a particular state of affairs such that it can genuinely be called or labeled (an instance of) depression. It is no small matter since each claim says something different about what the individual *possesses*. The first option is nonsensical since it suggests that a person uniquely possesses the entire kind to himself,[49] while the second, as I said above, is a common yet inexact way of speaking about depression; the third is ideal since it is a more exact way of speaking. Note that I do not get this third option with communicable diseases, bacteria, viruses, because in those cases, an individual actually does *possess* an instance of the kind in the form of a particular strain of the foreign substance that, once external to the body, has entered the body. This is not the case with depression. Therefore, when I say a person *has* depression, what he possesses is a certain state of affairs (i.e., the current state of his mental states, affects, neurochemistry, dispositions to interact with the world, and so on). Using shorthand, we can call this state of affairs his *condition* (used in the spirit of option three, rather than option two). Thus, one's condition, used in this sense, need not be pathological. One's condition might be such that we may call it normal sadness, or it might be such that we ought to call it depression. Another upshot of using this third option is that if theoretical concepts come to change, one's condition will not.[50]

This groundwork prepares the way for us to see how an instance of depression can also be an instance of *acedia*. We begin with the condition a person is in, the current state of his mental states, affects, neurochemistry, dispositions to interact with the world. Suppose that these are such that we can correctly call his condition (an instance of) depression. If the person has come to be in his state via some spiritual etiology, and some of his symptoms are the same as those of *acedia* as chronicled by the spiritual writers, then we can correctly call his condition (an instance of) *acedia*. Thus, our person has both an instance of depression and an instance of *acedia*[51] (or, we might say—though we would be going off-script from the DSM's descriptivism—that our person has a *religious kind, or form, of depression*, assuming by this that we incorporate into that term a robust understanding of *acedia*). Of course, I point here only to the cases in which they overlap. There are presumably several cases where they do not, where there is an instance of only one and not the other. We would need empirical data to determine the frequency of occurrences of each.[52]

Finally, recall Webb's concern with the dangers of associating sorrow with sin. This had led her to deny that sin causes psychological disorders categorically. This concern resonates with me, and I can see the harm it can cause. While well-intentioned, however, this categorical exclusion is much too hasty, for it may not be true. Webb is correct, citing Daly, that we cannot "simply identify" (2017, 77) *acedia* with depression (by this, I assume she means we cannot identify the concepts). But there are many relations beyond strict identity that Webb fails to consider. For example, we may have both an instance of depression and an instance of *acedia*, a possibility which I have described above. Or, at the very least, we may have an epistemically underdetermined situation. Even if sin does not cause psychological disorder properly, we can certainly admit that it can cause symptoms that mirror psychological disorder. Then, given that psychological disorders are notoriously difficult to conclusively diagnose, along with the difficulty inherent in discerning the etiology of a given set of symptoms, we cannot categorically rule out the possibility that a person's condition is an instance of *acedia*.

Conclusion

I have argued that while the concept of *acedia* is not identical to the concept of depression, the two may nevertheless overlap in their instances. Many concerns remain in light of what I have argued, most glaringly those involving *how* to diagnose *acedia*, how to address and treat cases in which both are present, and what potential harms this view may evoke. With space prohibiting a full discussion, here we may briefly catalogue some practical implications this has for clinicians who diagnose depression (and spiritual leaders who counsel on *acedia*), and for a proper theology of psychological disorder among laypersons in the church. (1) It brings into relief potential (indirect) agential culpability for one's depressive-like symptoms (assuming that that person's real diagnosis is instead *acedia*, or more appropriately speaking *acedia*, or an instance of both). You may be wondering—rightly—how we are to know when and how often this parenthetical clause gets triggered. The truth is, more often than not, we do not know. Since it is so difficult in practice to discern, this (2) epistemic opacity forces us to be cautious and kind in going about making both lay-judgments and any formal judgment (e.g. diagnosis). This, I anticipate, should steer off many potential harms or abuses we fear, if we maintain a serious epistemic humility about whether a particular person has depression or *acedia* or both. This goes not only for those in lay contexts, but also for religious workers and mental health workers, who would benefit significantly from increased communication and translation between their disciplines. Further, depending on what one's condition truly is, we may be invited to (3) recast how we interpret our suffering in light of our condition or symptoms. Depending on what one's condition truly is, there may be no difference in phenomenological experience or the actual badness of the suffering, but there will no doubt be a difference in how one conceptualizes the suffering, and perhaps also in how one comprehends, accepts, and resolves to move forward in the suffering. Finally, (4) it prompts us to reexamine the lingering issues of pathologization and the pharmaceuticalization of depressive-like symptoms. On a more practical level, for instance, we need to wrestle with questions like whether someone who is ostensibly experiencing *acedia* should be treated with antidepressant medication. These and many other nearby issues must be the subject of further rigorous and charitable thinking.[53]

Notes

1. Robert L. Spitzer says as much from his time as chair of the Task Force on Nomenclature and Statistics (later renamed Work Group to Revise DSM-3): "Our advisory committee on affective disorders … took an atheoretical descriptive approach—one that does not prevent anyone from further speculation or classification on the basis of presumed etiology." (1984, 547) I have doubts about whether these descriptions are truly *atheoretical.* Janet Stoppard (2000) shares doubts specifically about the DSM-4, arguing that the definition of *mental disorder* is not *purely descriptive* and *atheoretical*, as is usually claimed. See also Radden (2017, 99 n.30), as well as Horwitz et al. (2016), for more on this descriptivist approach.
2. Possible etiologies or causal origins of depression might be: biological (familial and genetic influences, endocrine system, circadian rhythms, neurotransmitters), psychological (stress and allostatic load, negative ideation, learned helplessness), social-cultural (marital relations, lack of social support). This list is certainly not exhaustive (Barlow et al. 2017, 238–250).
3. Or, we could say, between a description of the thing and the thing itself.

4. Below, I return to a weaker version of this question, namely the qualitative similarity between the concepts of *acedia* and depression.
5. In Irvine's words, "It is my argument that the fragmentation of the subject occasioned by the new phase of modernity (sometimes called 'high modernity' or 'post-industrialism') *lies on a continuum with, but is qualitatively different from*, earlier states of subjective suffering." (1999, 7; emphasis added) These "earlier states of subjective suffering"? "Acedia, Tristitia and Sloth," as his title says.
6. Jehl (2005, 458) writes that *taedium vitae* and *tristitia* were "absorbed into the tradition of the concept of melancholy." Jehl's assessment seems to be merely descriptive of what has happened, but not normative.
7. The principal early theological and philosophical thinkers and texts where we first find *acedia* are: Evagrius of Pontus (1990a, 1990b), John Cassian (1894a, 1894b), Gregory the Great (1844), and Thomas Aquinas (2003, 2010–2011).
8. To the monastic type, we can assign Evagrius and perhaps Cassian. Gregory the Great, himself a former monk—"the great pope who never lost his nostalgia for the monk's solitude" (Wenzel 1960b, 23)—fits somewhere in between the monastic type and the Scholastic type. Thomas Aquinas's treatment certainly is assigned to the Scholastic type, along with other *summae theologiae* of the 13th century. What is called the popular type is not merely the common or popular notion of *sloth*—though it indeed includes that—it is also marked by an emphasis on external, practical signs and effects. It is called *popular* in the sense of *populus*, since this kind of *acedia* was found in works written for laypersons, especially from the 13th to the 15th century, with emphasis on the practical religious life: catechetical handbooks, questionnaires, sermons, devotionals, confessional formulas, and encyclopedias. "This emphasis [on external faults as opposed to abstract states of mind] is so prominent as almost to determine the essence of the vice in the popular image after 1200; but it had occurred already earlier, in the works written for laymen during the eighth and ninth centuries." (Wenzel 1960b, 177) Some of these, like questionnaires and confessional formulas, can be seen as literary genres in their own right (see Wenzel 1960b, 83–84).
9. For an excellent conceptual history of *acedia*, Siegfried Wenzel's book (1960b) and dissertation (1960a) are frankly unrivaled for their scholarly depth, breadth, and integrity. Also of merit are Forthomme (2000), Nault (2005, 2006), Luciani-Zidane (2009), which concern *acedia* in particular, and Bloomfield (1952), and Newhauser (2007), which concern the Sins in general. See also chapter two of my dissertation (McAllister, forthcoming 2020) for a comparatively brief conceptual history of *acedia* and more on its relation to depression.
10. "[T]he *Collationes* [*Conferences*] treats of the monk's 'inner dispositions,' whereas the *Instituta* [*Institutes*] is concerned with the external regulations given to a [cenobitic] monastic community in need of a rule." (Wenzel 1960b, 22; see also Cassian 1894b, Pt. I preface).
11. As we are taught by Brother Lawrence, for instance. Outside of the religious life, one need only to think of C.S. Lewis's description in the sermon "Learning in War-Time" (2009), who likens the student to a priest: each has to undertake dreary, monotonous tasks which are far removed from, yet consistent with, the *telos* of his vocation.
12. "[I]f it is a question of the monastic life in general, *acedia* is not just one temptation among many, it is quite simply *the* temptation, the calling into question of one's entire existence, the major identity crisis, in which the very foundations of everything are

severely shaken." (Joest 2004, 144) It is the temptation for monastics, because in his day-to-day activities, the monk is starkly aware of God's claim and calling upon his life, and no aversion to his day-to-day activities can easily arise to a doubting of the rationale behind the life he has undertaken. The general contours of *acedia*, however, can still be seen regardless of the believer's vocation. The more aware an individual is of God's calling on his life, the more deeply the effects of *acedia* can penetrate.

13. A word study in *Moralia in Iob* (1844) reveals that the English word *sloth* (in John Henry Parker's 1844 English edition) is used as a fitting translation from at least six different Latin words: *torpor*, *pigritia*, *desidia*, *ignavus*, *hebetudo*, and *inertia*.
14. According to Wenzel (1960b, 165), Ælfric characterizes this vice as "unwillingness to do any good."
15. Thomas' proposal is a classic example of the Scholastic synthesis of disparate views. It is consistent with each of the previous views while offering a further nuanced distinction.
16. Even if we do not know the newly coined word, we are all familiar with the idea of *procrastibaking*, doing anything (in this case, baking) to avoid the more important work we are supposed to be doing.
17. Busyness, taken in one sense, can be considered an opposing virtue to *acedia*, so long as the work is important, meaningful, and tied to one's spiritual vocation, whatever that may be. This virtue is present not only in Cassian's remedies above but also is "fairly frequent in Middle English devotional literature and … allegorical works and medieval drama. Even Chaucer follows this trend: 'This firste stok was ful of rightwisnesse … and loved besinesse, Ayeinst the vyce of slouthe, in honestee'." (Wenzel 1960b, 89)
18. The Romance languages preserve this connection even more clearly: such as *divertir* (Fr., Sp., Pt.), from *divertere* (Lat.), which can mean variously *to divert/distract* or *to entertain*; as well as the derived adjectives *divertente* (It.) and *divertissant* (Fr.), which mean *entertaining*, *funny*, or *amusing*. A similar etymological connection may be preserved in the word *lustig* (Ger., Swed.) for *funny* or *amusing*, in the words *lustig* (Dut.) and *lystig* (Dan.) connoting *merry* or *cheerful*, and in the now-obsolete Middle English word *lusty* for *pleasant*, *merry*, or *delightful*. That is to say, given the clear connection to its other meaning *lustful*, each of these iterations can suggest the mind's fleeting away to pleasurable yet frivolous objects.
19. See Kierkegaard's 1839 journal entry, which directly touches upon this passage (1987, II, 381).
20. See Ferrall and Repp (1843, 197), for a Danish-English dictionary from Kierkegaard's time. Kierkegaard certainly knew the word *Melancholi*, as evidenced by a cursory search on http://sks.de, the Skrifter, the comprehensive and searchable online collected writings of Kierkegaard in Danish.
21. Earlier periods in the history of psychiatry were limited in their nosologies, often using either of the general categories *mania* or *melancholy*, then specifying further from there. Thus *melancholy* was previously understood to encompass a wide spectrum of disorders, not only excessive or prolonged sorrow (see Hosack 1821, 58).
22. Mark D. Altschule, M.D. (1906–1988) was a Clinical Professor of Medicine at Harvard. See Flanagan (1965a, 1965b) for direct responses to Altschule's work of 1965.
23. Plantinga (2011, 307) comments upon this selfsame attitude: "A particularly charming phrase, here, is the obligatory 'as we now know'; we were previously wallowing in ignorance and superstition, but now, thanks to science, we finally know the truth."

24. Lewis (1955, 207) coins "chronological snobbery" as "the uncritical acceptance of the intellectual climate common to our own age and the assumption that whatever has gone out of date is on that account discredited."
25. This includes human mental action (i.e., thoughts), as well as passions (emotions, feelings), though, technically speaking, a passion, since it is passive, is not properly an action.
26. Altschule's wording is this: "The gradual process by which the concept of sin came to acquire psychiatric connotations." (1965, 117n) But it is clear that he thinks that the sin paradigm for explaining human action has no place in psychiatry, saying "medicine does not concern itself with sin *per se*; accordingly, various items among those that an earlier age designated as sin might be regarded by a later era as either normal behaviour or neurotic or psychotic behaviour." (1965, 118n)
27. Hunter and MacAlpine's title for the excerpt from Scot's original *The diſcouerie of Witchcraft* (1963). Among all the 16th-century writers in this volume, which amounts to no more than twenty out of some 330 items total, this is the most obvious and plain example of witchcraft being subverted by melancholy or any other psychiatric concept in the 16th century. The only other entry which treats directly of witchcraft and melancholy is King James VI of Scotland and I of England's *The Description of Sorcerie and Witchcraft* (1963, 47). For his part, those who insist on "attributing their [accused witches'] confeſſions or apprehenſions, to a naturall melancholicque humour,… they ſall finde that that will be ouer ſhort a cloak to couer their knavery with." (1597, 29–30) For any reasonable person can see that their symptoms differ: melancholics are subject to "leannes, palenes, deſire of ſolitude: and if they come to the higheſt degree thereof, mere folie and *Manie*: where as by the contrarie, a great nomber of them that euer haue bene convict or confeſſors of Witchcraft,… ſome of them rich and worldly-wiſe, some of them fatte or corpulent in their bodies, and moſt part of them altogether giuen ouer to the pleaſures of the fleſh, continual haunting of companie, and all kind of merrines, both lawfull and vnlawfull, which are thinges directly contrary to the ſymptomes of Melancholie, whereof I spake." (1597, 30)
28. Scot writes of "How melancholie abuſeth old women," saying "I meane not of cooſening [cozening] witches, but of poore melancholike women, which are themſelves deceived. For you ſhall underſtand, that the force which melancholie hath, and the effects that it worketh in the bodie of a man, or rather of a woman … troubled with this diſeaſe, imagine manie ſtrange, incredible and impoſſible things …[such as] one that was in great perplexitie, imagining that his noſe was as big as a houſe." (Scot 1584, 52–53)
29. Or *coosening art*, a now obsolete term for *cozen* (to cheat or defraud).
30. Most likely, in this context, meaning foolish talk associated with old age or senility.
31. Simply note Scot's original (1584) title page, which cites 1 John 4:1, hinting at the rationale for his investigation: "*Beleeue not euerie ſpirit, but trie the ſpirits, 'whether they are of God; for manie falſe prophets are gone out into the world, &c'.*"
32. Scot enumerates each of these three in the opening epistle to, incidentally, his "couſen" Sir Thomas Scot Knight, &c.: "*See firſt whether the evidence be not frivolous, & whether the proofs brought against them be not incredible, conſiſting of gheſſes, preſumptions, & impoſſibilities contrarie to reaſon, ſcripture, and nature. See alſo what perſons complaine upon them, whether they be not of the baſeſt, the unwiſeſt, & most faithles kind of people. Alſo may it pleaſe you to waie what accuſations and crimes they laie to their charge, namelie: She was at my houſe of late, she would have had a pot of milke, she departed in*

a chafe bicaufe she had it not, she railed, she curffed, she mumbled and whifpered, and finallie she faid she would be even with me: and foone after my child, my cow, my fow, or my pullet died, or was ftranglie taken." (1584; see 1963, 32–33)

33. "Truelie I for my part cannot perceive what it is to go a whoring after strange gods, if this be not. He that looketh upon his neighbors wife, and lufteth after hir, hath committed adulterie [In the margin: 'To go to witches, &c. is idolatrie.']. And truelie, he that in hart and by argument mainteineth the facrifice of the maffe to be propitiatorie for the quicke and the dead, is an idolater; as alfo he that alloweth and commendeth creeping to the croffe, and fuch like idolatrous actions, although he bend not his corporall knees." (Scot 1584, 12)
34. "[T]hey can raife and fupreffe lightening and thunder, raine and haile, clouds and winds, tempefts and earthquakes. Others doo write, that they can pull downe the moone and the ftarres … that they can cure difeafes fupernaturallie, flie in the aire … They can raife fpirits (as others affirme) drie up fprings, turne the courfe of running waters, inhibit the funne, and ftaie both day and night, changing the one into the other … They can bring foules out of graves." (Scot 1584, 10)
35. "[N]either is there any mention made of these kinds of witches in the Bible. If Chrift had knowne them, he would not have pretermitted to invaie againft their prefumption, in taking upon them his office: as, to heale and cure difeafes; and to worke such miraculous and fupernaturall things, as whereby he himfelfe was fpeciallie knowne, beleeved, and publifhed to be God; his actions and cures confifting (in order and effect) according to the power by our witchmoongers imputed to witches." (Scot 1584, 11) Scot then doubles down, saying the mere belief itself is idolatrous: "In like maner I fay, he that attributeth to a witch, fuch divine power, as dulie and onelie apperteineth unto GOD (which all witchmongers doo) is in hart a blafphemer, an idolater, and full of groffe impietie, although he neither go nor fend to hir for affiftance." (1584, 12)
36. In response to a charge that "the study of medicine … favours a disposition to materialism," Feuchtersleben replies that this charge is "unjust." (1847, 8) "No one has more occasion than the physician, to recognise the power of mind and the perishable nature of matter; and if he do not attain to this recognition, the fault is not in the science, but in himself, in not having thoroughly studied it, for here, we may say as Bacon did of philosophy, 'when superficially studied it excites doubt, when thoroughly explored it dispels it'." (1847, 8) Sir Francis Bacon, whom he favorably quotes, was a devout Anglican.
37. "The effects of the passions of the soul are sometimes named metaphorically because of a likeness to sensible bodies, given that the movements of an animal appetite are similar to the inclinations of a natural appetite. It is in this way that intense heat (*fervor*) is attributed to love, being widened (*dilatatio*) is attributed to pleasure, and being weighed down (*aggravatio*) is attributed to sadness." (2010, I-II.37.2.co)
38. Marcia Webb has both a M.Div. theology degree and a Ph.D. in clinical psychology. She is presently an Associate Professor of Psychology at Seattle Pacific University.
39. "I have remained immobile in the early stages of goodness, and I have not progressed … I have often given way to frivolous and empty thoughts, and have permitted my mind to wander in such things." (qtd. in Webb 2017, 77)
40. Robert W. Daly, M.D. is Professor Emeritus of Bioethics and Humanities and Professor Emeritus of Psychiatry at SUNY Upstate Medical University.

41. We need only something like the following more general principle to be true, that one can, through actions for which he can be held responsible, contribute to his psychological distress or disordering to the point that he develops a diagnosable condition.
42. Jennifer Radden, D.Phil. Oxon. is Professor Emerita at UMass Boston.
43. The late Stanley W. Jackson, M.D. (1920–2000) was Professor of Psychiatry and History of Medicine at Yale University School of Medicine.
44. The problem might resolve itself more easily if we were discussing depression from a clinical perspective and permitted to hazard and employ different theories concerning etiology. We could, for instance, come away with a handy category of *religious depression*, which might be closer to *acedia*.
45. By Leibniz's Law of the Indiscernibility of Identicals, $x=y \rightarrow \forall F(Fx \leftrightarrow Fy)$, if x and y refer to the same object, then x and y will not differ in any of their properties—it is somewhat strange to use *their*, since, in a case of numerical identity, there is only one object. Moreover, if there is some property that x has but y does not have, or vice versa (i.e., they are not qualitatively identical), then x and y are not the same object (i.e., not numerically identical). What goes for concrete objects also goes for abstract things lacking extension, like concepts or definitions. If two definitions differ in any respect, then they are not the same definition.
46. See Saul Kripke's (1980) *Naming and Necessity* for the distinction between rigid designators and definite descriptions.
47. We would never say that someone has *the E. coli*. This awkward construction seems to connote a reference to the genus; our acknowledgment that this is an incorrect way of speaking, likely reveals that we are not claiming the individual owns a genus.
48. A person can indeed be said to possess a kind by having an instance of that kind. I can say here only that I believe this is yet another case of speaking loosely; however, it may be correct to speak this way in some cases, as when discussing certain properties like *red*. In some manner, the kind *red* is truly fully present in an instance of *red* (i.e., it lacks none of its brilliance, hue, and shade); though in another sense, it is also true that the kind *red* is not fully present in an instance of *red* (i.e., one instance of *red* does not account for the entire kind of *red*).
49. This seems strange whether it be understood on a Platonist-type view, since a thing participates in a Form but never fully appropriates it; or on an Aristotelian-type view, where, even though a substantial form may be fully present in a thing, one instance of a substantial form rarely ever (unless, perhaps, it is *sui generis*) accounts for the entirety of that *kind* of form.
50. For instance, S. T. Coleridge does not cease to have melancholy when that concept becomes outdated. Some might object that this approach is too *reductionistic*, but I prefer to say it more accurately captures what a person *has*. In any case, I am not opposed to using terms and labels like depression and *acedia*; this so-called *reductionistic* descriptive account would only be initial, a diagnostic first step before we apply our conceptual terms *du jour*. It is especially useful for comparing conditions across history and cultures.
51. I say *some* because it is reasonable to think, concerning both depression and *acedia*, that a person may present with only some of the characteristic symptoms and yet the corresponding term would still correctly apply. One certainly need not check off all the symptoms.

52. A certain stripe of Kierkegaardian might venture to say that all instances of depression are instances of *acedia*, since all of life is to be lived before God. However, that is a topic for another paper (1993, 124).
53. My special gratitude goes to C. Stephen Evans, Nick Colgrove, and Harrison Lee for providing me with a friendly conversation about these important topics. Also, I am grateful for the lively sharing and interaction with the participants of *The Faces of Depression in Literature* seminar at the 2019 ACLA National Meeting at Georgetown University, as well as the participants of the 2019 Annual Conference on Medicine and Religion at Duke University. Finally, I owe the editor of this volume, Josefa Ros Velasco, an enormous thanks for her gracious spirit and her vision, hard work, and ambition to see this project through.

References

Ælfric. 1966. *Lives of Saints: Being a Set of Sermons on Saints' Days Formerly Observed by the English Church*. London: Trübner & Co.

Altschule, M. D. 1965. "Acedia: Its Evolution from Deadly Sin to Psychiatric Syndrome." *The British Journal of Psychiatry* 111: 117–119. https://doi.org/10.1192/bjp.111.471.117.

American Psychiatric Association. 1980. *Diagnostic and Statistical Manual of Mental Disorders*, 3. Arlington, VA: American Psychiatric Publishing.

American Psychiatric Association. 2013. *Diagnostic and Statistical Manual of Mental Disorders*, 5. Arlington, VA: American Psychiatric Publishing.

Aquinas, T. 2003. *On Evil [de malo]*. Oxford: Oxford University Press.

Aquinas, T. 2010. *Summa Theologiæ. Prima Secundae*. Lexington, KY: Nov Antiqua.

Aquinas, T. 2011. *Summa Theologiæ. Secunda Secundae*. Lexington, KY: Nov Antiqua.

Azzone, P. 2012. "Sin of Sadness: Acedia vel Tristitia between Sociocultural Conditionings and Psychological Dynamics of Negative Emotions." *Journal of Psychology and Christianity* 31: 1.

Barlow, D. H., V. M. Durand, and S. G. Hofmann. 2017. *Abnormal Psychology: An Integrative Approach*. Wadsworth, OH: Cengage Learning.

Bloomfield, M. W. 1952. *The Seven Deadly Sins: An Introduction to the History of a Religious Concept, with Special Reference to Medieval English Literature*. East Lansing, MI: Michigan State College Press.

Boudon, H. M. 1683. *L'homme de Dieu en la Personne du R. Pere J.-J. Seürin*. Chartres: Claude Peigné Imprimeur.

Cassian, J. 1894a. "Institutes of the Coenobia." In *A Select Library of Nicene and Post-Nicene Fathers of the Christian Church, XI*, edited by P. Schaff and H. Wace, 201–290. New York, NY: The Christian Literature Company.

Cassian, J. 1894b. "The Conferences." In *A Select Library of Nicene and Post-Nicene Fathers of the Christian Church, XI*, edited by P. Schaff and H. Wace, 291–546. New York, NY: The Christian Literature Company.

Daly, R. W. 2007. "Before Depression: The Medieval Vice of Acedia." *Psychiatry* 70 (1): 30–51.

Evagrius of Pontus. 1990a. *Antirrhetikos.* Accessed June 10, 2019. http://ldysinger.stjohnsem.edu/Evagrius/07_Antirrhet/00a_start.htm.

Evagrius of Pontus. 1990b. *Praktikos.* Accessed June 10, 2019. http://evagriusponticus.net/cpg2430.html.

Ferrall, J. S., and Þ. G. Repp. 1843. *A Danish-English Dictionary.* Copenhagen: Gyldendal.

Feuchtersleben, B. E. 1847. *Principles of Medical Psychology.* London: C. and J. Adlard.

Flanagan, H. M. 1965a. "Acedia: Its Evolution from Deadly Sin to Psychiatric Syndrome." *The British Journal of Psychiatry* 111 (475): 550. https://doi.org/10.1192/bjp.111.471.117.

Flanagan, H. M. 1965b. "Acedia." *The British Journal of Psychiatry* 111 (478): 909. https://doi.org/10.1192/bjp. 111.478.909.

Forthomme, B. 2000. *De L'acédie monastique à l'anxio-dépression: histoire philosophique de la transformation d'un vice en pathologie.* Paris: Sanofi-Synthélabo.

Gregory the Great. 1844. *Moralia in Iob.* London: J. G. F and J. Rivington.

Horwitz, A. V., J. C. Wakefield, and L. Lorenzo-Luaces. 2016. "History of Depression." In *The Oxford Handbook of Mood Disorders*, edited by R. J. DeRubeis and D. R. Strunk, Chapter 2. New York, NY: Oxford University Press. https://doi.org/10.1093/oxfordhb/9780199973965.013.2.

Hosack, D. 1821. *A System of Practical Nosology, to Which Is Prefixed, a Synopsis of the Systems of Sauvages, Linnaeus, Vogel, Sagar, Macbride, Cullen, Darwin, Crichton, Pinel, Parr, Swediaur, Young, and Good, with References to the Best Authors on Each Disease.* New York, NY: C S Van Winkle.

Hunter, R., and I. MacAlpine. 1963. *Three Hundred Years of Psychiatry, 1535–1860: A History Presented in Selected English Texts.* London: Oxford University Press.

Irvine, I. 1999. "Acedia, Tristitia, and Sloth: Early Christian Forerunners to Chronic Ennui." *Humanitas* 12 (1): 89–103.

Jackson, S. W. 1981. "Acedia the Sin and Its Relationship to Sorrow and Melancholia in Medieval Times." *Bulletin of the History of Medicine* 55 (2): 172–185.

James VI of Scotland and I of England. 1597. *Dæmonologie, in forme of a dialogue.* Edinburgh: Waldegrave.

Jehl, R. 2005. "*Acedia* and Burnout Syndrome: From an Occupational Vice of the Early Monks to a Psychological Concept in Secularized Professional Life." In *In the Garden of Evil*, edited by R. Newhauser, 455–476. Toronto: Pontifical Institute of Mediaeval Studies.

Joest, C. 2004. "The Significance of *Acedia* and *Apatheia* in Evagrius Ponticus Part I." *American Benedictine Review* 55 (2–3): 121–150.

Kierkegaard, S. 1987. *Either/Or: Part II. Kierkegaard's Writings, 4.* Princeton, NJ: Princeton University Press.

Kierkegaard, S. 1993. *Upbuilding Discourses in Various Spirits. Kierkegaard's Writings, 15.* Princeton, NJ: Princeton University Press.

Kripke, S. A. 1980. *Naming and Necessity*. Cambridge, MA: Harvard University Press.

Lewis, C. S. 1955. *Surprised by Joy: The Shape of My Early Life*. New York, NY: Harcourt, Brace, and World, Inc.

Lewis, C. S. 2009. "Learning in War-Time." *The Official Website of C.S. Lewis*. Accessed June 10, 2009. http://www.cslewis.com/learning-in-war-time/.

Lim, J. Y., J. W. Yoon, and C. J. Hovde. 2010. "A Brief Overview of *Escherichia coli* O157:H7 and Its Plasmid O157." *Journal of Microbiology and Biotechnology* 20 (1): 1–10.

Luciani-Zidane, L. 2009. *L'acédie: Le vice de forme du christianisme, de saint Paul à Lacan*. Paris: Éditions du Cerf.

McAllister, D. 2020. "Fallow Season: An Historical Case for a Spiritual Etiology of Depression." Ph.D. Diss., Baylor University, Texas.

Nault, J. C. 2005. "L'héritage monastique et patristique du thème de l'acédie chez les Premiers Chartreux." In *Tristesse, acédie, et médecine des âmes dans la tradition monastique et cartusienne: anthologie de textes rares et inédits (XIIIe-XXe siècle)*, edited by N. Nabert, 37–59. Paris: Beauchesne.

Nault, J. C. 2006. *La saveur de Dieu: l'acédie dans le dynamisme de l'agir*. Paris: Cerf.

Newhauser, R. 2007. *The Seven Deadly Sins: From Communities to Individuals*. Leiden: Brill.

Plantinga, A. 2011. *Where the Conflict Really Lies: Science, Religion, and Naturalism*. Oxford: Oxford University Press.

Radden, J. 2002. *The Nature of Melancholy: From Aristotle to Kristeva*. Oxford: Oxford University Press.

Radden, J. 2017. *Melancholic Habits: Burton's Anatomy and the Mind Sciences*. Oxford: Oxford University Press.

Scot, R. 1584. *The discouerie of Witchcraft*. London: William Brome.

Scot, R. 1963. "Not Witchcraft but Melancholie." In *Three Hundred Years of Psychiatry, 1535–1860: A History Presented in Selected English Texts*, edited by R. Hunter and I. MacAlpine, 32–37. London: Oxford University Press.

Spitzer, R. L. 1984. "First Rebuttal." *American Journal of Psychiatry* 141 (4): 546–547. http://dx.doi.org/10.1176/ajp.141.4.54.

Stoppard, J. 2000. *Understanding Depression: Feminist Social Constructionist Approaches (Women and Psychology)*. New York, NY: Routledge.

Surin, J.-J. 1829. *Triomphe de l'amour divin sur les puissances de l'enfer ... Avec le moyen facile d'acquérir la joie du cœur*. Avignon: Seguin Aîné.

Taylor, C. 1908. "Accidie." In *Encyclopedia of Religion and Ethics, I*, edited by J. Hastings and J. A. Selbie, 66. New York, NY: Charles Scribner's Sons.

Webb, M. 2017. *Toward a Theology of Psychological Disorder*. Eugene, OR: Cascade Books.

Wenzel, S. 1960a. "*Acedia* and Related Terms in Medieval Thought with Special Emphasis on Middle English Literature." Ph.D. Diss., Ohio State University, Ohio.

Wenzel, S. 1960b. *The Sin of Sloth:* Acedia *in Medieval Thought and Literature*. Chapel Hill, NC: University of North Carolina Press.

2 *Depression in Ricardian Dream Visions*

Nancy Ciccone
University of Colorado

In Chaucer's dream vision known as the *Book of the Duchess* (c. 1368), the narrator wonders how he can still be alive: "I have gret wonder, by this light,/ How that I live, for day ne night/I may not slepe." ["I am amazed, by this light,/how I am still alive for neither day nor night/can I sleep."] (1987, 1–3)[1] He complains of idle thoughts continuously plaguing his mind (1987, 4). Having suffered for eight years, he has lost all discernment: "Joye or sorowe, wherso hyt be/For I have felynge in nothyng." ["Everything seems the same to me—whether joy or sorrow, wherever it comes from—because I don't feel anything."] (1987, 10–11) Whereas modern analyses might consider him suffering from clinical depression, the narrator diagnoses himself as suffering from "melancolye." (1987, 23) According to Medieval medical discourses, he is correct. Among his ailments is "sorwful imaginacioun" (1987, 14), a primary symptom of the disease.

Most literary scholars, however, diagnose him with lovesickness because Chaucer's dream visions borrow from French sources that designate unrequited love as causing their narrators' depressive melancholia. As Peter Toohey (1992, 267) has found, such a medical identification reaches back at least to Galen (c. 130–200 CE). He diagnosed it when an emaciated, feverish woman, who has insomnia, quickened her pulse at the mention of a particular dancer. Galen and other early medieval humoralists from the 3rd through the 5th centuries note that lovesickness presents symptoms likened to melancholia but indicative of a depressive state not based on the excess of black bile, the root definition of the humor (Toohey 1992, 267–268). According to Toohey's research, "descriptions of melancholia as a depressive disease seem to begin seriously about the same time as do descriptions of depressive lovesickness." (1992, 283)[2] Later, medieval medical texts treat lovesickness, translated as *hereos* or *amor heroes*, as a subset of melancholia. Lowes (1914) has traced the influence of works by al-Razi (c. 860–925) and by Avicenna (980–1037) on 14th-century practitioners. Although various physicians add commentary to their received translations, Lowes's lengthy quotations demonstrated that identification and treatments coalesce. One of Chaucer's contemporaries, John of Tornamira (1330–c. 1396), for example, treats lovesickness as a species of melancholia: "amor heroes cum sit una species melancoliae." (qtd. in Lowes 1914, 504) Bernardus Gordonis (fl. end of 14th century) clarifies: "Love is diseased blood/unwholesomeness of the mind." ["Amor est mentis insania."] (qtd. in Lowes 1914, 502) By the time we reach the literature of the 14th century, lovesickness proliferates to a near "textual epidemic." (Lowes 1914, 226) In the long and late periods, the depression accompanying melancholia and lovesickness binds them together. They flourish in the literary genre of dream visions.

In the *Duchess*, Chaucer's narrator tackles his *sorrowful imagination* by reading Ovid. In another of his dream visions, *Parliament of Fowls* (c. 1382), Chaucer's narrator finds Cupid incomprehensible. He begins with a dictum cadged from Horace to the effect that a lifetime is too short to perfect the writing of poetry. Chaucer applies the principle to the understanding of love (1987, 1–7). Knowing nothing of it except what he reads in books, the narrator turns away from the topic to read *Scipio's Dream* (1987). In so doing, Chaucerian narrators, perhaps unwittingly, follow medical advice. As Olson has argued (1982, 46), reading literature can be prescribed to treat melancholia, one of the extreme emotions of the *accidentes animae*, because it provides therapeutic pleasure. For Chaucer's narrators, however, reading also lulls them to sleep and so, at least, relieves their insomnia. In Chaucer's *Parliament* and *Duchess*, the narrator's dreams investigate love. However, ambiguous their conclusions on the topic, the sleep that ensues restores balance, the key to maintaining good health among the four medieval humors (Avicenna 2013, 68). Although lovesickness survives as a staple in literature, if not its centerpiece, the genre of the dream vision does not thrive after this period. However, over 200 were written between the 16th and the 15th centuries (Lynch 1988, 1). Our most famous secular English authors—Chaucer, Langland, Gower—rely on it during the last quarter of the 14th century under Richard II's tumultuous reign (1367–1400), which engenders the term Ricardian literature (Burrow 1971). In keeping with French versions, many of the English dream visions entail an ethical debate to foster appropriate behavior for the lovesick. The popularity of the genre, however, accompanies another medieval development. As Steven Kruger (1999, 55) has pointed out, the influx of medical texts during the later Middle Ages further enables the genre to become a place for the merging of medical and moral discourses: "A new somatic treatment of dreaming is in the way it enables a bringing together of a different kind of dream—internally and externally motivated, celestial and mundane, angelic, demonic, and human." (1999, 62) Kruger's insights called for "recognizing the somatic possibilities" of the literary dream vision, in order "to move away from the simple allegorizing and spiritualizing tendencies" in the critical literature (1999, 62). A focus on depression fosters a response to Kruger's suggestion because medieval melancholia entails the somatic.

Along with the merging of medical and moral discourses and lovesickness and melancholia, I focus here on another merging: that between lovesickness and grief. Since we grieve the loss of what we love, medieval medical discourses treat both types of depression as heart ailments. For comparison with the Chaucerian lovesick, I turn to a grieving narrator in another Ricardian dream vision, the anonymous *Pearl* (c. 1360–1395). This comparison is, admittedly, somewhat unfair. The *Pearl* is overtly theological in contrast to Chaucerian dream visions. Chaucer always has his tongue in his cheek. His narrators protest too much, and his literary antics may, in turn, alleviate sufferers of depression by entertaining them.

In contrast to the narrators in Chaucer's dream visions, *Pearl*'s gravity invites empathy for the narrator even as he too distracts fellow sufferers with a narrative. In short, the poets rely on entirely different registers. Whereas the *Duchess*'s narrator fails to feel anything, grief overwhelms the *Pearl*'s narrator. However, he too finds himself stymied. In turn, medieval therapies for these forms of depression differ despite presenting similar symptoms. Treatments for lovesickness include frequent coition, declarations of love, even flagellation (Lowes 1914, 501, 506). Assuaging grief, however, depends on religious belief and the passage of time to ease it, rather than precise action. To explore the representation of grief, I first address the *Pearl* narrator's symptoms. I then consider them in light of treatments from medieval medical discourses. Finally, I take an even more comprehensive view by contextualizing the significance of merging the medical and moral, lovesickness, and grief, within the late 14th-century social context.

In *Pearl*, grief first presents as lovesickness. The narrator claims he is "fordolked of luf-daungere/Of that privy perle withouten spot." ["grievously wounded by love's power for [his] own spotless pearl."] (Gordon 1974, 11–12) Conforming to its French dream vision models, the narrative furthermore begins in a *locus amoenus*, frequently a setting for courtly romance. However, the beautiful garden turns out to also be a graveyard.

The jeweler who lost his precious pearl there turns out to be a father who lost his two-year-old daughter named Pearl. As in Chaucer's dreams, the *Pearl*'s dream will investigate the topic that causes depression. No matter whether the narrators in Ricardian dream visions seek a requited love or a dead daughter, their subsequent dreams somewhat miss the mark. Pearl's ghost-image will assure her father that she is okay. She attempts to mitigate his grief by teaching him Christian doctrine. Whereas literary scholars debate whether or not those teachings comfort him, the focus on depression highlights an equal consideration overlooked in the critical literature: the *Pearl*-poet sprinkles medications for melancholia throughout the narrative. In other words, the narrative images themselves provide somatic treatment to moderate the narrator's grief.

The entire narrative of the *Pearl* centers on the heart. Marti (1991, 83) has found the narrative to be "a body structured around the formal and thematic nucleus of the heart—a heart that is literal as well as metaphorical"; it spatially and temporally centers the poem in the shape of a pearl (1991, 143). Marti correlated the heart with the pearl the Pearl-Maiden wears and with the heart of the Lamb. Among the literal correspondences, however, is the narrator's heart. For the narrator, it is the location of his grief: "devely dele in my hert denned." ["a desolating grief lay deep in my heart."] (Gordon 1974, 51) The 11th-century physician Avicenna locates the life force, the animalistic faculty, in the heart which manages the breath (2013, 89). In the 7th century, Isidore of Seville's chapter on medicine, "Entymologia," clarifies the connection through anatomy: the heart is next to the lungs so that the heart controls breathing (1964, I.118). Avicenna, however, provides a blueprint describing the characteristics of melancholia and remedies for those who come after him. He prescribes "pearl and silk," to counteract difficult things and improve the breath needing adjustment in the treatment of depression (Gruner 1930, 9.1119, 547). For Avicenna, *breath* refers to a vitality, which is constrained in depression and grief (Gruner 1930, IV.16, §134). The lost pearl suggests the *Pearl* narrator's inability to follow Avicenna's prescription of the materials to improve his breath. He initially describes the pearl as that which had granted him happiness and well-being: "al [his] hele." ["all [his] health."] (Gordon 1974, 16) Avicenna further distinguishes between fear and depression, which fall together under "contraction of the chest or heart." (Gruner 1930, 7.1116, 544) "Depression has much to do with saddening things and the heart does not tolerate them much." (1930, 7.1116, 544) The condition "impels one to stand still for the purpose of either resisting or repelling." (1930, 7.1116, 544) For diagnosis, depression (oppression of the chest) exhibits "(a) sense of threatening injury" and "(b) no desire to flee." (1930, 7.1116, 544) Having lost all his well-being, the *Pearl* narrator's laments and efforts to retrieve his pearl attest to a *threatening injury*. He also returns to the very place he lost his pearl: "I lest hyr in on erbere"; "I entred in þat erber grene." ["I lost her in an arbor"; "I entered into that green arbor."] (Gordon 1974, 9, 38) The narrative indicates the speaker's psychological stasis through geography. Returning to the place of his loss, he is unable to move on. He has no desire to flee, nowhere else to go. Stillness will also enter into his dream. His heart is stunned when he first views the Pearl-Maiden (1974, 176, 179). In awe, he famously stands "as hawk in halle" (1974, 184) and later in the narrative, "as stylle as dased quayle." (1974, 185) The figurative language of birds emphasizes his inability to fly, to flee. Whereas Chaucer's narrator in the *Duchess* complained of psychological paralysis, the *Pearl*'s narrator exhibits it physically. In both cases, the narrators' depression presents as being arrested in the progress of their lives.

According to Avicenna (2013), seasonal changes factor into the causes of disease. Summer "breaks downs humors and weakens strength and natural functions due to its excessive disintegration. It reduces blood and phlegm and increases the bitter yellow bile, then at its tail end, black bile increases." (2013, 131) The *Pearl* narrative begins in August, probably the Feast of the Assumption, August 15. While the feast day complements the overall Christian message, the time of year also contributes to an excess of the black bile, the melancholia, complementing the father's *care ful colde*, usually translated as sorrow. In other words, the poet's word choice for the narrator's sorrow suggests the coldness characteristic of the melancholic, unable to be warmed by the weather.

Nevertheless, the environment also offers treatment. The narrator collapses from his grief upon a "flowery turf" with "suche odour to my hernes shot." ["with the fragrances shooting into his brains."] (Gordon 1974, 58) Firing into his *brains*, the aromas target the site where Avicenna located depression in contrast to fear, which affects the body (Gruner 1930, 7.1116, 544). However, reminiscent of the *locus amoenus* of courtly romance, the catalog of garden flowers also conveys their particular medicinal benefits. The gillyflower constitutes a "healing clove"; the ginger fosters an "energizing anti-irritant; the gromwells' 'stony nutlets' resemble pearls"; the peony emblematizes "*Παιάν*, the Greek god of healing." (Stern 1970, 76) In addition to their symbolic meanings, the flowers accord with Avicenna's prescription: "sweet aromatics [to] strengthen the breath." (Gruner 1930, 2.119, 547) Davenport (1978, 11) has further pointed out that the spices enthrall all of the narrator's senses: "involving not only sight," but also "touch," "sound," "taste and smell." (27–28, 6, 19, 29) While the narrator's reason has set him at peace—"Though resoun sette myselven sight" (Gordon 1974, 52)—his "wreched wylle" (1974, 56) continues suffering. In effect, the narrative distinguishes between the intellect located in the narrator's *resoun* and his *wylle*. The spices bypass both as they shoot into the physiology of his *brains*.

The narrator, furthermore, acknowledges the comfort Christianity offers: "kynde of Kryst me comfort kenned." ["the nature/mercy of Christ has been taught to me."] (Gordon 1974, 55) It just does not help. As a result, some literary scholars find the narrator lacking faith, his stasis indicative of *acedia*. The depth of the narrator's grief suggested to Hillman (1970, 10) the sin of covetousness. Scholarly debate has ensued as to whether the sin of *stultitia*, foolishness, needs to be added to that of covetousness, and whether sinfulness resulted from loving earthy goods too much or from mistaking the daughter as an object (see Cherniss 1987, 158). Among his critics, Nolan (1977, 160) characterized the narrator's error as the sin of pride, hubris, and in so doing, addressed the problem of his self-absorption. Depression entails for the *Duchess*'s and the *Pearl*'s narrators an obsession with their feelings. However, whereas the *Pearl* narrator's grief speaks of sins, they also indicate symptoms of depression rather than a moral failing.

Distracting him from melancholy, medieval aromatherapy substitutes for the books Chaucerian narrators read. Each provides relief from being overwhelmed by self-absorption. Such distractions invite sleep. Collapsing to the ground, the *Pearl* narrator's "spyryt þer sprang in space." ["spirit springs into space."] (Gordon 1974, 61) On one level, the garden of flowers that die and are reborn mimic the cycle of life and death that grieves the narrator. On another level, sleep is the vehicle by which healing progresses as it does in Chaucer's dream visions. The garden hosts prescriptions for ailments to testify to the somatic healing the Christian God bestows on mortals. Among other embedded images that aided healing and discussed below, sleep eventually enables the narrator to move on from the garden/graveyard.

As the dreamer dreams, the vision of the Pearl-Maiden, her splendor, and the richness of the landscape provide additional antidotes to his grief: "The adubbemente of þo downeȝ dere/Garten my goste al greffe forȝete." ["The adornment of those glorious hills/made my spirit forget all grief."] (Gordon 1974, 85–86) However, much the landscape reflects the dreamer's projection of aristocratic opulence; it accords with Avicenna's instructions. The "crystal klyffeȝ" ["crystal cliffs"] (1974, 74), silver leaves (1974, 77), "emerad, saffer, oþer gemme gente" ["emerald, sapphires, or noble gem"] (1974, 118) aim to counteract "disagreeable things" (1974, 118) and to release vital breathing. Crystal, in particular, elicits physical effects through sensory perception.

Although hard and cold, it refracts light and therefore provides heat. Galvez (2014, 18) has argued for the literary image to convey an intense moment of subjectivity due to its use in mirrors. Applying her findings to the *Pearl* suggests that the narrator's gaze becomes ours; even if the Pearl-Maiden represents his wish fulfillment, we share in the reflection. The gems and stones further signify various meanings for the original audience of the poem, and as Stern (1970, 82) has noted: "Gemology was so common in the exegetical tradition that it is hardly possible that the poet did not take his jewel symbolism for granted"—especially pearls.

Much of the interpretative literature treats pearls in terms of either their religious or courtly significance.[3] Nevertheless, they also cure melancholy. The narrative pivots on the image of the pearl; it slides in its denotations of meaning, sometimes literal and sometimes figurative. However, whether akin to the Matthew's Pearl of Great Price (13:45–46) or Anne's adornment as Richard's queen, literal pearls also figure in pharmacology. Not only does Avicenna specifically single them out to alleviate depression (above), but the *Legenda Aurea* (c. 1275) introduces Saint Margarita, whose name derives from the Persian word for pearl, with a description of the jewel's properties "to be contrary to the heart's passion, and to comfort the spirit." ["Virtus autem hujus lapidis diciture esse contra cordis passionem, et ad spiritus confortationem."] (Gordon 1974, 28) The actual pearl occurs in the medieval pharmacopeia as an essential cure for a host of diseases. The *Cyrurgie of Guy de Chauliac* (c. 1363; Getz 1991) lists the "margary perles, ben colde and drye" are known for "cleren and conforten." ["Margery pearls, being cold and dry" are known "to purify and to comfort."] (Ogden 1971, 624)[4] The pearl is especially prescribed for heart ailments and melancholy: "And if it þe cardiacle comeþ of malencoly and of coler togedir … let him vse oftetymes in his metis lymail of golde and þe poudir of margerie peerless þat ben good for þe cardiacle þat is with a feuer also." ["And if heart disease [caused by excessive emotion] comes from melancholy [black bile] and colic [yellow bile] together, make the medicine of gold filings and powdered pearl that are also good for the passion that is with a fever."] (Getz 1991, 146, f.187v, 19–21)[5] The apothecary Richard de Montpellier who sent a prescription including pearls to Edward I (1237–1307), suffering from dysentery (Getz 1991, 19), believes that such remedies were copied *pro forma*. For its pharmaceutical effects, the pearl needs to be ground to a powder, and the first description of the dream landscape includes "precious perleȝ of oryente" on the ground (Gordon 1974, 82). Cherniss (1987, 158) has pointed out the irony here due to "the narrator's grief over the loss of a single gem" when they appear in abundance. However, the poet's word choice—"Þe grauayl þat on grounde con grynde" ["The gravel on the ground, ground"] (Gordon 1974, 81–82)—also brings to mind the grinding of the pearls as if for a prescription. Within this landscape, the dreamer subsequently "al greffe forȝete," as if momentarily cured of his melancholy (Gordon 1974, 86).

Despite the Pearl-Maiden's lessons on Christian doctrine, her father continues to question her well-being. How can she be one of the 144 thousand saved? When she was so young at death, how can she appear as a maiden? The narrator responds to Matthew's parable of the laborers in the vineyard as "unresounable" (Gordon 1974, 590), "bot a fable." (1974, 592) His mercantilism insists each be rewarded according to the hours of work (1974, 595). Perhaps he cannot grasp a situation so different from his experiential one. He wants to know what her castle looks like, where she lives. She finally reveals to him a vision of the New Jerusalem. At this point in the narrative, the narrator disregards the Pearl-Maiden's warnings that he must keep his distance. He wants to reach her and splashes into a river separating them. The movement wakens him. He sums up his dream experience: "If it be veray and soth sermoun/That thou so stykes in garlande gay/So wel is me in thys doel-doungoun/That though art to that Pryces paye." ["if it be [an] actual and true account/that you are set in a fair garland/it is well for me in this sorrowful dungeon/That you are in the Prince's pleasure."] (1974, 1185–1188) The conditional sentence somewhat undermines the dream's religious comfort. Nevertheless, despite such shortcomings in his understanding and along with the gift of Christ's grace, the images of somatic healing and the relief of sleep assist in putting him back on his feet. After waking, he goes to church to receive communion. Alone at the beginning of the narrative, he now rejoins the Christian community. Even if still grieving, even in some doubt about the veracity of his dream, he is able to act, to leave the gravesite.

Medieval scholars argue over whether or not the dream comforts the *Pearl*'s narrator and relieves him of his depressive melancholia. Some interpreters attempt to reconcile the narrative's two primary perspectives: Christian spirituality, represented by the Pearl-Maiden and humanistic grief, represented by the jeweler-father. In her introduction to the TEAMS edition of *Pearl*, Stanbury (2001, part 10) has articulated the interpretative conundrum with a question: "does the poem resolve in an aristocratized and utopic vision, or is there a remnant, the narrator himself, not totally encapsulated within a formal sacramental or courtly system?" Gilbert (2011, 187–189), for another example, deployed Lacan's concept of anamorphosis to posit a rapprochement between the mortal and heavenly spheres, so that each sphere animates the other. By way of contrast, Davenport (1978, 51) has found the poet's answer to grief to be "by believing in an existence other than the earthly."

Attributing comfort to the narrator, Hillman (1945 [1970], 14) has asserted a kind of conversion resulting from the jeweler's comprehension of the Pearl-Maiden's teachings.[6] If nothing else, these viewpoints taken together reveal the narrative gap between a faith-based religious ideology and the emotional grief of loss, dependent on the audience/reader. In effect, the *Pearl* evidences a textual indeterminacy comparable to that found in Chaucer's dream visions, however much they differ. However, with its complex concatenation, symbolic numbers, elaborate punning, sophisticated semiotics, this jewel of a poem also contributes to the images of somatic healing that may constitute a prescription for its original audience. They, too, are Christians, familiar with the doctrine the Pearl-Maiden reiterates. Moreover, they, too, have endured loss and hardship resulting from Richard's governance and the ravaging plagues.

Although we do not know the exact date in which the *Pearl* was written, we do know something about the late 14th-century English audience. Even at the risk of over-simplifying, two social crises warrant mention. In terms of economics, Richard II was emptying the British coffers. He taxed the populace to support the 100 Years War (1337–1453), and to the aristocracy's disappointment, was losing their French properties. Also, the Pole Tax was the final straw that led to the Peasant's Revolt of 1381, the first recorded social revolution in England that produced little actual change. The rebels notably rallied around another dream vision, Langland's *Piers Plowman* (c. 1370), however much they may have misinterpreted it. Richard also added economic insult to such injury by entertaining lavish courts. The *Pearl*'s glittering descriptions of the dream landscape and especially of the New Jerusalem suggest that such lavishness belongs in dreams and heaven, not decorating the court and the king's favorites, even if the poet himself was a royalist. In the last twenty years of the century, power shifts from the King to the Lord's Appellant and somewhat back to the king, which must have affected the social structure as armies were raised and battles fought within England and France until Richard was deposed in 1399.

The other major social crisis the *Pearl* evokes is that of the Bubonic plague. In 1348–1349, it had decimated England, and it returned in waves throughout that century. Moldering bodies (Gordon 1974, 306, 320, 857, 958) recur throughout the *Pearl* narrative. The white and pure jewel is muddied by the ground in which it is lost: "Thy corse in clot mot calder keye." ["Your body in clay must colder sink."] (1974, 320) The narrator mourns the marring of his "pryuy perle wythouten spot" ["his own spotless pearl"] (1974, 12), "To þenke hir color so clad in clot." ["to think her complexion so clad in clay."] (1974, 22) In that the Pearl-Maiden's "flesch be layde to rote" ["flesh is laid to rot"] (1974, 958), he lets his imagination intensify his grief.

Within the dream, the narrator even refers to himself as "bot mokke and mul." ["muck and dust."] (1974, 905) David Coley (2013, 231) has associated the different valences in "the spotty and the clean" with the plague symptoms. As Coley argued, "*Pearl* heightens its affective potential by absorbing the language and imagery of the pestilence into its mingled allegorical and elegiac narratives." (2013, 241) These insights complement the images of somatic healing in *Pearl*, for they represent a prescription for a traumatized, surviving audience. An entire population, already aware of the Christian afterlife, needs to begin the process of recovery, to re-enter the quotidian demands of continuing their lives after experiencing the losses brought on by economic instability and by plague.

Whether Chaucer's or the *Pearl*-Poet's narratives, the medieval dream vision suggests an appeal beyond that of courtly romance with its focus on *fin'amors*, fine love, and beyond that of Christian faith with its attention to moral behavior. The *Pearl*, for one example, provides a place of empathy for a community in times of crisis. Much literature arguably does that, but the dream vision mainly fills a gap because it targets cultural issues in an imaginary landscape in much the same as some science fiction does today wrestling with inequality, global warming, apocalyptic visions, and even love. Imagining shows us how some people, who may not know what to do, yet find a way to act, whether it is the practice of reading that produces relief from anxiety or the ideas from reading that furnish strategies enabling us to sleep and to rise the next morning.

Notes

1. I have placed the modern English translations after the Middle English quotations. All translations are mine unless otherwise noted. The line number following the quotations refers to their respective Middle English narratives. The *Pearl* vocabulary usually alludes to more than one meaning, so we have relied on the forward-slash to indicate alternatives.
2. For a recent medical finding on the connection between lovesickness and the brain, see Templin et al. (2019).
3. The critical literature is vast. Examples include Ackerman (1964), Gatta (1974), Arthur (1987), Clopper (1991), Hatt (2015) for religion; Bennett (1992), Barr (2000), Bowers (2001) for the aristocratic court; Muscatine (1972) for the combination of the two.
4. The *Cyrurgie* is an anonymous translation of Guy's *Inventarium sui collectorium in parte cyryrgicali medicine* thought to have been written in Avignon, 1362 (p.v.). Benjamin Lee Gordon (1959, 383) credits John of Gaunt with having made the text available to English surgeons during the One Hundred Year's War after he noted the skill of the French surgeons responding to battle injuries.

5. Although the Middle English version is a translation from the 15th century, it is based on the *Compendium medicinae*, written about 1250. See also Anna Nardo (1985, 34–36) for a history of the pearl as a cure for melancholy.
6. Aers (1993, 55–56) provides a summary of those literary critics, before his writing, who advocate for the narrator's reclamation of his faith and those who read the conclusion skeptically.

References

Ackerman, R. W. 1964. "The Pearl Maiden and the Penny." *Romance Philology* 17: 615–623.

Aers, D. 1993. "The Self Mourning: Reflections on *Pearl*." *Speculum* 68 (1): 54–73. https://doi.org/10.2307/2863834.

Arthur, R. G. 1987. "The Day of Judgment is now: A Johannine Pattern in the Middle English *Pearl*." *American Benedictine Review* 38: 227–242.

Avicenna. 2013. *Avicenna's Medicine*. Rochester, VT: Healing Arts Press.

Barr, H. 2000. "*Pearl* or the Jeweler's Tale." *Medium Ævum* 69: 59–79.

Bennett, M. 1992. "The Court of Richard II and the Promotion of Literature." In *Chaucer's English Literature in Historical Context*, edited by B. Hanawalt, 3–20. Minneapolis, MN: University of Minnesota Press.

Bowers, J. 2001. *The Politics of Pearl: Court Poetry in the Age of Richard II*. Cambridge: D. S. Brewer.

Burrow, J. 1971. *Ricardian Poetry: Chaucer, Gower, Langland, and the 'Gawain' Poet*. New Haven, CT: Yale University Press.

Chaucer, G. 1987. *Riverside Chaucer*. Boston, MA: Houghton Mifflin.

Cherniss, M. D. 1987. *Boethian Apocalypse*. Oklahoma, OK: University of Oklahoma Press.

Clopper, L. 1991. "*Pearl* and the Consolation of Scripture." *Viator* 23: 231–245. https://doi.org/10.1484/J.VIATOR. 2.301282.

Coley, D. K. 2013. "*Pearl* and the Narrative of Pestilence." *Studies in the Age of Chaucer* 35 (1): 209–262. https:/doi.org/10.1353/sac.2013.0022.

Davenport, W. A. 1978. *Art of the Gawain-Poet*. London: Athlone Press.

Galvez, M. 2014. "Dark Transparencies: Crystal Poetics in Medieval Texts and Beyond." *Philological Quarterly* 93 (1): 15–42.

Gatta, J. 1974. "Transformation Symbolism and the Liturgy of the Mass in *Pearl*." *Modern Philology* 71 (3): 243–256. https://doi.org/10.1086/390487.

Getz, F. M. 1991. *Healing and Society in Medieval English, a Middle English Translation of the Pharmaceutical Writings of Gilbertus Anglicus*. Wisconsin, WI: University of Wisconsin Press.

Gilbert, J. 2011. *Living Death in Medieval French and English Literature*. Cambridge: Cambridge University Press.

Gordon, B. L. 1959. *Medieval and Renaissance Medicine*. New York, NY: Philosophical Library.

Gordon, E. V. 1974. *Pearl.* New York, NY: Oxford University Press.

Gruner, O. C. 1930. *A Treatise on the Canon of Medicine of Avicenna.* London: Luzac & Co.

Hatt, C. A. 2015. *God and the Gawain-Poet.* Cambridge: D.S. Brewer.

Hillman, S. M. V. 1945. "Some Debatable Words in *Pearl* and Its Theme." *Modern Language Notes* LX: 241–248.

Hillman, S. M. V. 1970. "Some Debatable Words in *Pearl* and Its Theme." In *The Middle English Pearl Critical Essays*, edited by J. Conley, 9–17. Notre Dame: University of Notre Dame Press.

Isidore of Seville. 1964. *Isidore of Seville: The Medical Writings.* Independence Square, PA: American Philosophical Society.

Kruger, S. 1999. "Medical and Moral Authority in the Late Medieval Dream." In *Reading Dreams*, edited by P. Brown, 51–83. New York, NY: Oxford University Press.

Lowes, J. L. 1914. "The Loveres Maladye of Hereos." *Modern Philology* 11 (4): 491–546.

Lynch, K. 1988. *High Medieval Dream Vision.* Stanford, CA: Stanford University Press.

Marti, K. 1991. *Body, Heart, and Text in the Pearl-Poet.* Lewiston/Queenston/Lampeter: Edwin Mellen Press.

Muscatine, C. 1972. *Poetry and Crisis in the Age of Chaucer.* Notre Dame: University of Notre Dame Press.

Nardo, A. 1985. "'Here's to Thy Health': The Pearl in Hamlet's Wine." *English Language Notes* 2: 34–36.

Nolan, B. 1977. *Gothic Visionary Perspective.* Princeton, NJ: Princeton University Press.

Ogden, M. 1971. *The Cyrurgie of Guy de Chauliac, 1.* New York, NY: Oxford University Press.

Olson, G. 1982. *Literature as Recreation in the Later Middle Ages.* Ithaca, NY: Cornell University Press.

Stanbury, S. 2001. "Introduction to *Pearl.*" *TEAMS, Consortium for the Teaching of the Middle Ages.* Accessed June 9, 2019. https://d.lib.rochester.edu/teams/text/stanbury-pearl-introduction.

Stern, M. R. 1970. "An Approach to the *Pearl.*" In *The Middle English Pearl Critical Essays*, edited by J. Conley, 73–85. Notre Dame: University of Notre Dame Press.

Templin, C., J. Hänggi, C. Klein, M. S. Topka, T. Hiestand, R. A. Levinson, S. Jurisic, T. F. Lüscher, J. R. Ghadri, and L. Jäncke. 2019. "Altered Limbic and Autonomic Processing Supports Brain-Heart Axis in Takotsubo Syndrome." *European Heart Journal*: ehz068. https://doi.org/10.1093/eurheartj/ehz068.

Toohey, P. 1992. "Love, Lovesickness, and Melancholia." *Illinois Classical Studies* 17 (2): 265–286. http://hdl.handle.net/2142/12941.

3 *Giambattista Vico and the Melancholy of History*

Miriam Muccione
University of Chicago

The present chapter aims to reconstruct the role of melancholy in the work of the 18th century Neapolitan philosopher Giambattista Vico (1668–1744), the *New Science* (1725, 1730, 1744 [1984]), in the context of what Vico calls the *ideal eternal history*, the path of development common to all nations, melancholy emerges as the physical, emotional, and human mental responses that accompany the interventions of divine providence on the course of human civil life.

In his treatise dedicated to the health of the intellectual, *Three books on life* [*De vita libri tres or De triplici vita*] (1989), written between 1480 and 1489, the Neoplatonic philosopher, physician, and one of the most influential Renaissance interpreters of ancient medicine, Marsilio Ficino (1433–1499) refers to the link between melancholy and the intellectual achievements proposed by the Aristotelian tradition. Through a philosophical syncretism of Platonic metaphysics, Galenic medicine, magic, and astrology, Ficino supports the theory of the productive influence of the planet Saturn, associated with melancholy, on contemplative life. According to Ficino, all intellectuals are melancholy and, yet, only the very few who manage to reduce the paralyzing excesses of black bile, by keeping it at its natural temperature, can benefit from its positive influence on the contemplative life. As an intellectual, Ficino himself dealt with the unbalances of melancholy, a life mark that he traces back to his day of birth under the astrological influence of the planet Saturn. Through hygienic practices and attention to food, however, the propensity to negative melancholy, the one that leads to excesses of terror, paralysis, and madness, can be tempered and directed towards the zeal of intellectual work, hence, to reinvigorating the mind of the genius.[1]

The myth of the melancholic genius would consolidate throughout the centuries, representing, in particular, the spirit of Romanticism. An exception, instead, during the Enlightenment, the Neapolitan philosopher Giambattista Vico still showed full admiration for Ficino's reinterpretation of ancient medicine, which, according to him, had produced a school of great doctors, extinct by Vico's time. Vico refers to Ficino's medical tradition and, in particular, to his interpretation of the link between melancholy and philosophical greatness.

Like Ficino, Vico presents himself as a melancholy philosopher, from the first lines of his autobiography, *The Life of Giambattista Vico Written by Himself* (1728, 1731 [1944]), where he offers the genealogy of his melancholic predisposition. Both his father, who was of a *cheerful disposition*, and his mother, who was of a *very melancholy temper*, contributed to the development of his young personality, which was of *high spirits and impatient of rest* until a fall from a ladder at the age of seven bent his outwarded tendencies towards philosophical reflection. Contrary to the doctor's opinion, who predicted the child was either going to die or survive with intellectual deficiencies, Vico claims that after the fall he developed "a melancholy and irritable temperament such as belongs to men of ingenuity and depth," being ingenuity a form of intellectual sharpness that allows perceiving connection in things apparently unrelated to each other (1944, 111).

As the autobiography begins with Vico's melancholic premises, so his major philosophical work, the *New Science*, which aims to reconstruct the mythical beginnings of the human mind and civil institutions, begins under the influence of Saturn. The third and last edition of the *New Science* (1984), published in 1744, opens with an image, a frontispiece that functions both as a mnemonic map and pictorial synthesis of the work as a whole. In introducing the image, Vico compares it to the *Tablet of Cebes*, a painting discussed in the homonym moral treatise that stages the dialogue between a group of pilgrims who enter the temple of Saturn and ask an elderly man to explain the meaning of the image to them. The painting portrays the spiraled path that leads human beings to happiness and which only a very few can reach, whereas many stop before due to the moral obstacles they find on the way.[2] The tablet in the temple of Saturn signifies the temporal nature of human life, whose melancholic features lie in the fact that only a few can achieve happiness as time unravels under their feet. Thus, by claiming that "As Cebes the Theban made a table of things moral, we here offer one of things civil" (1984, 3), Vico intends to rescue the historical modifications of civil life from the erosive action of time and subsequent sink into oblivion.

Because no historiography exists from this remote stage of human history, Vico bases his theory on the testimonies of ancient fables and myths, which he interprets as *true and trustworthy histories*, and designates poets as the first real historians of humankind. Thanks to fables and myths, Vico can reconstruct the universal laws underlying human history. He defines his new historical science as *new critical art*, which combines the philological study of the *certum*, of human creations and volitions, with the study of the *verum*, of the universal and eternal laws of development. Through a philological and comparative study of ancient stories, when uniform features arise from different nations that were not in contact with one another, then the philosophical historian can elevate this pattern to the level of universal laws, which partake in the *ideal eternal history* common to all nations. Vico adopts ancient Egyptians' cyclical view of history and divides his ideal eternal history in a recursive cycle of three subsequent ages: the age of the gods, the age of the heroes, and the age of men. In all three, political creations and intellectual achievements mark the signs of progress and relapses of humankind, the study of which allow him to reconstruct the life course of birth, maturity, corruption, decadence, and death of a given civilization.

The epistemological value of human volitions and creations emerges in Vico's theoretical manifesto *On the Most Ancient Wisdom of the Italians* (1710 [2010]), in which he opposes to the Cartesian *cogito ergo sum* the principle of the *verum ipsum factum*, the true is the made. Through this principle, Vico contests the French rationalist philosopher's anti-skeptic value of the idea that man can doubt everything except the fact that he thinks, which, in turn, would prove the knowledge of one's existence. Counter to Descartes, Vico argues that the fact that man is conscious of thinking does not prove that he knows of it. Knowing something, in Vico's terms, means to be able to recollect the causes and conditions under which it first emerged. Since men are not conscious of the causes and modality of their thoughts, they do not know thought; hence, on the base of their thoughts, they cannot be sure of their existence. In Vico's theory of knowledge, the only way to refute skepticism is by claiming that "the criterion of the true should be to have made the thing itself." (2010, 56) As the one who begot the natural world and, with it, the human mind and body, only God has inner knowledge of human thinking and existence. Following the same principle, the privileged realm of human knowledge is that of history and human creations, what has been *done* as well as *made* over time. Vico's *scienza nuova* is, therefore, a philosophy of history as well as the rehabilitation of historical knowledge as the intellectual struggle to save the beginning of the most outstanding human creations that is civic life, as life with others, from oblivion.

In Vico's reconstruction of the course of human sociability, "the order of ideas must follow the order of institutions" (1984, 239), which means that the rise of new social structures generates in men the necessity of forming a new intellectual representation or adjusting old ones. By reconstructing the order in which human civil institutions appear in the ancient fables, Vico can track the transformations of the human mind. From the state of nature to the age of popular commonwealths, the order in which civil institutions appear in ancient narratives unravels as follows: "First the forest, after the huts, then the villages, next the cities, and finally the academies." (1984, 240) In the same way in which the establishment of new political institutions, such as the village, the city or universities, transforms the civil order, so at the level of the history of the mind, new faculties emerge corresponding to each new stage of civil life: "Men at first feel without perceiving, then they perceive with a troubled and agitated spirit, finally they reflect with a clear mind." (1984, 218) At the level of the mind, people first feel through their senses, then they confusedly apprehend through imagination, and finally, they reach a rational form of understanding. In this genealogical perspective, clear ideas are a later achievement of the human mind, whereas the very first epistemological medium between the individual and the world lies in the body, in which, during the state of nature, the mind is completely absorbed.

In this process, human civil advancement is the sum of two wills, of the particular one of human will and the universal one of God, which operates on the natural world through providential interventions. In opposition to the stoic belief in fate and epicurean emphasis on chance—the first having a deterministic view of human history and the second enslaving men to their passions—Vico states the influence of divine guidance on human affairs, which is providence, divine law in nature. In Vico, providence has the educational purpose of introducing limits of sorts to human volition, with the scope of moderating excessive passions and gradually transforming them into virtues. At each stage of development, providence intervenes by disrupting the status quo. The perturbing consequences of divine action on the human world generate melancholic responses of enduring fear and terror in the individuals, who feel themselves and their institutions at risk. Nevertheless, because providence applies regulative restrictions to the specific social structures and mental representations typical of a certain age, in turn, the melancholic responses of the individuals reflect the order of things and order of ideas predominant at each stage. In this regard, Vico not only provides an account of the unsettling effects of time and history on the human mind, but he also offers a genealogical account of melancholy itself, starting with its primeval manifestations, which marked the passage from the state of nature to the formation of early communities.

In his work *Beginnings* (1975), Edward Said, author of *Orientalism* (1978), defines Vico the first *philosopher of beginnings*, as opposed to *origin*. As Said points out, rather than subsuming the plurality of historical manifestations under a single linear path and a common point of origin, Vico defines the movement of history in terms of the coexistence of a plurality of adjacent trajectories, arising independently from one another, advancing next to each other, hence, converging and diverging with the mobility of a complex organism. In this respect, Vico is among the first philosophers who supported the idea that each community owns its narrative, which is built on the creation of its mythical beginning. In reconstructing the mythical beginning of Ancient Western civilizations, Vico starts by dividing the course of history into two parallel trajectories and narrative threads, that of the Hebrews and that of the gentiles, whose divergent paths are exemplified, first and foremost, by the *physical histories* of their bodies:

> The entire original human race was divided into two species: the one of giants, the other of men of normal stature; the former gentiles, the latter Hebrews. Also … this difference can only have come about as the result of the savage education of the former and the human education of the latter. Hence that the Hebrews had a different origin from that of the gentiles. (1984, 172)

What differentiates the Hebrews from the gentiles, inscribed here in the history of their bodies, lies in their understanding of the nature of God. While the Hebrews received revelation directly from God and truthfully represented his being as pure intelligence, the religion of the gentiles is false, as they attributed first natural, then, human features to the divine. Besides, because through the direct revelation of the true God, the Hebrews were gifted with the knowledge of the eternal laws of sociability, their civilization is not subjected to historical modifications but rather is built upon the truthfulness of their traditions. The gentiles, who refused the laws of the true God, are thrown into the melancholic course of time and history, a process of tangential approximation to the truth.

The history of the gentiles begins as a distancing from the Hebrew tradition as it is the outcome of a rebellion, when three children of the Hebrew patriarch Noah refused their father's religion and, one after another, left their family and wandered alone across the four corners of the untamed forest that was the earth. By rebelling, the sons of Noah went from the state of civilization back to the state of nature and regressed to a bestial condition. Back into the forest, they gradually lost all sense of belonging to their customs and started to mate with wild women outside the institution of marriage. The mothers abandoned the children born from these encounters on the ground, and, when the natural event of the universal flood occurred, the water transported them to different parts of the world, where their bodies, nourished by the soil, which was abundant in minerals and nutrients, grew bigger and bigger. In Vico's mythical reconstruction of the history of the gentile nations, the first offspring of the gentiles were, therefore, giants, proto-human creatures, *sons of the earth*, whose selves coincided entirely with their physical existence. As colossal sequoias, the giants were independent of one another, did not speak, were only driven by physical needs and individual biological survival; they did not build civilizations, create art, nor any other form of human endeavor. Such was the wild mythical state of the gentile nations, which preceded any form of social and political life. The *New Science* examines the *physical histories* of the gentile nations in order to reconstruct the genealogy of the becoming human of the giants.

In opposition to social contract theorists, such as Grotius and Hobbes, Vico supports the idea that natural laws fail to explain the process of collective departure of early societies from the state of nature. Rather than being a progressive, natural process, in Vico's understanding of human nature, something extreme had to occur for the giants to awake from the primeval torpor of their wild, self-absorbed, solitary life, a crisis, so to speak, that propelled the necessity of gathering in communities and launched the process of civilization of the gentiles:

> It was necessary that just so much time should pass before the earth, having at last dried off from the wetness of the universal flood, could send off dry exhalations of the sort wherein lightning could be generated, which stunned and terrified men into abandoning them to the false religions of so many Joves. (1984, IX, 38)

It took hundreds of years for the earth to dry after the universal flood and to create the physical condition for the air to produce flashes of lightning. Only when the first thunderstorm with the first lightening occurred, the giants started to sense the presence of the sky, the existence of something above more powerful than themselves.[3] As they felt terror, their body started to shrink to average human dimensions, they felt the need to find shelter and gather with others, and create the basic form of community around their first false religions, in which the gods, whose father was Jove, were inhabiting the earth with men:

> A few giants, who must have been the most robust, and who were dispersed through the forests on the mountain heights where the strongest beasts have their dens, were frightened and astonished by the great effect whose cause they did not know, and raised their eyes and *became aware of the sky*. And because in such a case … the nature of the human mind leads it to attribute its own nature to the effect, and because in that state their nature was that of men all robust

> bodily strength, who expressed their very violent passions by shouting and grumbling, they pictured the sky to themselves as a great animated body, which in that aspect they called Jove, the first god of the so-called *gentes maiores,* who by the whistling of his bolts and the noise of his thunder was attempting to tell them something. (1984, 377)

With the first lighting, the ahistorical existence of the giants blended into the age of the gods, the first age of human civil institutions, resulting from the terror of the representation of superior authority (*timor dei*), false divinities in the shape of the revengeful Jove and his Olympus of gods: "It was … this fear of gods and of fathers—in both cases a fear we shall find amounting to terror in the earliest times—that the giants diminished to our normal stature." (1984, 371) The dryness of the sky, as opposed to the moisture of the soil, the frightful spectacle of the first thunder, marked the melancholic passage from life in the wilderness to that of the first societies, enabled by a change in the physical status, in both the sky and the body of the giants. This is a form of physical melancholy which propelled the first significant transformation in the course of human mind.

As Klibansky, Panofsky, and Saxl explain in their study on *Saturn and Melancholy* (1964, 32), Ficino represents the melancholic individual as continually juggling between two potential excesses, walking "a narrow path between two abysses of melancholy sickness, on the one hand that of depression and terror, and that of recklessness, on the other." Likewise, in Vico's *New Science*, the first occurrence of melancholy presents itself in the form of a metaphysical terror, provoked by the dryness of the atmosphere and absorbed by the body of the giants, which provoked the physical shortening of their colossal height to average human dimensions, a process that accompanied the creation of the first form of civil institution which is that of the family. In this context, the first thunderstorm is a providential intervention on the giants' unsocial existence, which "by awaking in them a confused idea of divinity" helped "stupid, insensate and horrible beasts" of the first humanity to exit the solitary state of nature and constitute early societies: "Thus through the terror of this imagined divinity, they began to put themselves in some order." (1984, 178) The setting in motion of some civil order is the positive outcome of such a physical form of melancholy, result of the providential action that modified the body of the giants.

After the terror that accompanied the first thunderstorm triggered the imagination of the many Joves, these first people extended divine features to other phenomena, which led to the progressive creations of twelve gods, "the ideas of whom were imagined by them from time to time on certain occasions of human necessity or utility." (1984, 392) With the thunderlight and the poetic creation of the twelve profane divinities, the state of nature of the giants gradually merged with the age of the gods, in which "Heaven began to reign on earth and to bestow great benefits on men." (1984, 399) Contrary to any form of idealization of antiquity, Vico shows that in these ancient societies, during the age of the gods, men still prove to be cruel and barbaric, along with their political institutions. Far from generating a humane order, which, in the third age, the age of men, will be based on civil equality, in these first societies a social split occurred based on the false sense of physical superiority held by some, which, in the world of the giants, had legitimized the political authority of the strong over the weak:

> Of the giants there were in turn two kinds: the first, the sons of Earth, or nobles, from whom, as being giants in the full sense of the term, the age of giants took its name, as we have said (and it is these whom sacred history defines as 'strong, famous and powerful men of the age'); the second, less properly so called, those other giants who were subjugated [by the former]. (1984, 372)

The first giants, who claimed to be saved by Jove, called themselves *sons of Jove*, claimed possession over the land where they settled, and gradually constituted an aristocratic order of the first fathers of the families. As the *physical histories* of the giants mark the formation of families in the terror of false divinities, the fables of the gods' age reflect the birth a of such political order, in which the fathers of the families—by imagining themselves as sons of Jove and holding privileges of marriage, religion, and propriety—protect their aristocratic order in opposition to the *famuli*, servants of the families who did not have civil rights and cultivated the land in exchange for the heroes' protection. The division of status between the fathers and the *famuli* defines the social structure of the gods' age, which corresponds to the beginning of agriculture or, in other words, of rural economy and trade. The myths of this age, narrated by the fathers, reflect the fear of losing their new aristocratic order at the hands of the servants.

Among the gods of this first age, Saturn plays a vital role as he represents the passage from the ahistorical life of the state of nature to history, marked by the beginning of agriculture and the calculation of time. In line with Renaissance interpretations, in the *New Science*, Saturn is both Chronos, the god of time, and Kronos, the god of sown fields.[4] In this regard, Saturn is the god of the beginning of history as he is the beginning of chronology, for each harvest cycle corresponded to one year. Vico postulates that in the Italian region of Latium, where early Romans settled, the Greek Chronos became Saturn from *sati*, which meant *fields*. Ancient poets, historians of early societies, referred to the age of Saturn as the *age of gold*, from the color of wheat, the first form of currency in goods exchange.

In such a political context, Vico tells the reader that the fears of the fathers come to a full poetical representation in the fable of Saturn attempting to devour his child Jove, saved by the priests of Cybele, who conceal his cry by clashing their weapons. In this poetic story, the character of Saturn represents the collectivity of the servants, while the child Jove personifies the new civil order of the fathers, who used their religious privileges to quell the rebellion of the servants, who began to demand equal civil rights. It is also out of fear of political subversion, of a plebeian takeover, that the fathers offered human sacrifices to Saturn, *Saturni hostiae*, Saturn's victims, to placate the god's voracity. In his commentaries on the practice of sacrifices, Vico pushes his contemporary readers to read such a horrific set of rituals as the products of false beliefs, which assigned frightful human qualities to the gods, so that the primeval fear of the sky gradually merged with the fear of enemies. In addition, Vico states that those terrible practices, as cruel as they were, "derive from the counsel of divine providence. For all this was necessary to tame the cyclopes' sons and reduce them to the humanity of an Aristides, a Socrates, a Laelius, and a Scipio Africanus," who are all examples of human virtues after the barbarism of the first ages (1984, 191). Consequently, because "fear first created gods in the world," Saturn and his victims embody the fear of the subversion of the political order by the collective body of the plebs (1984, 191). In his analysis of the role of the plebs in the *New Science*, in *The Plebian Experience* Breaugh pinpoints the essential transformative role of the *famuli* as follows:

> The plebs are collectively the actor ensuring change within human communities. Whenever the established order was altered, there are signs of plebeian action, as evidenced by the passage out of the age of the gods thanks to the impetus of the famuli's opposition to the order of the fathers. (2013, 65)

Indeed, it is thanks to the servants' destabilizing actions that the Roman aristocracy of the fathers/heroes, who believed to be superior in nature to the *famuli*, progressively opened up to popular representation and the popular commonwealth of the age of men built on civil equality—on the base of reason, as the faculty common to all men.

Similar to the transition from the state of nature to the gods' age, the process of political transformation that from the heroes' ages leads to the men's age is accompanied by fear and terror of destruction of the status quo. In Vico's interpretation of the characteristic features of humanity, he states that "the human mind is naturally impelled to take delight in uniformity," from which the intolerance of the unfamiliar derives: "It is another property of the human mind that whenever men can form no idea of distant and unknown things, they judge them by what is familiar and at hand." (1984,

122) Providence pushes men to ameliorate themselves by breaking with expectations. In this regard, it generates fear and terror in the human mind, which seeks uniformity and continuity, and spawns the human melancholic condition engrained in the transformative action of Chronos/time on human affairs. Going back to Vico's autobiographical account on the fall from the ladder, the doctor's incorrect predictions not only seem to advance a criticism towards the medical methodology of his own time, but also pinpoints to the general human tendency to seeking for uniformity in the various events of life. For Vico, human beings face the possibility of error every time they attempt to anticipate the outcomes of a given phenomenon based on uniformity in the natural world.

On the contrary, the *New Science* is the project of discovering the universal laws common to all nations, by assuming the influence of some higher intelligence, such as providence, in the natural domain, which, in turn, guides humans throughout the making of their civil world. If at the personal level, providence shapes Vico's predisposition towards the acute ingenuity proper to the melancholic, brilliant intellectual, at the collective level, it generates conditions for the gentile nations to outrun their barbaric beginnings and form human commonwealths. Nevertheless, how providence operates on the constitution of human communities generates terror in those who are not in the know of the cycle of history. Therefore, in order "To be useful to the human race the philosopher, just like providence, must raise and direct weak and fallen man, not rend his nature or abandon him in his corruption." (1984, V)

Because history is cyclical for Vico, all civilizations are subject to relapses and possible returns to barbarism. Far from being an indefinite form of progressive improvement, after the peak of the age of men and popular commonwealths, human history outlines a process of decay to a different form of barbarism, which brings the cycle of civilization to an end. Just like in the individual, in which the highest point of maturity leads to the conclusive chapters of one's own life, so do the cultural and political climax of a civilization start a new process of moral digression: "Men first feel necessity, then look for utility, next attend to comfort, still later amuse themselves with pleasure, thence grow dissolute in luxury, and finally go mad and waste their substance." (1984, 241) The return to barbarism, at the end of the age of men, is a *barbarism of reflection*, a corruption of the mind marked by a different melancholic state. Contrarily to the first barbarism, marked by fear and terror, the barbarism of reflection is instead a collective malady of rationality, in which humans are disconnected from concrete matters, and occupy themselves with completely abstract thinking and ruminations, such as the study of pure metaphysics or algebra or through luxury and excessive wealth, so much so that "they become overfine for life in their way of thinking and are rendered incapable of any great work" (1984, 59), hence, of any great achievement.[5] In axiom 243 of the *New Science*, which includes the return to a second barbarism, Vico describes the course of history as follows:

> In the human race first appear the huge and grotesque, like the cyclopes; the proud and magnanimous, like Achilles; then the valorous and just, like Aristides and Scipio Africanus; nearer to us, imposing figures with great semblances of virtue accompanied by great vices, who among the vulgar win a name for true glory, like Alexander and Caesar; still later, the melancholy and reflective, like Tiberius; finally the dissolute and shameless madmen, like Caligula, Nero, and Domitian. (1984, 243)

In the *New Science*, human societies are always walking the narrow path between the two abysses of obtuseness, as in the case of the giants in the state of nature, and madness of abstraction, shown as a violent disconnection of tyrants from the life of the political body. Even in this last case, where melancholy seems to conform more to the negative side of Saturn's influence on the mind, the metaphysical overview that Vico sustains in his work suggests that just when pure abstraction and selfish fantasies crush the life of the civilized world, providence intervenes to make humanity reconnect to their physical existence.

The barbarism of reflection, which precedes the death of an entire civilization and is accompanied by ferocious fear of the upcoming ending, still leads to a transcendent positivity. Only the melancholic philosophers, those who "take no pleasure in verbal cleverness or falsehood," venture to look in the terrific, saturnine duplicity of this process (1944, 111). Indeed, Vico contemplates the history and "never smiles," as there is no utopia in his understanding of the cyclical path of human history (Croce 1913, 257). As Verene points out, "with his melancholic temperament, Vico is a child of Saturn, destined to have a sense of rise and fall, of beginning and end." (2013, 237) History itself, with its ups and downs, unravels within the temple of Saturn, outlining the unsettling, melancholic course of human civil life.

Notes

1. In her work on *The Nature of Melancholy* (2002, 87–88), Radden emphasizes the autobiographical motives of Ficino's study of melancholy, tied to the production of great intellectual works, arises as the "compensating, positive outcome" of melancholic predisposition, a positive side of melancholy which, linked to notion of "genius," has been repeatedly reconsidered throughout the centuries.

2. Concerning the explanation of the *Tablet of Cebes*, see Verene's *Vico's "New Science": A Philosophical Commentary* (2016, 35).
3. On the relationship between melancholy and dryness, see Ficino (1989, 115): "The human cause, that which comes from ourselves, is as follows: Because frequent agitation of the mind greatly dries up the brain, therefore, when the moisture has been mostly consumed—moisture being the support of the natural heat—the heat also is usually extinguished; and from this chain of events, the nature of the brain becomes dry and cold, which is known as the earthy and melancholic quality."
4. For a comprehensive analysis of the question regarding the homophony between Chronos, the god of time, and Kronos, the god protector of agriculture, see Navet's essay "Le dieu saturne dans la «scienza nuova»." (2005, 37)
5. Ficino says (1989, 115): "But of all learned people, those especially are oppressed by black bile, who, being sedulously devoted to the study of philosophy, recall their mind from the body and corporeal things and apply it to incorporeal things. The cause is, first, that the more difficult the work, the greater concentration of mind it requires; and second, that the more they apply their mind to incorporeal truth, the more they are compelled to disjoin it from the body. Hence their body is often rendered as if it were half-alive and often melancholic."

References

Breaugh, M. 2013. *The Plebeian Experience: A Discontinuous History of Political Freedom.* New York, NY: Columbia University Press.

Burton, R., T. C. Faulkner, N. K. Kiessling, and R. L. Blair. 1989. *The Anatomy of Melancholy.* Oxford: Clarendon Press.

Croce, B., and R. G. Collingwood. 1913. *The Philosophy of Giambattista Vico.* New York, NY: Macmillan Co.

Ficino, M. 1989. *Three Books on Life.* Binghamton, NY: MRTS.

Grassi, E., and M. D. P. Lorch. 1986. *Folly and Insanity in Renaissance Literature.* Binghamton, NY: MRTS.

Jackson, S. W. 1986. *Melancholia and Depression: From Hippocratic Times to Modern Times.* New Haven, CT: Yale University Press.

Klibansky, R., E. Panofsky, and F. Saxl. 1964. *Saturn and Melancholy: Studies in the History of Natural Philosophy, Religion, and Art.* New York, NY: Basic Books.

Mazzotta, G. 2014. *The New Map of the World: The Poetic Philosophy of Giambattista Vico.* Princeton, NJ: Princeton University Press.

Middeke, M., and C. Wald. 2011. *The Literature of Melancholia: Early Modern to Postmodern.* New York, NY: Palgrave Macmillan.

Navet, G. 2005. "Le dieu saturne dans la «scienza nuova»." *Revue des études italiennes* 51 (1–2): 35–43.

Radden, J. 2000. *The Nature of Melancholy: From Aristotle to Kristeva.* New York, NY: Oxford University Press.

Ripa, C., and E. A. Maser. 1971. *Baroque and Rococo Pictorial Imagery. The 1758–60 Hertel Edition of Ripa's "Iconologia."* New York, NY: Dover Publications.

Sfez, G. 1995. “Machiavel: la raison des humeurs.” *Rue Descartes* 12 (13): 11–37.

Verene, D. P. 2013. “Giambattista Vico’s New Science of the Common Nature of the Nations.” In *A Companion to Enlightenment Historiography*, edited by R. A. Sparling, 217–246. Boston, MA: Brill.

Verene, D. P. 2016. *Vico’s “New Science”: A Philosophical Commentary*. Ithaca, NY: Cornell University Press.

Vico, G. 1944. *The Autobiography of Giambattista Vico*. Ithaca, NY: Cornell University Press.

Vico, G. 1984. *The New Science of Giambattista Vico*. Ithaca, NY: Cornell University Press.

Vico, G. 2010. *On the Most Ancient Wisdom of the Italians: Drawn out from the Origins of the Latin Language*. New Haven, CT: Yale University Press.

4 *Depression in the Literature of the Health Reform and Mental Hygiene Movement: An Example of Ellen G. White Writings*

PAWEL ZAGOZDZON
Medical University of Gdansk, Poland

Introduction

Ellen Gould White (1827–1915) was a productive author and Christian pioneer. Along with other Sabbath-keeping Adventist leaders, like Joseph Bates and her husband, James White, they formed what is now known as the Seventh-day Adventist Church. The health principles from Ellen G. White's writings contributed to give rise to one of the most extended living people groups in the world—The Seventh-day Adventists. The health and longevity of the Adventists have attracted the interest of many public health specialists, who incidentally tend to focus more on the dietary and psychosocial determinants of the Adventist lifestyle.

The aim underlying this work is to present the phenomenon of depression as discussed in the works of Ellen G. White, as well as confront it with the current understanding of depression determinants, as seen in their medical context.

In the course of preparation of this chapter, a review of Ellen G. White's works through the Ellen G. White Estate Writings Application (EGW Writings App) was carried out. The EGW Writings App enables one to read, annotate, and theme-search all the published writings of Ellen G. White online. It is available in 55 languages, including Polish, and it contains 122 books, 168 pamphlets, and hundreds of letters and manuscripts. The term depression, as the application calculates, occurs in this collection 843 times.

Depression and Spirituality

Depression understood as a particular type of mood is discussed or alluded by Ellen G. White, mainly in connection with one's spiritual aptitude and its impact on one's ability to keep a close relationship with God. A lack of that relationship, incapability of finding a practical path of communicating with God, and a loss of faith are both causes and results of depression. Ellen G. White many a time refers to biblical characters struggling with adversities. The case of Jacob, who was forced to leave his home turf and run for safety fearing the vengeance of his wronged brother Esau, is frequently mentioned by the author as an illustration of a state of those who are exposed to distress and loneliness due to their former mistakes, and hence are compelled to seek help with God:

> The second day of his journey is drawing to a close. He is weary, hungry, and homeless, and he feels that he is forsaken of God. He knows that he has brought this upon himself by his own wrong course. Dark clouds of despair enclose him, and he feels that he is an outcast. His heart is filled with a nameless terror, and he hardly dares to pray. But he is so utterly lonely that he feels the need of protection from God as he has never felt it before. He weeps and confesses his sin before God, and entreats for some evidence that He has not utterly forsaken him. But his burdened heart finds no relief. He has lost all confidence in himself, and he fears that the God of his fathers has cast him off. But God, the merciful God, pities the desolate, sorrow-stricken man, who gathers the stones for his pillow and has only the canopy of heaven for his covering. (White 1885, 465.1)

The overwhelming feeling of loss and loneliness is deepened by the sense of guilt resulting from his having cheated on the father, too. However, the burden of sin is somewhat alleviated as Jacob confesses his sin to God, who, in turn, assures him of His presence and mercy. Circumstances of this type, leading to a low or depressed mood, are a frequent theme of White's writings. Many studies on depression found a positive correlation between religiosity and distress, a correlation we can observe in studies of prayer and mental health, as well as studies linking emotional distress to an increased likelihood of a future religious conversion. Some authors address the possibility of reverse causation when examining the relationship between religious engagement and health outcomes (Maselko et al. 2012).

Depression and Physical Health

Depression is seen as not only associated with spirituality but also potent in influence on physical health. The book *Ministry of Healing* (White 1905, 241.1) contains a statement that could serve as a declaration of the fundamental principle of the Adventist health reform upholding a link between mental health and physical diseases:

> The relation that exists between the mind and the body is very intimate. When one is affected, the other sympathizes. The condition of the mind affects the health to a far greater degree than many realize. Many of the diseases from which men suffer are the result of mental depression. Grief, anxiety, discontent, remorse, guilt, distrust, all tend to break down the life forces and to invite decay and death. Disease is sometimes produced, and is often greatly aggravated, by the imagination. Many are lifelong invalids who might be well if they only thought so. Many imagine that every slight exposure will cause illness, and the evil effect is produced because it is expected. Many die from disease the cause of which is wholly imaginary. Courage, hope, faith, sympathy, love, promote health and prolong life. A contented mind, a cheerful spirit, is health to the body and strength to the soul. 'A merry [rejoicing] heart doeth good like a medicine.' Proverbs 17:22. In the treatment of the sick the effect of mental influence should not be overlooked. Rightly used, this influence affords one of the most effective agencies for combating disease.

Medicine, in its current state of development, is capable of specifying the channels through which depression influences one's physical health. In a bout of depression, the immune system falls short of effectiveness, inflammatory processes, as well as the level of cortisol, are enhanced, and metabolical changes leading to an elevated risk of diabetes and cardiovascular conditions occur (Penninx et al. 2013). Epidemiological studies provide clear evidence for higher mortality in individuals with contracted depression in comparison to the general population (Gilman et al. 2017). Psychologists in their attempts at specifying the interdependence of depression and reduced body's adaptive response have employed, among others, the concept of allostasis. Allostasis involves the physiological or mental balance of the body and acts on them via physiological or behavioral channels. Allostasis is a dynamic process that promotes and uses an adaptation of the organism to outward changes daily, and, in this way, prepares it to cope with significant changes and adversities as they come. We can understand depression as a result of stress overload, which affects the effectiveness of the allostatic response of the organism adversely. Religion, faith in God and His promises constitute ways in which one can cope with allostatic load. It is based on this model that a considerable number of research projects on the role of religiosity in upholding health are currently conducted (Lee et al. 2009). This defensive mechanism, as presented in the writings of Ellen G. White, is striking in its simplicity and naturalness: "A contented mind, a cheerful spirit, is health to the body and strength to the soul. Nothing is so fruitful a cause of disease as depression, gloominess, and sadness." (1868, 702.1)

Positive Mental Attitude as a Defense against Depression

The role of positive thinking and optimism in upholding good health seems obvious, and the physiological mechanisms connected with this process, based mostly on the immunological response, have been well addressed in the medical literature (Brydon et al. 2009). Optimism, as presented by Ellen G. White, is based on readiness to accept and enjoy the current situation in life. This attitude goes, however, far beyond the epicurean idea of satisfaction from the very fact of existing and giving up on the urge to change the things which one cannot influence. The Adventist author encourages us to embark on something more advanced: on determining to be grateful for all that one currently possesses. Should traces of dissatisfaction appear one must do everything to reject these thoughts, as the primary target for a Christian is to assert eternal life, and thus complaining does not go well together with his/her effort claim that ultimate objective:

> Nothing tends more to promote health of body and of soul than does a spirit of gratitude and praise. It is a positive duty to resist melancholy, discontented thoughts and feelings—as much a duty as it is to pray. If we are heaven-bound, how can we go as a band of mourners, groaning and complaining all along the way to our Father's house? (White 1905, 251.3)

Nutrition and Depression

What makes Ellen G. White's writings, however, particularly distinct from the ranks of all the 19th-century health reform literature is her constant emphasis on the significant role of eating and living habits in ensuring good health and good mood. Unique, when compared to other specimens, the then health writings are those statements in which she attracted the readers' attention to the detrimental impact of stimulants on the general state of health and an increase of depression risk. She suggested that coffee, tea as well as meat—through stimulating appetite—are likely to promote depression:

> Intemperance commences at our tables in the use of unhealthful food. After a time, through continued indulgence, the digestive organs become weakened, and the food taken does not satisfy the appetite. Unhealthy conditions are established, and there is a craving for more stimulating food. Tea, coffee, and flesh meats produce an immediate effect. Under the influence of these poisons the nervous system is excited, and, in some cases, for the time being, the intellect seems to be invigorated and the imagination to be more vivid. Because these stimulants produce for the time being such agreeable results, many conclude that they really need them and continue their use. But there is always a reaction. The nervous system, having been unduly excited, borrowed power for present

> use from its future resources of strength. All this temporary invigoration of the system is followed by depression. In proportion as these stimulants temporarily invigorate the system will be the letting down of the power of the excited organs after the stimulus has lost its force. The appetite is educated to crave something stronger which will have a tendency to keep up and increase the agreeable excitement, until indulgence becomes habit, and there is a continual craving for stronger stimulus, as tobacco, wines, and liquors. The more the appetite is indulged, the more frequent will be its demands and the more difficult of control. The more debilitated the system becomes and the less able to do without unnatural stimulus, the more the passion for these things increases, until the will is overborne, and there seems to be no power to deny the unnatural craving for these indulgences. (White 1875, 487.2)

The above quotation constitutes, as a matter of fact, a perfect illustration of the psychological system of positive reinforcement leading to the rise of behaviors linked with basic urges. Our current understanding of those phenomena confirms a connection between intemperate eating, alcohol drinking, and an increased risk of depression (Chua et al. 2019; Martino et al. 2019). Research also acknowledges the existence of the reward system as well as sexual urge and appetite stimulation, which occurs through fantasizing about or even looking at an object (Demos et al. 2012).

On the other hand, Ellen G. White (1905) kept emphasizing the significance of a meat-free diet for upholding one's health. She stated that grains, fruits, nuts, and vegetables constitute the diet chosen for us by our Creator. In recent years evidence to this end has been produced by randomized experimental research presenting positive results of diet change in the non-pharmaceutical treatment of depression (Opie et al. 2015; Jacka et al. 2017). The assertion of positive effects of a vegetarian diet has been confirmed by large-scale epidemiological research projects focusing on vegetarians with marked participation of the Seventh-day Adventist community, which proved decreased mortality in persons avoiding meat consumption (Orlich et al. 2013).

Physicians' Attitude towards Depression Care

Taking into account Ellen G. White's views on health and stimulants, the following pledge to doctors should not be surprising:

> When a physician sees a patient suffering from disease caused by improper eating and drinking or other wrong habits, yet neglects to tell him of this, he is doing his fellow being an injury. Drunkards, maniacs, those who are given over to licentiousness, all appeal to the physician to declare clearly and distinctly that suffering results from sin. Those who understand the principles of life should be in earnest

in striving to counteract the causes of disease. Seeing the continual conflict with pain, laboring constantly to alleviate suffering, how can the physician hold his peace? Is he benevolent and merciful if he does not teach strict temperance as a remedy for disease? (White 1905, 114.1)

Air Pollution and Depression

Another area of environmental impact on health, which occupies considerable space in the health precursors' works, is the theme of clean air. It is worthwhile to quote an extensive passage devoted solely to the importance of staying in well-ventilated spaces:

> Mental depression is terrible. You all suffer from it. The daughter is fretful, partaking of the spirit of the father; and then the heated, oppressed atmosphere, deprived of vitality, benumbs the sensitive brain. The lungs contract, the liver is inactive. Air, air, the precious boon of heaven which all may have, will bless you with its invigorating influence if you will not refuse it entrance. Welcome it, cultivate a love for it, and it will prove a precious soother of the nerves. Air must be in constant circulation to be kept pure. The influence of pure, fresh air is to cause the blood to circulate healthfully through the system. It refreshes the body and tends to render it strong and healthy, while at the same time its influence is decidedly felt upon the mind, imparting a degree of composure and serenity. It excites the appetite, and renders the digestion of food more perfect, and induces sound and sweet sleep. The effects produced by living in close, ill-ventilated rooms are these: The system becomes weak and unhealthy, the circulation is depressed, the blood moves sluggishly through the system because it is not purified and vitalized by the pure, invigorating air of heaven. The mind becomes depressed and gloomy, while the whole system is enervated; and fevers and other acute diseases are liable to be generated. Your careful exclusion of external air and fear of free ventilation leave you to breathe the corrupt, unwholesome air which is exhaled from the lungs of those staying in these rooms, and which is poisonous, unfit for the support of life. The body becomes relaxed, the skin becomes sallow, digestion is retarded, and the system is peculiarly sensitive to the influence of cold. A slight exposure produces serious diseases. Great care should be exercised not to sit in a draft or in a cold room when weary, or when in a perspiration. You should so accustom yourself to the air that you will not be under the necessity of having the mercury higher than sixty-five degrees. (White 1868, 702.1)

Clean air has very rarely been studied in the context of its potential impact on depression. Modern air pollution monitoring systems enable constant measurement of fine dust (fine particulate matter) and chemical substances concentration in the air. Owing to this it has been proved that poor quality air with high concentration rates of fine particulate matter (PM2.5 that is below two and one-half microns or less in width) increases the risk of cardiovascular diseases and general mortality (Scheers et al. 2015; Achilleos et al. 2017). It was quite a surprise when a connection between air quality and mental health in general, as well as the risk of depression and suicide rates, in particular, were observed (Gładka et al. 2018; Newbury et al. 2019). It seems that Ellen G. White was right also in this respect. It has turned out that nervous system disorders, including depression, may result from minor inflammation processes caused by breathing with contaminated air (Jayaraj et al. 2017).

Burnout Syndrome and Depression

In the writings of Ellen G. White, there is also a description of another potential cause for depression: overworking and fatigue. The problem of burnout and its potential connection with depression is currently perceived as significant risk factors for workers' health. Proper levels of rest and fatigue avoidance are crucial for better work efficiency and mental balance. How Ellen G. White describes the state of increased emotional tension accompanying fatigue and resulting in irritability is remarkable:

> You should labor with care and observe periods of rest. By so doing you will retain your physical and mental vigor, and render your labor much more efficient. Brother F, you are a nervous man and move much from impulse. Mental depression influences your labor very much. At times you feel a want of freedom and think it is because others are in darkness or wrong, or that something is the matter, you can hardly tell what, and you make a drive somewhere and upon somebody, which is liable to do great harm. If you would quiet yourself when in this restless, nervous condition, and rest and calmly wait on God and inquire if the trouble is not in yourself, you would save wounding your own soul and wounding the precious cause of God. (1868, 622.1)

Ellen G. White implies that overworking can be a cause of depressed mood, lack of efficiency, and an increasing lack of tolerance towards others. The appearance of cynical attitudes towards others as well as towards one's work value are typical syndromes of burnout and, as such was, in principle, included in the category of potential depression risk factors by Ellen G. White (Maslach et al. 1996). A lack of clear differentiation between the fatigue syndrome and depression, as well as problems in specifying the direction of a causative relationship/interdependence between these two sets of clinical symptoms can be generally observed in the research devoted to this field (Koutsimani et al. 2019). The course of changes taking place in one's attitude towards his/her professional duties under the pressure of fatigue is aptly described in the following address to a particular minister:

> The Lord would have you, my brother, reform in your method of labor, that you may have a well-balanced mind, a symmetrical character, and spiritual strength

> to counsel wisely. Men who have experience in the knowledge of the truth are too few for you to be sacrificed. You are almost constantly overtaxing both your physical and mental powers, because you allow yourself to feel too intensely. You have a vivid imagination, and put much intensity into your preaching, which keeps the mind on a constant strain, with the voice raised to a high pitch, and not only are you wearied, but the people are annoyed and their interest lessened. The reaction is sure to come; for you do not know how to let yourself down gradually from such a strain, and the poor mortal body feels the wear. A corresponding depression follows the high pressure. (White 1946, 658.6)

The author addresses the sequence of events in the cause-and-effect chain of action as she manifestly points to first an overload of work, then fatigue, and a decreased mental efficiency caused by keeping the brain for prolonged stint of time under overt pressure, which, in the end, leads to a lack of mental powers and a depression. In this context, the appeal that Ellen G. White makes towards the man sounds rational, even if it also contains a reference to God: "Labor Intelligently—Every worker should labor intelligently, with an eye single to the glory of God. He should take special care not to abuse any of his God-given faculties." (1946, 658.5) This call expresses another important principle pervading the works of the Adventist author: a particular respect for the body and its abilities (talents) which are not the property of a human, but his/her Creator.

Salvation and Depression

Trusting in God is an ever-present undergirding principle of Christian life, which should be in use, especially in times of dejection and depression. It is those who have a settled hierarchy of values and whose priority is to serve God, who find making use of the potential existing in religious faith the most straightforward task:

> 'The humble shall see this, and be glad: and your heart shall live that seek God' Psalm 69:32. It is your privilege to be glad in the Lord, and to rejoice in the knowledge of His sustaining grace. Let His love take possession of mind and heart. Guard against becoming overwearied, careworn, depressed. Bear an uplifting testimony. Turn your eyes away from that which is dark and discouraging, and behold Jesus, our great Leader, under whose watchful supervision the cause of present truth, to which we are giving our lives and our all, is destined to triumph gloriously. (White 1976, 159.2)

Experiencing adversities and obstacles in one's pursuit of life goals is usually a source of frustration and, thus, a potential stimulus of depression. A religious person's natural reaction is to ask a question of why events of this kind take place in a world created by a perfect and loving God. The answer to this question that Ellen G. White provides will not be seen as a novelty by a seasoned Christian. Facing adversities is an opportunity for one to turn to God. We generally seek God when the available assistance from individuals and institutions is not satisfactory or sufficient, and it seems clear that our situation will not be improved by human intervention. It is those who have been afflicted who are compelled to adjust to new unfitting circumstances. This change, however, is an opportunity for an individual to learn a new lesson—a lesson of reacting to new challenges—and thus to build openness to still further unexpected events. It is then through this experience that one generates an attitude of a mature understanding of his/her relationship with God. A Christian is a matter molded by events that are not necessarily a fulfillment of his/her desires and expectations. He/she learns to accept these events as he/she understands that they occur with the Creator's consent. This God is the one who created each individual, and the only solution for a Christian individual is to accept His will. This way of reasoning, however, paradoxically draws us nearer to God, as the only other way out is rebellion against God, which is no solution at all. This is how the Adventist author describes this process of alteration in a Christian under challenging circumstances:

> The Saviour's words have a message of comfort to those also who are suffering affliction or bereavement. Our sorrows do not spring out of the ground. God 'doth not afflict willingly nor grieve the children of men' Lamentations 3:33. When He permits trials and afflictions, it is 'for our profit, that we might be partakers of His holiness' Hebrews 12:10. If received in faith, the trial that seems so bitter and hard to bear will prove a blessing. The cruel blow that blights the joys of earth will be the means of turning our eyes to heaven. How many there are who would never have known Jesus had not sorrow led them to seek comfort in Him! The trials of life are God's workmen, to remove the impurities and roughness from our character. Their hewing, squaring, and chiseling, their burnishing and polishing, is a painful process; it is hard to be pressed down to the grinding wheel. But the stone is brought forth prepared to fill its place in the heavenly temple. Upon no useless material does the Master bestow such careful, thorough work. Only His precious stones are polished after the similitude of a palace. (White 1956, 10.2)

Behavioral Cognitive Therapy, Dreams, and Depression

Frequently, the reason why people are perplexed are their own mistakes. The advice to focus on the positive aspects of life constitutes an essential principle in cognitive behavioral therapy—a fundamental non-pharmaceutical therapy for depression. Among the gifts that the Adventist writer possessed was undoubtedly an ability to discern cognitive distortions in the thinking processes of her neighbors submerged in a depressive mood:

> Disappointed hopes have made you both completely wretched. You will have no reward for your suffering, for you have caused it yourselves. Your own words have been like deadly poison upon nerve and brain, upon bone and muscle. You reap that which you sow. You do not appreciate the feelings and sufferings of each other. God is displeased with the hard, unfeeling, world-loving spirit you possess. Brother C, the love of money is the root of all evil. You have loved money, loved the world; you have looked at the illness of your wife as a severe, a terrible, tax, not realizing that it is your fault in a great measure that she is sick. You have not the elements of a contented spirit. You dwell upon your troubles; imaginary want and poverty far ahead stare you in the face; you feel afflicted, distressed, agonized; your brain seems on fire, your spirits depressed. You do not cherish love to God and gratitude of heart for all the blessings which your kind heavenly Father has bestowed upon you. You see only the discomforts of life. A worldly insanity shuts you in like heavy clouds of thick darkness. Satan exults over you because you will have misery when peace and happiness are at your command. (White 1868, 696.2)

Extensive thinking about life failures is never bound to improve one's mood. When Ellen G. White wrote/spoke to people with depression she many a time uttered words of bitter truth and sometimes reproof, if seen as beneficial for an individual, yet she was also ever generous with words of comfort designed to do the ultimate task—lift the person's spirit to empower him/her to improve. According to her, many a time the wisdom needed to address a problem of a particular person as she was asked to give them advice, came not through an analytical process, but a night dream:

> Many, walking along the path of life, dwell upon their mistakes and failures and disappointments, and their hearts are filled with grief and discouragement. While I was in Europe, a sister who had been doing this, and who was in deep distress, wrote to me, asking for some word of encouragement. The night after I had read her letter I dreamed that I was in a garden, and one who seemed to be the owner of the garden was conducting me through its paths. I was gathering the flowers and enjoying their fragrance, when this sister, who had been walking by my side, called my attention to some unsightly briers that were impeding her way. There she was mourning and grieving. She was not walking in the pathway, following the guide, but was walking among the briers and thorns. 'Oh,' she mourned, 'is it not a pity that this beautiful garden is spoiled with thorns?' Then the guide said, 'Let the thorns alone, for they will only wound you. Gather the roses, the lilies, and the pinks.' (White 1921, 116.3)

This enigmatic and somewhat poetic description of the dream offers still a considerably clear set of symbolic imagery. The owner of the garden, who serves here as the tour-guide attracting the visitors' attention to its most beautiful areas, can be no other than Jesus.

Women and Depression

The place of women in society was, at that time, far from privileged. In this context, it is worth saying that Ellen G. White was a true pioneer not only, as I have already demonstrated, in her approach to health reform, but also in marking equality in her treatment of men and women. Several times she stood up for women who were particularly exposed to work overload and pleaded with men to treat their wives with respect and love:

> Infirmities and disease especially affect women. The happiness of the family depends much upon the wife and mother. If she is weak and nervous, and is suffered to be overtaxed with labor, the mind becomes depressed, for it sympathizes with the weariness of the body; and then she too often meets with cold reserve from the husband. If everything does not move off just as pleasantly as he could wish, he blames the wife and mother. He is almost wholly unacquainted with her cares and burdens, and does not always know how to sympathize with her. He does not realize that he is aiding the great enemy in his work of tearing down. He should by faith in God lift up a standard against Satan; but he seems blinded to his own interest and hers. He treats her with indifference. He knows not what he is doing. He is working directly against his own happiness and is destroying the happiness of his family. The wife becomes desponding and discouraged. Hope and cheerfulness are gone. She goes her daily rounds mechanically because she sees that her work must be done. Her lack of cheerfulness and courage is felt throughout the family circle. There are many such miserable families all through the ranks of Sabbathkeepers. Angels bear the shameful tidings to heaven, and the recording angel makes a record of it all. (White 1868, 306.1)

Estimates show that women suffer from depression twice as frequently as men. It is believed that the cause of this situation lies in the impact of estrogens—the *sex hormones* as well as in *gender-related environmental experiences*, which should be explained in the light of the socially determined position of women, position that has persevered right through to today (Kessler 2003).

Neurobiology and Depression

Comprehension of psycho-pathological phenomena in terms of brain activity surely was not a popular concept at the end of the 19th century. However, Ellen G. White refers to that. She describes the electrical activity of the brain as a power activating the entire body by providing it the right rhythm:

> The influence of the mind on the body, as well as of the body on the mind, should be emphasized. The electric power of the brain, promoted by mental activity, vitalizes the whole system, and is thus an invaluable aid in resisting disease. This should be made plain. The power of the will and the importance of

> self-control, both in the preservation and in the recovery of health, the depressing and even ruinous effect of anger, discontent, selfishness, or impurity, and, on the other hand, the marvelous life-giving power to be found in cheerfulness, unselfishness, gratitude, should also be shown. (White 1942, 197.2)

Ellen G. White does not, however, attribute causes of depression and other diseases to a malfunctioning brain—malfunctioning concerning its electrical activity. Human thought produces the electric power of the brain, and this is what exercises control over the mood and emotions. As a concept, it comes close to the view held by that part of psychiatry, which calls into question the so-called theory of brain chemical imbalance, according to which depression occurs whenever there is serotonin deficiency in the brain (Lacasse and Leo 2015). In principle, Ellen G. White never refers to depression as an identified, separate mental health disorder functioning in seclusion from one's somatic and spiritual state. The terms depression or mental depression always occur in the context of deep sadness and depressed mood or worsened mental health. In the current debate on depression, there is a tendency to withdraw from treating it as a medical condition with clear cut borders, or as homogenous symptomatology, and attempt at placing it in the broad continuum between fundamental sadness and serious mental syndrome/condition (Maj 2016). Ellen G. White's approach to depressive mood disorders inclines more to the sociological aspect of the condition rather than to its biomedical concept (Horwitz and Wakefield 2007).

Conclusions

Depression in the works of Ellen G. White is described not so much as a disease than as a particular state of mind, depressed mood, deep sadness, which influences the manner how an organism functions, as well as its effectiveness. In this outlook, depression is a state resulting from the impact of various factors and circumstances, including those not immediately apparent, for instance, lack of access to clean air. It results from decisions spanning virtually all aspects of life: diet, taking stimulants, committing immoral acts, *sinful behaviors*, spending time with the wrong company of people, overworking, and fatigue. Simultaneously, Ellen G. White points, indeed, in opposition to most if not all representatives of her era, to a strict connection between body and mind, holding that many diseases may be a result of depression-related conditions. According to her advice to those who suffer from depression and depression-related conditions, the best remedy for this state is a pursuit of hope in the gift presented to humanity by Jesus of Nazareth. Insistence on upholding one's faith in God's forgiveness, respect to one's body which belongs to God, and trust in a significant change of circumstances when Jesus returns to this earth, are all elements Ellen G. White perceives as crucial for recovering from as well as keeping away from all depression-related conditions.

References

Achilleos, S., M. A. Kioumourtzoglou, C. D. Wu, J. D. Schwartz, P. Koutrakis, and S. I. Papatheodorou. 2017. "Acute Effects of Fine Particulate Matter Constituents on Mortality: A Systematic Review and Meta-Regression Analysis." *Environment International* 109: 89–100. https://doi.org/10.1016/j.envint.2017.09.010.

Brydon, L., C. Walker, A. J. Wawrzyniak, H. Chart, and A. Steptoe. 2009. "Dispositional Optimism and Stress-Induced Changes in Immunity and Negative Mood." *Brain, Behavior, and Immunity* 23 (6): 810–816. https://doi.org/10.1016/j.bbi.2009.02.018.

Chua, Y. W., G. Lewis, A. Easter, G. Lewis, and F. Solmi. 2019. "Eighteen-Year Trajectories of Depressive Symptoms in Mothers with a Lifetime Eating Disorder: Findings from the ALSPAC Cohort." *British Journal of Psychiatry* 1–7. https://doi.org/10.1192/bjp.2019.89.

Demos, K. E., T. F. Heatherton, and W. M. Kelley. 2012. "Individual Differences in Nucleus Accumbens Activity to Food and Sexual Images Predict Weight Gain and Sexual Behavior." *Journal of Neuroscience* 32 (16): 5549–5552. https://doi.org/10.1523/jneurosci.5958-11.2012.

Gilman, S. E., E. Sucha, M. Kingsbury, N. J. Horton, J. M. Murphy, and I. Colman. 2017. "Depression and Mortality in a Longitudinal Study: 1952–2011." *Cmaj* 189 (42): E1304–E1310. https://doi.org/10.1503/cmaj.170125.

Gładka, A., J. Rymaszewska, and T. Zatoński. 2018. "Impact of Air Pollution on Depression and Suicide." *International Journal of Occupational Medicine and Environmental Health* 31 (6): 711–721. https://doi.org/10.13075/ijomeh.1896.01277.

Horwitz, A. V., and J. C. Wakefield. 2007. *The Loss of Sadness: How Psychiatry Transformed Normal Sorrow into Depressive Disorder.* New York, NY: Oxford University Press.

Jacka, F. N., A. O'Neil, R. Opie, C. Itsiopoulos, S. Cotton, M. Mohebbi, D. Castle, S. Dash, C. Mihalopoulos, M. L. Chatterton, L. Brazionis, O. M. Dean, A. M. Hodge, and M. Berk. 2017. "A Randomised Controlled Trial of Dietary Improvement for Adults with Major Depression (The 'SMILES' Trial)." *BMC Medicine* 15 (1): 23. https://doi.org/10.1186/s12916-017-0791-y.

Jayaraj, R. L., E. A. Rodriguez, Y. Wang, and M. L. Block. 2017. "Outdoor Ambient Air Pollution and Neurodegenerative Diseases: The Neuroinflammation Hypothesis." *Current Environmental Health Report* 4 (2): 166–179. https://doi.org/10.1007/s40572-017-0142-3.

Kessler, R. C. 2003. "Epidemiology of Women and Depression." *Journal of Affective Disorders* 74 (1): 5–13.

Koutsimani, P., A. Montgomery, and K. Georganta. 2019. "The Relationship between Burnout, Depression, and Anxiety: A Systematic Review and Meta-Analysis." *Frontiers in Psychology* 10: 284. https://doi.org/10.3389/fpsyg.2019.00284.

Lacasse, J. R., and J. Leo. 2015. "Antidepressants and the Chemical Imbalance Theory of Depression: A Reflection and Update on the Discourse." *The Behavior Therapist* 38 (7): 206–213.

Lee, J. W., K. R. Morton, J. Walters, D. L. Bellinger, T. L. Butler, C. Wilson, E. Walsh, C. G. Ellison, M. M. McKenzie, and G. E. Fraser. 2009. "Cohort Profile: The Biopsychosocial Religion and Health Study (BRHS)." *International Journal of Epidemiology* 38 (6): 1470–1478. https://doi.org/10.1093/ije/dyn244.

Maj, M. 2016. "The Continuum of Depressive States in the Population and the Differential Diagnosis between 'Normal' Sadness and Clinical Depression." In *Sadness or Depression?*, edited by J. C. Wakefield and S. Demazeux, 29–38. Dordrecht: Springer.

Martino, F., G. Caselli, E. Fiabane, F. Felicetti, C. Trevisani, M. Menchetti, C. Mezzaluna, S. Sassaroli, I. P. Albery, and M. M. Spada. 2019. "Desire Thinking as a Predictor of Drinking Status Following Treatment for Alcohol Use Disorder: A Prospective Study." *Addictive Behaviors* 95: 70–76. https://doi.org/10.1016/j.addbeh.2019.03.004.

Maselko, J., R. D. Hayward, A. Hanlon, S. Buka, and K. Meador. 2012. "Religious Service Attendance and Major Depression: A Case of Reverse Causality?" *American Journal of Epidemiology* 175 (6): 576–583. https://doi.org/10.1093/aje/kwr349.

Maslach, C., S. E. Jackson, and M. P. Leiter. 1996. *Maslach Burnout Inventory*. Palo Alto, CA: Consulting Psychologists Press.

Newbury, J. B., L. Arseneault, S. Beevers, N. Kitwiroon, S. Roberts, C. M. Pariante, F. J. Kelly, and H. L. Fisher. 2019. "Association of Air Pollution Exposure with Psychotic Experiences during Adolescence." *JAMA Psychiatry*. https://doi.org/10.1001/jamapsychiatry.2019.0056.

Opie, R. S., A. O'Neil, C. Itsiopoulos, and F. N. Jacka. 2015. "The Impact of Whole-of-Diet Interventions on Depression and Anxiety: A Systematic Review of Randomised Controlled Trials." *Public Health Nutrition* 18 (11): 2074–2093. https://doi.org/10.1017/s1368980014002614.

Orlich, M. J., P. N. Singh, J. Sabaté, K. Jaceldo-Siegl, J. Fan, S. Knutsen, W. L. Beeson, and G. E. Fraser. 2013. "Vegetarian Dietary Patterns and Mortality in Adventist Health Study 2." *Jama Internal Medicine* 173 (13): 1230–1238. https://doi.org/10.1001/jamainternmed.2013.6473.

Penninx, B. W., Y. Milaneschi, F. Lamers, and N. Vogelzangs. 2013. "Understanding the Somatic Consequences of Depression: Biological Mechanisms and the Role of Depression Symptom Profile." *BMC Medicine* 11: 129. https://doi.org/10.1186/1741-7015-11-129.

Scheers, H., L. Jacobs, L. Casas, B. Nemery, and S. Nawrot Tim. 2015. "Long-Term Exposure to Particulate Matter Air Pollution is a Risk Factor for Stroke." *Stroke* 46 (11): 3058–3066. https://doi.org/10.1161/STROKEAHA.115.009913.

White, E. G. H. 1868. "Testimonies for the Church, vol. 1." *Ellen G. White Estate, Inc.* Accessed July 25, 2019. https://media2.egwwritings.org/pdf/en_1T.pdf.

White, E. G. H. 1875. "Testimonies for the Church, vol. 3." *Ellen G. White Estate, Inc.* Accessed July 25, 2019. https://media2.egwwritings.org/pdf/en_3T.pdf.

White, E. G. H. 1885. "Testimonies for the Church, vol. 4." *Ellen G. White Estate, Inc.* Accessed July 25, 2019. https://media2.egwwritings.org/pdf/en_4T.pdf.

White, E. G. H. 1905. *The Ministry of Healing*. Washington, D.C.: Review and Herald Publishing Association.

White, E. G. H. 1921. *Steps to Christ*. Washington, D.C.: Review and Herald Publishing Association.

White, E. G. H. 1942. *Education*. Mountain View, CA/Brookfield, IL: Pacific Press Publishing Association.

White, E. G. H. 1946. "Evangelism." *Ellen G. White Estate, Inc.* Accessed July 25, 2019. https://media2.egwwritings.org/pdf/en_Ev.pdf.

White, E. G. H. 1956. *Thoughts from the Mount of Blessing*. Mountain View, CA: Pacific Press Publishing Association.

White, E. G. H. 1976. "Maranatha." *Ellen G. White Estate, Inc.* Accessed July 25, 2019. https://media2.egwwritings.org/pdf/en_Ma.pdf.

Part II Secularization of Depression in Modern and Contemporary Literature

5 *Nihilism, Depression, and Wholeheartedness. Metacognitive Strategies in 19th-Century Literature*

Søren Harnow Klausen
University of Southern Denmark

Introduction: Nihilism and Depression

It is a commonplace that one of the most pervasive topics of 19th-century literature was the specter of nihilism. What has been much less widely observed—apart from the fact that the concept of nihilism emerged already at the end of 18th century, and should not be associated too narrowly with figures from the second half of the 19th century, like Turgenev or Nietzsche—is the close link between nihilism and depression. In textbooks and encyclopedias, nihilism is usually presented as a philosophical viewpoint, that is, as an articulated belief system, a deliberate and reasoned rejection of traditional beliefs in the meaningfulness of life, objective morality, or religious doctrines. However, when 19th-century intellectuals described a worrying tendency towards nihilism, they were not so much concerned with a theoretical stance or *Weltanschauung* as with a kind of mood or mental disease, a condition that befell individuals regardless of their explicit attitudes or intentions. While this condition was undoubtedly seen as connected to the rise of a more or less scientific, disenchanting world-view, the focus was on the psychological and existential ramifications. What was diagnosed in the literature of the time was a lack of ability to believe (and act, and feel), rather than a rational decision not to believe.

I will highlight the connection between nihilism and depression by considering two exemplary literary treatments of the subject from around the middle of the 19th century. In Kierkegaard's "Crop Rotation" (from *Either/Or*, 1843 [1992]), the principal challenges to a meaningful life are diagnosed as boredom and indifference. Through its style and implicit contradictions, the text provides indirect evidence for the pathological condition of its pseudonymous author and the limitations of the otherwise ingenious techniques he devises for overcoming boredom (some of which resemble what is now referred to as *metacognitive* strategies). I will further illustrate this view of depression with Tolstoy's description in *War and Peace* (1868–1869 [2006]) of the main character, Pierre Bezukhov, as suffering from a lack of orientation and self-accept, which at times takes on pathological forms—as well as with the description of Pierre's friend, Prince Andrey Bolkonsky, who, in spite of having a very different personal constitution, likewise battles with depression.

In both Kierkegaard and Tolstoy, existential emptiness is seen as stemming from the lack of not only a stable value system but still more of a wholehearted endorsement of oneself. Moreover, both writers describe the cure to this condition as being in some respects very similar to, but in others markedly different from, current therapeutic approaches. In line with current standard views on depression, they see metacognitive habits and abilities (which, of course, they do not identify as such, *metacognition* being a much more recent terminological invention) as central to both the disease and the cure. Depression is connected to distraction, boredom, rumination, absent-mindedness, lack of self-esteem, and motivation; it can be prevented by strengthening concentration, self-control, emotional regulation, self-accept, and sense of self. That is, in many ways, similar to the ideas underlying the current use of mindfulness or cognitive therapy to counter depression.

The main difference is—unsurprisingly, if one takes into account their more philosophical and religious orientation—that Tolstoy and Kierkegaard believe that overcoming depression requires more than merely a mastery of psychological skills. They warn that a partial, or even nearby, implementation of the metacognitive strategies recommended by themselves might not only fail to work, but can even lead to further depression. Moreover, they are less confident that there is a complete solution for depression, seeing it as a condition that might be handled more or less successfully, but has to be fought perpetually.

This does not merely reflect a difference in ideology or time-specific worldviews. Kierkegaard and Tolstoy describe how it is possible to get (almost) everything right and still fail to come decisively to terms with depression; how one might remain haunted by the shadow of depression even when things seem to run smoothly, or when one has adopted a seemingly different attitude to life or reshaped one's personality. They both develop a theme that was brought up when the very notion of nihilism first emerged: that emptiness or loss of meaning may be caused by a theoretical stance, in the broadest sense of the word; not just by the adoption of a scientific worldview, but also by the apparently more appropriate forms of *theorizing* designed to compensate for the limitations of such a worldview, like religious or moral convictions, or merely personal habits of treating matters of life abstractly or reflectively. Hence, science and theory do play a constitutive role for nihilism but in terms of their psychological or existential, rather than their epistemic or doxastic effects.

Although there is a good reason to not take Kierkegaard and Tolstoy's descriptions at face value—they do indeed have their idiosyncrasies—their understanding of depression is of more than historical interest. Both writers display acute psychological insight, sometimes also describing patterns that do not merely follow from, and perhaps even seem contrary to, their more general philosophical views. If read and used with care, their texts can shed light on aspects of depression that are real and pertinent to current attempts to come to terms with it.

The Emergence of Nihilism

The concept of nihilism was introduced almost a century before it was raised to prominence in connection with the nihilist movement in Russia and the writings of Nietzsche. The German critic of Enlightenment, Jacobi, initiated the so-called *Nihilismusstreit* in 1799 with a lengthy letter to Fichte, in which he attacked not just the latter's influential philosophy of pure subjectivity in the form action and will to self-realization [*Tathandlung*], but almost all the dominant philosophical systems of his time, including the pantheism inspired by Spinoza.

Jacobi saw nihilism as stemming, at least in part, from demands for rational justification typical of the Enlightenment—demands that could not, eventual, be met, and so forced their proponents into a position of ultimate groundlessness. Even less rationalist philosophies like Fichte's exhibited the same fundamental flaw. They were all attempts to control reality by intellectual means and impose on it a meaning it was not assumed to have in itself. Fichte took the philosophical stance to its utmost consequence, affirming the meaninglessness of every pre-given reality and resorting to the notion of a will that does not really will anything in particular (Jacobi 2009, 44). Thus to Jacobi, idealism was also at bottom nihilism (2009, 50). The root of the problem was the endless searching and examining taken to constitute the spirit of science and philosophy. Scientific thinking might have legitimate applications, but, in the form of philosophical speculation, it degenerates into mere play, a tool for diversion (2009, 33). Hence, it is not just the content of philosophy, but the very activity of speculating and balancing different views, the mental gymnastics, which threatens to make life meaningless. Only by humbly accepting one's fundamental non-knowledge (something very different from the probing Socratic ignorance) and taking reality for granted, can nihilism be overcome (2009, 57).

Nihilism as a Condition

In the wake of the first *Nihilismusstreit*, there emerged in European literature several expressions of a general condition of despair, dissatisfaction, or sadness. Byron introduced the moody, disillusioned hero, and the topic was taken up by Lermontov in his *Hero of Our Time* (1841 [2009]), whose protagonist is brooding, alienated, and almost obsessively self-occupied, without being able to come to terms with himself.

Common to many intellectuals of the time was the experience of a tragic mismatch between the deep longings and expectations that had been nurtured by reading and speculation, and the mundane realities with which they sooner or later had to come to terms. There was a general mistrust of the too-good-to-be-true, grand solutions, like the classicist idea of self-realization and emotional fulfillment through cultivation and immersion in civic life. Even projects, like the educational journey or the commitment to just social causes or warfare, eventually led to the same basic disillusion. Resorting to decisionism (like Fichte can be said to have done) or conservatism proved no better. A fundamental dissatisfaction remained and expressed itself sometimes in quiet melancholy, sometimes in the form of more outright despair.

This should already suffice to highlight the connection between nihilism and depression. Nihilism is felt, rather than thought; it is the experience that nothing has real value or motivational power. Furthermore, nihilism in the Romantic age was often described as a condition of *indifference*: Byronic heroes turn into villains because there is no reason why they should not; no other way of life is any better. In Heine's poetry (1827), scenes and situations usually considered gripping or beautiful are presented as boring clichés or merely *old news*, on par with mundane facts, and so unable stir any deeper emotions, apart from sadness and sentimental longing for something that is no longer to be found.

Boredom and Nihilism in Kierkegaard

Kierkegaard's "Crop Rotation" is one of many pseudonymous texts that make up the first volume of his highly complex philosophical novel *Either/Or*. It is characteristic of the whole work that Kierkegaard lets a variety of fictive characters present their different attitudes towards life in matching styles and genres. There are aphorisms in the style of Schlegel, different varieties of the epistolary novel, and even a sermon at the end, signaling the emergence of the religious standpoint of Kierkegaard's later works. However, although the literary means are chosen to match the views and temperaments of the fictive authors, there is, in many cases, a tension between what the authors want to convey—their *official* or explicit points of view—and the way it is said and experienced by the reader. In "Crop Rotation," there is an obvious, intended contrast between genre and the actual point of view, as the text is a deliberate parody or pastiche. Nevertheless, even considered as such, as a piece of romantic irony, it also harbors a more subtle, but more profound tension, as the very ironic stance comes across as less appropriate, and the author's attempt to take command of the genre and exploit it for his particular purposes does not quite succeed.

That "Crop Rotation" parodies the self-help genre or *conduct book* can be seen from its subtitle, "An Attempt at a Theory of Social Prudence." The idea of a theory of prudential rationality—or *Klugheitslehre*—goes back at least to Aristotle's ethics. However, it became particularly influential during the 18th century, as some writers achieved a broad readership by shifting the focus of the genre from the theoretical understanding of prudential rationality to practical guidelines or rules of conduct (Grunert 2016). Famous examples include Christian Thomasius' *On the Art of Loving Reasonably and Virtuously* (1692), Christoph August Heumann's *The Political Philosopher. Rational Prescriptions for Prudence in Ordinary Life* (1714), and John Fielding's *The Universal Mentor* (1763).

The anonymous author of "Crop Rotation" (hereafter referred to simply as *the aesthete*) adopts the goals and conventions of the genre by offering the reader guidance in the form of basic principles for life. However, he quickly shows his contempt for the genre and the conventional lifestyle it embodies by choosing as his basic principle the observation that "all men are boring." (1992, 227) That is not just a minor quibble; the aesthete is sincere in presenting it as having fundamental importance. For he considers boredom *the root of all evil*, and the typical reactions to boredom as merely aggravating the misery because it makes people embark on pointless projects. Going deeper into the nature of boredom, the aesthete makes an implicit reference to the *Nihilismusstreit* by characterizing it as "demonic pantheism." (1992, 231; 2013, II, 279) Whereas pantheism is normally characterized by "fullness," boredom is based on "emptiness"; it "rests upon the nothingness that winds its way through existence." (1992, 232; 2013, II, 280)

That is obviously about nihilism, but in how far is it about depression? Both folk and contemporary scientific psychology distinguishes boredom from depression (Goldberg et al. 2011). While the similarities between the two states seem obvious enough, one would normally say that boredom is a much less serious and also more transient condition. Boredom might trigger depression, and it can be part, or symptom, of a more general state of depression (Farmer and Sundberg 1986), but depression is deeper and more comprehensive; besides, *genuine* depression, depression in the *clinical* or *major* sense, is a pathological phenomenon, an affective *disorder*, and not just a particular emotion or mood among others.

Nevertheless, Kierkegaard uses a more general notion of boredom, which admits of considerable subdivisions and gradations (1992, 230; 2013, II, 278). Moreover, as is typical of his thinking—which in some respects anticipates something like the psychoanalytical notion of the unconscious—he takes certain superficial phenomena to be symptoms or expressions of deeper and much more severe conditions, of which the subject herself may be unaware. This also goes, for example, for despair or anxiety, which Kierkegaard takes to be present in otherwise self-content and busily occupied persons (this is in line with the contemporary view of depression as a state that can easily go undetected—see e.g. Gillihan 2017).

The aesthete takes boredom to be a deep phenomenon, a serious condition not easily shaken off. It is not merely the result of living an ordinary life. It cannot be kept at bay by adopting an unconventional bohemian lifestyle. Paraphrasing Heine, the aesthete notes that one becomes *europamüde*, but then finds no real diversion in going to America (1992, 233; 2013, II 281). No kind of superficial diversion, no external or *eccentric* activity can be sufficient. Moreover, in trying to avoid boredom by such means, "one only works oneself further into it." (1992, 232; 2013, II, 281)

The aesthete agrees with the commonplace that one needs some diversion or change to overcome boredom (1992, 232; 2013, II, 281). However, he departs from the common understanding of it by recommending that one should change not the soil, but the "method of cultivation." (1992, 233; 2013, II, 281) It is not the content of one's experiences or the events in one's life that matter, but the ability to adopt a *flexible attitude* and see the same things in a different light. Central to this strategy is the employment of the faculties of *remembering* and *forgetting:*

> Every life-situation must possess no more importance than that one can forget it whenever one wants to; each single life-situation should have enough importance, however, for one to be able at any time to remember it … One must keep reins on the enjoyment from the beginning. (1992, 234; 2013, II, 282f.)

"The art of remembering and forgetting will then also prevent one's sticking fast in some particular circumstance in life and ensure perfect suspension."

(1992, 236; 2013, II, 284) According to recent studies, depression is characterized by *negative memory bias.* People suffering from depression tend to overestimate the experience of negative emotion (Urban et al. 2018). However, the response favored by the aesthete is not simple *positive psychology* or an attempt to forget about sorry events in one's past. An overprotective attitude to one's emotional life may fuel depression by rendering one insensitive to whatever meaning one's experiences still do or could have. Hence, what is needed is a measured and flexible response. One must invest oneself in life up to a certain point but remain able to withdraw and avoid becoming too deeply affected by the losses and disillusions that will inevitably occur.

Depression, like melancholy, involves a letting go of oneself—Seligman (1975) speaks of *giving up.* It is a kind of negative *oceanic* feeling, as the boundaries and structures of the self are dissolved (Luyten and Fonagy 2016), but with this leading to a sense of estrangement rather the satisfaction and sense of belonging or connectedness usually associated with this kind of experience (compare the aesthete's notion of *demonic pantheism*). The aesthete of "Crop Rotation" tries to avoid falling into this abyss not by staunchly resisting melancholy or clinging to civic life, but by *going with the flow* in a controlled fashion. He is not a slave of his emotions, but neither is he their complete master. He does speak of "playing battledore and shuttlecock with the whole of existence." (1992, 234; 2013, II, 283) However, that does not mean that the aesthete wants to play with his existence as an object to be controlled from an external, sovereign standpoint. He does not believe this to be possible but instead tries to play with existence from the inside, taking for granted that he will be in the grip of fortuitous circumstances, but trying to mitigate their impact by turning the very experience of responding to contingencies as a source of diversion. One example of this is the advice that one must necessarily gain *control of moods*; this does not imply the impossible task of producing moods at will, but merely that one should learn "to make use of the instant." (1992, 239; 2013, I, 287)

The approach of the aesthete in "Crop Rotation" resembles contemporary cognitive therapeutic strategies in many ways. It employs—and aims at training—metacognitive skills. It focuses on the ability to harness positive emotions, to use remembrance and forgetfulness constructively. Despite both the heavily ironic tone and the self-critical counterpoint that can be felt throughout the text, this should not be dismissed as mere satire. The aesthete has experience with fighting boredom, and assuming that it is a fundamental condition and alternative solutions are hard to come by, his advice should be taken seriously, even though it appears less than ideal. He is himself explicitly aware of the risk of becoming bored by constantly seeking change:

> The acquired form of boredom is usually a product of a mistaken attempt at diversion. That the remedy for boredom can bring boredom about in this way seems doubtful, but it does so only to the extent that it is incorrectly applied. (1992, 232; 2013, II, 282)

However, it is not just mistaken attempts at a superficial diversion that may cause boredom; even the calculated, meticulous approach—based on *cool deliberation* (1992, 232; 2013, II, 282)—advocated by the aesthete as a way of avoiding becoming bored with one's activities may eventually do so. The literary features of the text indicate the risk and limitations of the approach it seemingly recommends. Most significantly, the very project of playing with existence itself becomes boring. Though the text takes up a mere thirteen pages, and the aesthete is witty and inventive, it soon becomes *too much*, and too much of the *same*, and thereby also less aesthetically pleasing, thereby failing to satisfy the aesthete's fundamental requirement. The aesthete, it seems, eventually falls into the trap of the *Klugheitslehren*: its self-assured insistence and stylistic monotony compromise his prose. It also takes on an obsessive quality. The aesthete is carried away by his thoughts and expressions, and so effectively loses the control that he wanted to maintain.

Contemporary cognitive approaches to depression recommend that one should *cultivate awareness* (Lu 2015). Kierkegaard's aesthete gives the same advice but worries that the attempt might backfire. This worry is also present in current approaches. Mindfulness therapists point to the risk that reflection might "perpetuate, rather than … resolve depression" (Segal et al. 2018, 34) and recommends "distancing" from negative thoughts and getting "perspective." (2018, 36) Kierkegaard's aesthete acknowledges the power of perspective—and of re-contextualizing experiences—but sees that too much distancing can make it impossible to maintain the emotional attachment that is also necessary for finding meaning in life. Moreover, Kierkegaard himself (or his text) indicates, by literary means, that the very instrumental, systematic approach to one's existence may also be experienced as displeasing and engender an even stronger sense of futility and helplessness. Some of this is echoed in contemporary criticism of cognitive-behavioral therapy as being too *technique* (Nydegger 2008). As we shall see, the approach ultimately advocated by Kierkegaard entails not a reduction, but rather a heightening and purification of self-awareness and desire. The perils of reflection should be handled by more, and more qualified, reflection.

Nihilism and Depression in Tolstoy

I find in Tolstoy the same complex response to the challenge of nihilism and depression as in Kierkegaard. Because Tolstoy wrote at a time when nihilism had begun to take the form of a political movement, especially in Russia, the scholarly focus has been on his attitude to towards nihilism in this more specific sense, and in his later, more socially concerned works (see, e.g. Heier 1969). However, nihilism is a pervasive theme already in *War and Peace*, as many of the characters in the novel struggle with finding meaning in life. One might think of the debaucherous Anatole Kuragin, a character very similar to the less sophisticated aesthetes presented in the first sections of Kierkegaard's *Either/Or*, or of society ladies like Anna Pavlovna, who, without seemingly recognizing it themselves, live a life of emptiness and superficial glamour. But the subtler aspects of nihilism and its connection to depression are chiefly exemplified by the main protagonist of the novel, Pierre Bezukhov, and to certain extent also by his friend, Prince Andrey Bolkonsky (though it might be argued that all the main characters of the novel, including its heroine, Natasha, show signs of depression). The two are described as having very different personalities. Pierre is unsure about himself and his place in the world. He behaves erratically, lacks a sense of societal conventions, and gets along merely due to his wealthy background and ability to arouse sympathy in spite, or perhaps because, of his awkward appearance. He is absentminded and regularly gets lost in speculation, and he is unable to make up his mind and decide on a course of action.

Andrey, by contrast, makes a much more controlled and mature impression. Pierre himself notes that Prince Andrey "combine[s] in the highest degree all the qualities he himself lack[s]" and that they can be "summed up in a single concept: will power." (Tolstoy 2006, 31) However, subsequent events reveal that Prince Andrey is not that different from Pierre. Prince Andrey seems to exhibit will power since he forces himself to fulfill his societal obligations. However, he becomes depressed no less than Pierre does. His apparent strength of will does not make him able to break free of a life that he finds confining and pointless. Moreover, while he has no penchant for philosophical speculation, he does take refuge in abstract thought, especially about the military organization (2006, III, 3). He seeks refuge in the country, then comes to find country life *tedious*. His former interests comes to "lose their appeal," and when sitting in his study, he often goes to the mirror and "stare[s] at his own face for minutes on end"; he spends "long minutes pacing up and down the room, frowning one moment and smiling the next, brooding on a series of strange ideas that [lie] beyond words." (2006, 459f.)

Andrey seems to have gone further than Pierre in terms of disillusion. Whereas Pierre constantly deliberates and pursues ideas and projects, Andrey no longer believes that there is something to search for. His response to Pierre's forcedly enthusiastic exposure of masonic teachings is a telling: "Yes, if only it was true." (2006, 420)

Tolstoy connects nihilism and depression very explicitly. Pierre is described as battling depression with mental techniques very similar to those recommended by modern psychotherapy. He tries to avoid certain lines of thought, which he knows would likely trigger negative emotions, and attempts to concentrate on a project that appears more meaningful:

> Ever since the night of the ball Pierre had been aware of an impending bout of nervous depression, and had been trying desperately to struggle against it … he had felt a growing sense of weariness and embarrassment in court society, and his old thoughts about the vanity of all human life began to resurface more and more often … He made equal efforts to avoid two lines of [disconcerting] thought … Once again, everything seemed meaningless on the scale of eternity; once again he faced the question 'What is it all about?' Day after day, he forced himself to concentrate on masonic work. (2006, 516)

A central source for nihilism and depression among the characters in *War and Peace* is the comparison with eternity, that is, the measurement of one's accomplishment according to a universal standard. More mundane, but still overly ambitious standards of comparison also fuel Pierre's gloomy mood, as when Prince Andrey shows himself to have suddenly allayed his depression by falling in love with Natasha (whom Pierre also loves, without having realized it entirely):

> His friend was now … a new man, utterly changed. Where had his depression gone, his contempt for life, all his disillusionment? … [Pierre's] eyes brimmed with sweet sadness. The brighter Prince's fate became, the gloomier his own seemed to be. (2006, 517f.)

Prince Andrey, in turn, is also affected by experiencing the seemingly uncomplicated happiness of his female companions (like Kierkegaard, Tolstoy generally tends to depict women as being, for good and for bad, less given to reflection and more absorbed in their dealings and immediate situation than men). He notes how Natasha is "laughing and enjoying herself," wondering "What's in her mind? What is it that she is so glad about?" (2006, 456), before eventually becoming so charmed with her, and so fascinated with her ability to take happiness from simple things and enjoy the beauty around her, that this gives him a new motivation for returning to an "active life," even though he conceals the source of his decision by "dreaming up" apparently more logical reasons (2006, 459).

The understanding of depression in *War and Peace* resembles that of "Crop Rotation" in that it takes the content of one's belief, as well as the systematic approach, as such, to be ultimately insignificant. Almost all the elements of what turns out to be, eventually, the solution to Pierre's troubles, could be found in his earlier beliefs and practices. The teachings of the freemasons do seem noble and sensible (though Tolstoy also makes them seem like too much of good thing, and overly moralizing, in a manner reminiscent of Kierkegaard's ambivalent depiction of the ethical standpoint in *Either/Or*, II). However, Pierre is unable to adopt the masonic teachings wholeheartedly. They remain to him a mere system of thought, and the fact that Pierre knows that he ought, for both moral and prudential reasons, to believe in them, but is incapable of doing so, makes him despair even more strongly.

There is a parallel here, not as much to cognitive therapy in general, but to *meta*cognitive therapy in particular, which is "based on the principle that it is not merely *what* a person thinks but *how* he or she thinks that determines emotions and the control one has over them" and warns against "unhelpful self-regulatory strategies." (Wells 2009, 1f.) However, Kierkegaard and Tolstoy are more radical, also pointing to the dangers of going *meta-*, both in terms of exaggerated detachment and the risk that the very controlling attitude to life might itself come to appear distasteful and futile. One of the most pervasive themes of *War and Peace* is the ultimate futility of "arrangements, efforts and plans" (2006, 1117) in history as well as personal life. It is also telling that when Pierre finally seems to have overcome depression, after having experienced near-execution at the hands of the French occupying forces, one sign of this is his ability to re-establish immediate contact with reality, to again have "intensely pleasurable sensations" and revel in the satisfaction of his basic needs "without having to qualify it." (2006, 1125f.)

In another respect, however, Tolstoy's description of Pierre's ways in and out of depression does concur with the metacognitive approach. It dwells recurrently on Pierre's attentional habits. During the depression, he is mentally restless, unable to concentrate or take in the qualities of a situation. However, already during his near-execution, his experiences become more vivid and focused: "all he could do was look and listen." (2006, 1070) At first, his attitude is described as marked by "curiosity and emotion," and he seems baffled at what is happening with himself (2006, 1072). Still, curiosity is a sign of motivation; and when Pierre has later come more definitely to terms with himself, he can control even his forgetfulness, albeit by "sticking to a list supplied by his wife." (2006, 1297) Thus, Pierre's recovery is about metacognition—but it takes the form of a restoration of his instinctive mental habits, which is described as resulting not from training or conscious effort, but from particularly remarkable experiences, which, like an external force, mold them into a more harmonious shape.

Wholeheartedness, Passion, and Accept of Reality

Kierkegaard eventually agrees that the radical change in self-attitude needed for overcoming depression must be imposed from the outside. In the second volume of *Either/Or*, he presents what seems at first a superior alternative to the approach of the aesthete. His ethical character, Judge Wilhelm, diagnoses the fundamental cause of depression (*Tungsind*; heavy mind) as "the sin of not willing deeply and inwardly." (1992, 499; 2013, III, 183) By way of positive contrast, the Judge claims that *self-choice* "essentially cancels"[1] depression (though he also admits, interestingly, that "a little of it will remain," because human nature makes it impossible to become entirely transparent for oneself[2]—but at the same time rejects that depression should be seen as a "bodily ailment," with the argument that physicians are not able to cure it (1992, 499f.; 2013, III, 184).

This crucial act of self-choice should not, however, be understood as an abstract choice of idealized self-image, which would merely lead to further depression (as exemplified by Pierre). It consists of wholeheartedly endorsing one's *concrete self*, and with it all the mundane circumstances of one's life. Judge Wilhelm makes the critical concession to the aesthete that this attitude has to be esthetically satisfactory; in the very title of his letter, he speaks of an "equilibrium" between the esthetic and the ethical, and he praises his own, apparently bourgeois and humdrum existence as "beautiful." (1992, 584; 2013, III, 306) This again resembles Tolstoy's description of Pierre's recovery. In both cases, wholehearted self-acceptance is seen as enabling one to take pleasure from the simple things in life, no longer measuring them by unrealistic standards, and so ultimately dispensing with the need for cultivating or controlling experiences. Furthermore, in both cases, the experience that self-acceptance need not be an unpleasant act of duty, that accepting and enjoying oneself and one's circumstances go hand in hand, is seen as enabling the protagonists to achieve this ideal finally and not only strive for it.

Conclusion: Strengths and Limitations of Metacognitive Strategies

Kierkegaard and Tolstoy anticipate the contemporary understanding of depression in many ways. They see it as linked to an attentional syndrome, and as something that calls for an attempt to control and cultivate emotions and cognitive processes. They anticipate recent *meta*cognitive approaches by pointing out how self-regulatory strategies can be unhelpful or counterproductive, and emphasizing *how* one thinks and feels rather than the content of thought and feelings. Nevertheless, they go beyond even the most sophisticated contemporary approaches by showing how metacognitive strategies can backfire, and by insisting that the change in self-attitude must be brought about from without. Like nihilism and depression, it *befalls* the individual; it cannot be initiated at will.

This touches upon a problem that is also well known from contemporary cases of depression: how to engage in countermeasures to depression when depression prevents one from engaging in or willing anything? In Kierkegaard's (i.e., the Judge's) expression, one must *choose to choose oneself* (1992, 513; 2013, III, 203). It is one of the first signs that the approach of the Judge is not necessarily superior that he quickly suppresses the question of how to avoid this, leading to an infinite regress (e.g. 1992, 483ff.; 2013, III, 161). The Judge wrongly believes being able to keep depression at bay by his strength of will and other mental powers. He does, however, admit that traces of it will remain. Moreover, his advocacy of passionate self-choice also becomes too much of a good thing; he is too brashly insisting, too pleased with himself and his attitude towards life, and so in the end also falls short of meeting his esthetic standard of success. Tolstoy likewise describes, in the Epilogue to *War and Peace*, how Pierre is, after some time, again carried away by lofty ideas and has to be kept in check by the more down-to-earth Natasha.

This is typical of how Tolstoy and Kierkegaard ultimately view nihilism and depression: There is no prospect of overcoming them once and for all; and as far as they can be reined in, this cannot be done by one's own devices, but requires external stimulation and support, be it in the form authentic personal relationships or emotional contact with a religious power (which, again, is something altogether different from subscribing to religious teachings). Kierkegaard would later speak of *indirect communication* as a way of fostering self-choice without compromising the autonomy of the recipient (see Klausen 2018, 62ff.).

While this may sound like a rather pessimistic and at least not very practical conclusion, I hope to have nevertheless shown how the writings of Kierkegaard and Tolstoy can contribute to contemporary attempts to understand and handle depression, both by suggesting self-therapeutic strategies and by highlighting their eventual ramifications. That there is no quick fix should come as no surprise to professionals working in the field or those who have themselves been victims of depression. However, literature is capable of drawing attention to the subtler, almost paradoxical aspects of living with and battling this condition. Moreover, laying out the existential and esthetic costs and benefits of tinkering with metacognition may serve as a timely reminder in the face of current therapeutic approaches.[3]

Notes

1. Author's translation. Hannay imprecisely translates this into "the effect is removed." (1992, 499)
2. Again, this is not adequately rendered by Hannay's translation.
3. This paper has benefited very much from interaction with the participants of *The Faces of Depression in Literature* seminar at the 2019 ACLA National Meeting at Georgetown University, for which I am grateful. I would also like to thank the editor Josefa Ros Velasco, for her encouragement and dedicated work on this volume.

References

Farmer, R., and N. D. Sundberg. 1986. "Boredom Proneness: The Development and Correlates of a New Scale." *Journal of Personality Assessment* 50: 4–17. http://dx.doi.org/10.1207/s15327752jpa5001_2.

Fielding, J. 1763. *The Universal Mentor*. London: A. Millar.

Gillihan, S. J. 2017. "Can You Be Depressed Without Knowing It? I Was." *Psychology Today*, May 2, 2017. https://www.psychologytoday.com/intl/blog/think-act-be/201705/can-you-be-depressed-without-knowing-it-i-was.

Goldberg, Y. K., J. D. Eastwood, J. Laguardia, and J. Danckert. 2011. "Boredom: An Emotional Experience Distinct from Apathy, Anhedonia or Depression." *Journal of Social and Clinical Psychology* 30 (6): 647–666. http://dx.doi.org/10.1521/jscp.2011.30.6.647.

Grunert, F. 2016. "Feindschaft, Freundschaft, Sicherheit. Zur Klugheitstlehre von Cristoph August Heumann." In *Literatur und praktische Vernunft*, edited by F. Ammon and C. Rémi, 295–316. Berlin: De Gruyter.

Heier, E. 1969. "Tolstoi and Nihilism." *Canadian Slavonic Papers* 11 (4): 454–465. https://doi.org/10.1080/00085006.1969.11091175.

Heine, H. 1827. *Buch der Lieder*. Hamburg: Hofmann und Campe.

Heumann, C. A. 1714. *Der politische Philosophus. Das ist vernunfftmäßige Anweisungen zur Klugheit im gemeinen Leben*. Frankfurt am Main/Leipzig: Renger.

Jacobi, H. J. 2009 [1799]. *Brief über den Nihilismus*. Stuttgart/Bad Cannstatt: Fromann-Holzbog.

Kierkegaard, S. A. 1992. *Either/Or. A Fragment of Life*. London: Penguin.

Kierkegaard, S. A. 2013. *Søren Kierkegaards Skrifter*. Copenhagen: Søren Kierkegaard Forskningscenteret.

Klausen, S. H. 2018. *Kierkegaard: Educating for Authenticity*. New York, NY: Springer.

Lermontov, M. 1840 [2009]. *A Hero of Our Time*. London: Penguin.

Lu, S. 2015. "Mindfulness Holds Promise for Treating Depression." *APA Monitor on Psychology* 46 (3): 50.

Luyten, P., and P. Fonagy. 2016. "The Self in Depression." In *The Self in Understanding and Treating Psychological Disorders*, edited by A. Beck, M. Kyrios, R. Moulding, G.

Doron, S. S. Bhar, M. Nedeljkovic, and M. Mikulincer, 71–81. Cambridge: Cambridge University Press.

Nydegger, R. 2008. *Understanding and Treating Depression.* London: Praeger.

Segal, Z. V., J. M. G. Williams, J. D. Teasdale, and J. Kabat-Zinn. 2018. *Mindfulness-Based Cognitive Therapy for Depression.* New York, NY: Guilford.

Seligman, M. E. P. 1975. *Helplessness: On Depression, Development and Death.* San Francisco, CA: Freeman.

Thomasius, C. 1692. *Von der Kunst Vernünfftig und Tugendhafft zu lieben. Als dem eintzigen Mittel zu einen glückseligen/ galanten und vergnügten Leben zu gelangen/Oder Einleitung Zur Sitten Lehre.* Halle: Salfeld.

Tolstoy, L. 2006 [1868–1869]. *War and Peace.* London: Penguin.

Urban, E., S. T. Charles, L. J. Levine, and D. M. Almeida. 2018. "Depression History and Memory Bias for Specific Daily Emotions." *PLoS ONE* 13 (9): e0203574. https://doi.org/10.1371/journal.pone.0203574.

Wells, A. 2009. *Metacognitive Therapy for Anxiety and Depression.* New York, NY: Guilford.

6 *Can Melancholy Be Heroic? Walter Benjamin and the Vicissitudes of Melancholy*

SHANNON HAYES
Tennessee State University

In this chapter, I explore the vicissitudes of melancholy in the works of 20th-century German intellectual and critical theorist Walter Benjamin. *Melancholy* is a central affect woven throughout his texts. It connotes a depressed mood, a feeling of withdrawal, alienation, passivity, inertia. Despite the long-standing association of melancholy with creative, poetic activity, melancholic depression remains chastized as a nonpolitical mode of existence associated with stagnancy, paralysis, and a willful alienation. If we follow the insights of Marxist critical theory, and it remains true that, under capitalism, we are already dismembered and distanced in our strategic relations, then melancholy is a mood that unmasks our present situation. In the fatigue and weariness of the melancholic body, there is an insight into the decay and fragmentation that characterizes social existence. In the melancholic, attention to destruction is a spirit of resistance. It is a mood capable of revealing the eschatological structure of historical existence—an insight which can transform political struggles—and it has the potential to reconcile the tensions necessary for political struggles. In other words, melancholy bears political potential, and it can be put to work for both emancipatory and reactionary political projects.

This chapter aims to illuminate the differences between a nihilistic *left-wing melancholy* and an emancipatory *heroic melancholy*. The difference between these types has to do with the object toward which their destructive energies are directed. Although left melancholics espouse emancipatory political ideals, their destructiveness is directed toward that which threatens the preservation of their way of life, and thus is directed toward the audience that would be the source of radical political change in the present. At the heart of left melancholy is a desire to preserve the material conditions that give them the gift of their sorrow. In contrast, heroic melancholy gives voice to the historical forces and material conditions that sustain suffering so that the sensitivity might organize the audience to the injustice that plagues the melancholic. As this includes the conditions of the work's production and reception, heroic melancholy aims its destructive energy toward its image. For Benjamin, melancholy is not heroic through the exaltation of the melancholic subject, but through the dissolution of melancholy for the sake of social transformation: it is heroism without a hero.

Poetic Melancholy

Throughout his works, Benjamin looks to the past, without nostalgia, for the creativity of those whose melancholy gave them, in exchange for their sorrow, the gift of distance from their historical world. The melancholic subject is a *flâneur*, akin to Nietzsche's *wanderer*. In order to gaze soberly at one's historical time, one must take some distance from it. "One must do as the traveler who wants to know the height of the towers of a city: he leaves the city." (Nietzsche 1974, 342) Like the one who wants to see their town clearly, such a view can only be accomplished by gaining some distance from the town. From a distance, its general forms and tendencies can come into focus. The activity of melancholy similarly occurs at such a distance from the town. Even as a melancholic strolls its streets and simulates its rhythms, it is the historical tendency of the town that comes into focus, and, with it, the nature of their historical experience is illuminated, albeit in allegorical fashion.

It is the insight into the general tendencies of a historical moment that sparks Benjamin's interest in the melancholy of poets. Melancholy is an affect of inwardness that entails feelings of disconnection and disenchantment with the historical, social world. What Benjamin recognizes is that the movement away from everything historical is, at the same time, a movement toward the nature that remains. Melancholic poets look to nature, with a gaze both micrological and empathetic. "All nature would begin to lament," writes Benjamin, "if it were endowed with language." (2004, 72) Contained within poetic expressions of natural forms and natural beauty is an insight into the losses that nature would mourn, and thus, melancholic poets offer insight into the *truth-content* of their historical period—the catastrophe that defines its tendency: the direction of its unfolding.

In *The Origin of German Tragic Drama* (2009), Benjamin explores the work of melancholic poets from 16th and 17th century Germany as he offers a re-evaluation of the oft-maligned *Trauerspiels* (mourning-plays) from that era. His interest in *Trauerspiels* did not stem from his appreciation for the baroque prolixity of the plays, or the excessive feeling of their language, which was charged with seriousness and solemnity. He was drawn to these plays, as to other forms of maligned art, because of their reception in German literary history as failures and expressions of a period in decline. Until Benjamin's text, the artistic form shared by these plays had been mainly derided by critics and historians as a farcical double of Ancient Greek tragedies. Not merely derivative of tragedies, *Trauerspiels* committed the even graver sin of being unenjoyable for its spectators and thus marked an "incompetent renaissance of tragedy." (2009, 50) Such an interpretation recalls Marx's oft-cited claim in *Eighteenth Brumaire* (1984). He writes, "Hegel remarks somewhere that all great, world-historical facts and personages occur, as it were, twice. He has forgotten to add: the first time as tragedy, the second as farce." (1984, 584) As a farce, *Trauerspiels*, as well as perhaps all creations beleaguered by this designation, become located within a linear narrative of world history. What is remarkable about *Trauerspiels* and other expressions of decline is precisely the distance they keep from the historical progress that characterizes modernity. Such forms are remarkable because they emerge within a given historical period, but do so as if from outside, disconnected from its values and biases; they are untimely, unfashionable, and bear a spirit of resistance to everything modern. It is this *outside-within* that characterizes melancholic distance, and that guarantees the truth-content of melancholic insight. The task of the critic is to wrest *Trauerspiels* from its superficial identification with tragedy and rescue it as a form whose truth-content is disruptive of world-historical narratives.

By their melancholic gaze, which was attentive to misery and suffering—both past losses and those still to come—*Trauerspiel* poets were able to apprehend their historical experience in nature in allegorical fashion. On these poets, Benjamin writes, "nature was not seen by them in the bud and bloom, but in the over-ripeness and decay of her creations." (2006, 179) With a saturnine vision, they saw their experience reflected in the *eternal transience* of nature, and it is this nature which was then reflected in the lyricism of the *Trauerspiel*. It was the timelessness of nature that these poets mourned, and it is this loss which is given voice in the characters through their prolix solemnity, endless prattle, and empty declarations. Although the character of melancholy is variable to particular historical conditions, what melancholic poets share is an attitude to the past and present. Attentive to the experience that is lost and now belongs more to the past than to the present, this is an attitude that knows "nothing of nostalgia." (2005b, 190) Their lyricism bears destructive energy—neither toward the past nor present, but toward the false idea of nature that haunts the present.

The Decay of the Aura

In order to illuminate the destructive attention that Benjamin attributes to melancholy, we turn to his enigmatic concept of the aura. Benjamin's aura is often taken up as an aesthetic category that refers to the features of traditional art (authority, authenticity, uniqueness) that stand in antithetical relation to the productive forces. The decay of the aura marks the felt experience of the decay that is concomitant with the development of the productive forces and expansions of the empty time of progress to every realm of life. Rather than limit the auratic experience to works of art, we approach the decay of the aura as a melancholic experience of the present, which extends to all *sensuous objects*, including other persons.

Following Marx's materialist historiography, nature is the "sensuous external world," the material of human social activity (1984, 60). The activity of subjects always mediates nature; nature insofar as it can be known is historical. The way a historical period perceives nature is revelatory of the perceiver's sensory-apparatus, which is itself historical and technologically-mediated. Nature is not reducible to the activity of subjects, but bears an independent material existence, an *aura* that Benjamin points to when he writes,

> What then is the aura? A strange tissue of space and time: the unique apparition of a distance, however near it may be. To follow with the eye—while resting on a summer afternoon—a mountain range on a horizon or a branch that casts its shadow on the beholder is to breathe the aura of its mountain. (2008, 23)

Importantly, when nature is historicized, it is brought out of the realm of timeless nature and into historical time, which is, for Benjamin, the empty, homogenous, repetitive time of progress that characterizes modernity.

When nature is historicized, the aura—the experience of uniqueness and permanence that one may encounter in a moment of the mountain's contemplation—undergoes a process of decay. In Benjamin's "Work of Art" (2008) essay, he attributes the aura's decay to the technological reproducibility of art. "By replicating the work many times over, it substitutes a mass existence for a unique existence." (2008, 22) What is lost in the mechanical reproduction of images is the occasion to encounter the referent of the image, which is unique and singular. Ernst Bloch illustrates the decay of the aura by pointing to Goethe's description of the Alps. One senses Goethe's uneasiness when he writes, "the moon rose and shone on uncanny things." (Bloch 2000, 435) While the Alps may have been uncanny for Goethe, it evoked fear in his predecessors. Faced with the sublimity of nature's magnitude, "even Caesar shrank from it and had himself carried over the Alps in a closed sedan chair." (Bloch 2000, 435) That the aura of the Alps has decayed is further evidenced by the "over-friendly approach taken by picture postcards and cellophane-wrapped souvenirs that hide nature's true strangeness and terror." (2000, 435) The decay of the aura marks a forgetting in the present of the *independent material existence* of nature—its otherness, and the authority of the other's singular existence.

As a melancholic attitude, one expects it to be one of ambivalence, and Benjamin maintains an ambivalence toward the loss of the aura in his writing. In one sense, the decay of the aura marks the loss of a kind of historical experience—that of the authenticity and authority that belongs to ritual and tradition; this is a loss that is worthy of being mourned. In another sense, the decay of the aura is the emancipation of the object from the conditions of its production and the significance that belongs to its historical context. It is only by becoming a ruin, vulnerable to the decay of historical time, that the historical object can release its significance and reveal the truth-content of the object.

Adorno's Melancholy

In Theodor Adorno's 1932 lecture, "The Idea of Natural-History" (2006), he reimagines the Hegelian dialectic in a way that incorporates the melancholic insights into the aura's decay. That such a reformulation is necessary is due to the status of the particular, which "has been reduced and … is increasingly defined as a mere object belonging to the universal without being able to affect it." (Adorno 2009, 30) The idea of natural-history is the "retransformation of concrete history into dialectical nature," a dialectic of identity and non-identity (2006, 260). Adorno identifies precursors to his idea of natural history in the thought of Benjamin and Georg Lukàcs. To Lukàcs, he attributes the insight that modern capitalism produces the world of commodities as a reified *second nature*: "a world of things, created by man, yet lost to him." (Adorno 2009, 264) This is an effect of capitalism's totalizing processes of rationalization and fragmentation. In Benjamin, he finds a model for transforming the world of *second nature* into an object of philosophical investigation. Benjamin "brought the resurrection of second nature out of infinite distance into infinite closeness." (Adorno 2009, 264) Toward the historical objects, he directed his *Medusan* gaze and sought to mortify the elements that appeared to be living, that still bore traces of organic unity. Doing so revealed the historical object as a ruin and released it from the historical determinations that obscure its truth. Unfailingly "micrological and fragmentary," Adorno criticizes Benjamin for failing to elucidate the phenomena as products of a social whole. Instead of relating them to universal history, he attempted to relate them "directly, in their singularity, to material tendencies and social struggles." (1997, 235) In the end, Benjamin winds up disavowing the world for the sake of its dead objects: a criticism summed up in Adorno's view that Benjamin is too melancholic.[1]

To counter Benjamin's inwardness, Adorno takes the allegorical gaze of Benjamin's melancholy and erects it into a model of philosophical investigation. In later writings, he claims *natural-history* to be synonymous with his notion of "interpretation" as a critical Marxist methodology.[2] In a reified world, philosophical thought and language are tasked with disrupting the frozen phenomena of second nature and giving back to them their dynamism and fluctuations. This aim motivates his development of *parataxis* as a philosophical style of writing. Theresa Kelly explains the appeal of parataxis for Adorno in a way that illuminates his commitment to difference and contingency over identity and argumentative clarity. Parataxis is a mode of presentation, she writes, that

> insists, by its very awkward unassimilation of one view to the next, that the intelligibility of the truth on offer lies in the cavities between statements, not zipped up inside the seams of the discourse, like a French seam of a fine garment that folds the rough outside edge inside and then seams it shut. (2009, 102)

While the drive for clarity in philosophical writing winds up subordinating the thing to the concept, writing that brings to the fore the nonidentity of thing and concept by making visible the fraying of the concept's edges does not preserve the particular but gives back to the phenomena their death—the transience and contingency which is the truth of both nature and history.

Like Benjamin, Adorno finds in poetry a melancholic gaze that illuminates the transience of nature. He writes that Hölderlin's late poem "Shelter at Hardt" exemplifies "the interlocking of nature and history" (2008, 134): "The forest sinks off/And like buds, the leaves/Hang inward, to which/The valley floor below/Flowers up, far from mute,/For Ulrich passed through/These parts, a great destiny/Often broods over his footprint,/Ready, among the remains." (qtd. in Adorno 2008, 135) According to Adorno, interpretation of the poem should reveal the way history merges into the natural setting, and this requires knowledge of the historical events, which the poem allegorizes.[3] It is this history that lends to the natural formation of its beauty.

Importantly, for Adorno, nature is not beautiful because it is inscribed with myth by history. "In natural beauty," he writes, "natural and historical elements interact in a musical and kaleidoscopically changing fashion." (2004, 71) Interpretation returns the dynamism to the phenomenon. Through interpretation, the natural elements appear as historical elements ("The valley floor ... far from mute"), and, in the next moment, the historical elements vanish again into nature through their transience. Although nature and history merge in the phenomenon, its existence exceeds what we assume it to be. Adorno writes, "the negativity of natural history—which always discovers what the phenomena used to be, what they have become and, at the same time, what they might have been—retains the *possible* life of phenomena as opposed to their actual existence." (2009, 138) The possible life of phenomena always exceeds actual life, and it is this moribund attention that retains possible life, which piques Adorno's interest in melancholy. While the value of melancholy lies in the way the gaze can penetrate second nature through insight into the decay of everything quasi-natural, thus releasing the phenomenon from the realm of myth, putting melancholy to work means giving back to the phenomenon what exceeds its historical determination—in this lies the transience of nature.

Heroic Melancholy

The decay of the aura is the fading phenomenon of something that is both lost and not yet lost. To be faithful to the "productive instability of [Benjamin's] exploratory vocabulary," Georges Didi-Huberman writes that the aura is an "'uncompleted' and 'always open' phenomenon." (2005, 5) In the wake of its loss, the aura of what-has-been continues to emit a dimming light upon the present. To recall Freud's theory of mourning,[4] we can say that melancholy is an affective response to the dimming light of what-has-been. Mourning works through the loss of the object and thereby completes the decaying process, divesting the present of its ghostly apparitions. Melancholy tends to be characterized by a refusal or inability to bury the dead, and, inchoate in the refusal, is a decision to choose the dead over the living. This is, at least, the risk of melancholy: that one will choose the dimming light of the past over and against the present and become a victim of a destructive, nihilistic nostalgia. By refusing to complete the loss, which would effectively let the other die a second time, the melancholic subject effectively chooses the second life of the lost object over and against their historical existence. In the context of Benjamin's political commitments, the danger of melancholy, at least for Adorno, is that the insights gleaned from melancholy's dialectical relation to its objects will resolve into inwardness and erect a new melancholic subjectivity.[5]

It is in this vein that Benjamin lauds the 19th-century French poet, Charles Baudelaire, who apprehends a disenchanted world of commodities. Instead of withdrawing from this world or re-enchanting it, he dwells there and makes his poetry at home in the heart of reification. In his work, images and ideas interweave to maintain the tension between idea and image as non-identical dialectical counterparts. In his poetry, the reified world is no longer made to speak in the name of progress and civilization. He makes the reified world reveal its deathly visage and speak in the name of that which underlies the idea of historical progress: the alienation and exploitation that makes every human and the whole of nature suffer in their particularity. The beauty of his poems is not attributed to the nostalgia of a romantic vision of nature. Benjamin writes that their beauty "lies in this: a rising up from out of the abyss." (2007, 134) More precisely, his beauty arises from his melancholic weariness. "When yawning, the human being himself opens like an abyss. He makes himself resemble the time stagnating around him." (2007, 160) His genius is in the pantomime of his lyricism, which exalts his historical experience—characterized by decay and destruction—as an expression of nature.

By dissociating melancholy from work, Freud erected a false dichotomy between mourning and melancholy. For Benjamin, the productive potential of melancholy lies in its being put to work. This requires first of all the dissolution of the melancholic subject for the sake of its objects. The objects are to be freed from their acquired significations, including the conditions of the work's production and its reception, and redeemed. In order to redeem the objects, this work can neither represent the objects as living nor efface the traces of their presence. Drawing on Benjamin's image of the mosaic as the product of philosophical work, Ferber points to the importance of the glue which holds together the fragments of the mosaic. She writes,

> Benjamin's manner of working through loss involves engagement with the loss itself, with the presentation of this loss. The glue's significance in the mosaic alludes to the importance of pointing out lacunae, the spaces missing and destined to be eternally unaccounted for. (2013, 66)

Unconcerned with making what-has-been again present, melancholy works toward bringing to present what has been lost *as* loss so that the audience can account for the weight of this absence in the present.

In summary, melancholy becomes *heroic* when melancholy is put to work. This means that the work of melancholy is in overcoming melancholy: the "mournful subjectivity, political paralysis, and contemplative fixity in which these insights are contained." (Pensky 2001, 140) As Max Pensky writes, "Overcoming melancholia without losing the redemptive relation to the thing: that is Benjamin's real interest." (2001, 140) Melancholy's objects are past and future losses that it encounters in the poet's sensitivity to his or her misery and suffering. *Redemptive* here does not mean either changing past injustices or finding justice in the future. Melancholy redeems its objects and becomes *heroic* through transforming its historical insight into something material to be shared with others so that they can feel the weight of history's losses, and be organized by sensitivity to its injustices.[6] Like the aura itself, the political tendency of melancholy's labors is incomplete and always open.

Left-Wing Melancholy

With the advance of the productive forces, the unfulfilled past, not entirely sublated, persists in the present. The implication of this is that "not all people exist in the same Now." (Bloch 1977, 22) People who share the same space nevertheless exist at different *Nows*: they live according to different rhythms, they hold the memories of other pasts, and dream of different futures. The present is constituted, according to Bloch, by a polyphonic, dialectical interplay of synchronous and nonsynchronous forces. Archaic ways of life, unable to be sublated entirely through the development of the productive forces, persist alongside synchronous ways of life, which reflect the present state of the economic mode of production. To extend Benjamin's characterization of melancholic insight as resistant to world-historical narratives, melancholy is a nonsynchronous mood, which affects various modes of existence. Under the category of nonsynchronism, Bloch includes the youth and the immiserated middle class, both of which include members who are homesick and untimely. Confronted with a barren present, the proletarian youth are disappointed and homesick for the naiveté and exuberance of an idealized youth. The immiserated middle class is homesick for the world whose comforts and securities they think themselves entitled to. Confronted with an empty present and impeded future, nonsynchronous types attempt to enter the future by detouring through the past.

Due to the reactionary appearance of nonsynchronous forces, the transformative energy of unfulfilled dreams is always at risk of being appropriated by fascist political interests that are counter to human interests. Such interests mobilize the nostalgic dreams of the immiserated by making these dreams appear to have a future in the present again. While looking to the past, Bloch remarks that Hitler was able to give to these dreams the false appearance of new life. He writes, "even the masses flock to it since the unbearable Now at least seems different with Hitler, who paints good old things for everyone." (1977, 25) When such types become conscious of their *objective contradictions* under pretenses, the result is not the revolutionary activity of the working class, but a destructive, nihilistic activity. These types do not seek to overcome the material conditions of their misery but turn their destructive energies toward the present. Theirs is a "torpid not wanting of the Now," which manifests as "*pent-up anger*." (1977, 31; italics in original) To reclaim the right to a future that will fulfill the promises of the unfulfilled past, the struggle is waged against those whose activity is synchronous, and reinforces the hegemony of the present: both the ruling class whose interest is in reproducing the status quo, and the class-conscious proletariat that spies the undoing of capitalism in the material contradictions of the present. "There is nothing more unexpected," writes Bloch, "nothing more dangerous than this power of being at once fiery and puny, contradicting and nonsynchronous." (1977, 22)

It is in this context that we should read Benjamin's writings on the political function of art and the dangers of melancholy. Although we find in the work of so-called *left-wing melancholy* claims of allegiance to the subjected underclass with which the artist empathizes, Benjamin spies the way this work sabotages its ideals. Since meaningful social transformation would transform the material conditions that justify the left-wing melancholic's creative outputs, their work has the effect of disrupting the critical capacities that such social transformation requires. Instead of presenting misery in such a way that it would inspire a call to action in the audience, it is presented as something to entertain and to be passively consumed.

A central insight of Benjamin's 1936 essay, "The Work of Art in the Age of Its Mechanical Reproduction" is into the fusion of art and politics that helps explain the rise of German fascism. Fascism reigns through the use of terror to control and subjugate all areas of life, but its real power lies not in the power it exerts over and against subjects, but in how it coerces its subjects to will their self-alienation. Fascism aestheticizes the political and becomes spectacular while organizing the masses as depoliticized spectators and consumers. Through the appearance of politics as an object meant to amuse or distract, fascism organizes its audience as passive subjects who absorb its messages, rather than become absorbed by them as may otherwise take place in the activity of contemplation. It is in this way that the depoliticized masses come to believe in the *beautiful illusion* offered by reactionary politics that espouse *socialist* visions of harmony, beauty, nature, and come to vote against their class interests. As Benjamin explains, "German fascism knew how to transfer all energies, wishes, yearnings, psychic drives, and phantasies into an aesthetic, socialistic illusion which worked to cover up the real causes of economic and psychic misery; indeed, it could even push for their continuation." (2008, 52) Although fascism aestheticizes politics, the continued organization of the masses as depoliticized spectators relies on the fiction of autonomous art. It is for this reason that, for Benjamin, it was no longer acceptable to believe in the autonomy of art—the idea that the artist's creative activity is free and need not be at the service of any class interests. All art has a political function. What, then, is it that makes a work of art *socialist* or *fascist*? What determines whether its destructive energies are directed toward what is useful for the bourgeois or proletariat in the class struggle? Rather than situate these questions in an ongoing debate between artistic form or content, Benjamin pursues the *tendency* of the work.

The political tendency of the work, the class interests that it serves, is not determined by the intentions of the artist or manifest content of the work. Art and artists that claim allegiance to emancipatory ideals may nevertheless enchain the viewer through their organization as a depoliticized spectator. The political tendency, then, is necessary but not sufficient to ensure that the work does not function in a counterrevolutionary way. The literary tendencies of the work determine the political tendency, and these can likewise be reactionary or progressive insofar as they are geared toward organizing the masses as consumers or producers. Thus, for Benjamin, the revolutionary work with the correct political tendency with also be literarily correct, and this constitutes the quality of that work. Socialist art is that art that uses advances in literary technique to make literary progress there where historical progress will also be made—through socializing the productive forces. For the author or artist as producer, "technical progress is … the foundation of his political progress." (2008, 87)

Benjamin aims to disentangle the types of leftist artists and intellectuals to reveal those whose leftist positions serve bourgeois class interests from those that serve proletariat class interests. Benjamin uses *hack writer* to designate those authors of the first type. A hack writer is one "who abstains in principle from alienating the productive apparatus from the ruling class by improving it in ways serving the interests of socialism." (2008, 86) In a 1931 essay, Benjamin coins the term *left-wing melancholia* to critique the poetry of Weimar poet, Erich Kästner and the work of those associated with the New Objectivism movement that gained prominence during the Weimar republic. In the cool, distanced, objective perspective that New Objectivism made fashionable, Benjamin spies a dangerous melancholy. Although it professes the use of this melancholic gaze as a critique of the material conditions of the present that sustain experiences of misery and suffering, the literary tendency of such works reveals another political tendency. Instead of politicizing the present's material conditions, it aestheticizes them and renders the material conditions an object of consumption.

In the poems of Kästner, one finds a melancholic gaze that is well-acquainted with misery and suffering. Of Kästner's despair, Benjamin derides it is a "tortured stupidity ... the latest of two millennia of metamorphoses of melancholy." (2005a, 426) If the melancholy of Kästner and other left-wing melancholics is dangerous, it is because it is dissociated from work. Left-wing melancholics do not want to transform the conditions of their melancholy but instead hold onto the melancholy, which has given them the gift of their sorrow. They raise their sorrow and poverty to the level of supreme aesthetic pleasure. In their lyricism, these types claim the interests of the working class, while being materially disconnected from those interests. Because the positions they espouse have "little to do with the labor movement," their positions are "lost." (2005a, 426) Reflecting nothing but its economic physiognomy, Kästner's lyricism serves to protect the bourgeois existence of his readers, and resolves the melancholic tension between idea and image, effectively divesting melancholy of the imperative to act and to transform the nature of things. "In short," Benjamin proclaims,

> this left-wing radicalism is precisely the attitude to which there is no longer, in general, any corresponding political action. It is not to the left of this or that tendency, but simply to the left of what is in general possible. (2005a, 425)

Instead of politicizing the emptiness of capitalist alienation, left-wing melancholia aestheticizes it and acts against the interests of the working class. If, as Benjamin recognized, the rise of fascism is intrinsically bound up with the transformation of subjects into spectators and consumers, then left-wing melancholy is not merely wrong or unsuccessful art, but art that works to reinforce the real material conditions that fascism requires.

Benjamin remarks at the difficult work one must undergo if they wish to aim their destructive energies at the conditions that sustain their everyday existence. This is the challenging work of heroic melancholy discussed in the previous section. It is one thing for a petit-bourgeois writer (like Kästner) to undergo proletarianization and ally themselves with the aims of the revolutionary working class. It is quite another thing for the writer to put their lives on the line for the radical positions they espouse. This is because proletarianization hardly makes one a proletarian. For left intellectuals, "the bourgeois class gave [them], in the form of education, a means of production that, owing to educational privilege, makes [them] feel solidarity with it, and still more it with him." (2008, 92) The left-wing melancholic is one who is unwilling to do this work, which entails the continual labor of critiquing and undoing their bourgeois education, and the privileges it continues to afford in their everyday life.

In "Resisting Left Melancholy," Wendy Brown (2003) extends Benjamin's critique of left-wing melancholia to analyze the failures of the contemporary left to actualize its progressive political visions. Drawing on the work of critical theorist Stuart Hall (1988), Brown characterizes the failures of the Left as anachronistic preservation of Marxist and intellectual orthodoxies that belong to a past epoch. These include outdated Marxist analyses of capital and the primacy of class, as well as materialism that fails to adequately account for the subject, experience, style, and the importance of language (Brown 2003, 464). Through the dogmatic preservation of these outdated formulas and formulations, the contemporary Left inscribes a conservatism at the heart of their political vision that inevitably sabotages the radicalism of political praxis. Towards answering the question of why the Left would aim its destructive energies toward its intended aims, Brown characterizes the self-sabotage as an effect of a lousy nostalgia and sentimentality for possibilities that no longer belong to the present. The Left's melancholic preservation of its political insights results in the erection of a substitutive object to denigrate, and Brown sees this object in the Left's frequent attacks of identity politics and poststructuralism, both of which are charged with fragmenting the Left and undermining the requisite solidarity for a radical politics. What undermines the Left is, instead, the melancholy that fetishizes dead objects over and against the living.

While Brown's analysis provides helpful insight into the hidden conservatism of leftist political projects, it elides the productive possibilities of leftist melancholy. As the insight into the nature of historical experience, the death and decay that belies the vitality of the present's appearance, melancholy can offer insight into the historical conditions that sustain experiences of misery and loss. When melancholy's destructive energies are directed towards these conditions, which are unevenly distributed, and disproportionately affect the marginalized and subjected underclasses, it directs itself toward emancipatory ends and holds open the possibility of heroism without a hero.

Conclusion

In this chapter, I explored Benjamin's interest in the melancholy of poets to whom he attributes a special knowledge. For these poets, their despair was not merely personal and subjective, but capable of revealing the nature of their historical experience, namely, the decay and transience of everyday life.

Benjamin reads this destructive attention as a sensitivity to the material conditions of the present that sustain the misery and suffering of others. Through its poetic transfiguration, melancholic attention can be made material and shared with others. In their work, poets offer a model for transforming the destructiveness of melancholic despair into productive, creative activity.

The dangers of melancholy, discussed concerning Adorno's concern with inwardness and the emergence of a new melancholic subjectivity, take on a new urgency in Benjamin's political writings of the 1930s. Melancholy is destructive, but toward what are its destructive energies aimed? As Benjamin illuminated in his critical text, "Left-Wing Melancholy," the art of melancholy, like the politics of melancholy, can bear a deep conservatism that belies the political positions the subject espouses. While left-wing melancholics claim to work in the name of emancipatory ideals to actualize progressive political visions, a sentimentality towards suffering and the social position suffering enables keeps them from attaining true heroism. That left-wing melancholy is counterrevolutionary is due to the preservation of the melancholic subject. Heroic melancholy is melancholy that aims its destructiveness towards those conditions without which it would not exist, and so, it is directed toward its alienated self-image. To return to the question posed in the title of the chapter: Can melancholy be heroic? Yes, melancholy can be heroic, but it is an absurd heroism without a hero.

Notes

1. For further discussion of Adorno's critique of Benjamin, see Feldman (2011) and Pensky (2001, 130–148).
2. "Interpretation … is criticism of phenomena that have come to a standstill; it consists in revealing the dynamism stored up in them, so that what appears as nature can be seen to be history. On the other hand, it ensures that what has evolved loses its appearance as mere existence as stands revealed as the product of history. This is essentially the procedure of Marxist critique." (Adorno 2009, 135)
3. The *shelter* refers to two slabs of sandstone resting upon one another near Hardt, Germany. This natural formation merged with historical events when Duke Ulrich hid in the shelter in the 1500s to escape persecution. According to folklore, a spider then spun a web over the entrance to the shelter, which hid him from his captors.
4. In "Mourning and Melancholia" (1957), Sigmund Freud presented mourning and melancholia are two distinct, affective reactions to loss. Mourning names a normal, conscious process of working through the loss, while melancholia indicates a refusal or unwilling on the part of the subject to properly mourn the loss. As a response, melancholia is pathological, unconscious, solitary, destructive, and dissociated from work.
5. On Adorno's critique of Kierkegaard's inwardness, see 1989 (29–35).
6. An example that illustrates the absurdity of heroic melancholy can be found in Franz Kafka's "In the Penal Colony." In this story, it is not the traveler who has insight

into the unjust laws of the penal colony. It is the officer, the one who watches as his beloved execution machine decays unceremoniously into a ruin. His melancholy, which appears to the reader as a defiant and solipsistic nostalgia, becomes heroic through the final act of the officer's self-sacrifice to the machine's unjust-justice (1995, 191–230).

References

Adorno, T. 1989. *Kierkegaard: Construction of the Aesthetic*. Minneapolis, MN: University of Minnesota Press.

Adorno, T. 1997. *Prisms*. Cambridge, MA: The MIT Press.

Adorno, T. 2004. *Aesthetic Theory*. London: Continuum.

Adorno, T. 2006. "The Idea of Natural-History." In *Things beyond Resemblance: Collected Essays on Theodor W. Adorno*, edited by R. Hullot-Kentor, 252–261. New York, NY: Columbia University Press.

Adorno, T. 2009. *History and Freedom*. Malden, MA: Polity Press.

Benjamin, W. 2004. *Selected Writings, 1, 1913–1926*. Cambridge, MA: Harvard University Press.

Benjamin, W. 2005a. *Selected Writings, 2, 1935–1938*. Cambridge, MA: Harvard University Press.

Benjamin, W. 2005b. *Selected Writings, 4, 1938–1940*. Cambridge, MA: Belknap Press.

Benjamin, W. 2006. *The Writer of Modern Life: Essays on Baudelaire*. Cambridge, MA: Belknap Press.

Benjamin, W. 2007. *Illuminations*. New York, NY: Schocken Books.

Benjamin, W. 2008. *The Work of Art in the Age of Its Mechanical Reproducibility and Other Writings on Media*. Cambridge, MA: Belknap Press.

Benjamin, W. 2009. *The Origin of German Tragic Drama*. London: Verso.

Bloch, E. 1977. "Nonsynchronism and the Obligation to Its Dialectics." *New German Critique* 11: 22–38. https://doi.org/10.2307/487802.

Bloch, E. 2000. *Literary Essays*. Stanford, CA: Stanford University Press.

Brown, W. 2003. "Resisting Left Melancholy." In *Loss: The Politics of Mourning*, edited by D. Kazajian and D. Eng, 458–465. Berkeley, CA: University of California Press.

Didi-Huberman, G. 2005. "The Supposition of the Aura: The Now, the Then, and Modernity." In *Walter Benjamin and History*, edited by A. Benjamin, 3–18. New York, NY: Routledge.

Feldman, K. 2011. "Not Dialectical Enough: On Benjamin, Adorno, and the Autonomous Critique." *Philosophy and Rhetoric* 44 (4): 336–362. https://doi.org/10.5325/philrhet.44.4.0336.

Ferber, I. 2013. *Philosophy and Melancholy: Benjamin's Early Reflections on Theater and Language*. Stanford, CA: Stanford University Press.

Freud, S. 1957. "Mourning and Melancholia." In *The Standard Edition of the Complete Psychological Works of Sigmund Freud, 14*, edited by J. Strachey, 243–258. London: Hogarth Press.

Hall, S. 1988. *The Hard Road to Renewal: Thatcherism and the Crisis of the Left*. New York, NY: Verso Books.

Kafka, F. 1995. "In the Penal Colony." In *The Metamorphosis and Other Stories*, edited by W. Muir and E. Muir, 191–230. New York, NY: Schocken Books.

Kelly, T. 2009. "Adorno—Nature—Hegel." In *Language without Soil: Adorno and Late Philosophical Modernity*, edited by G. Richter, 99–116. New York, NY: Fordham University Press.

Marx, K. 1984. *Karl Marx: Selected Writings*. Indianapolis, IN: Hackett Publishing, Inc.

Nietzsche, F. 1974. "The 'Wanderer' Speaks." In *The Gay Science*, edited by W. Kaufmann, 342–380. New York, NY: Random House, Inc.

Pensky, M. 2001. *Melancholy Dialectics: Walter Benjamin and the Play of Mourning*. Boston, MA: University of Massachusetts Press.

7 *Anhedonia, Dysthymia, and Tristasia: Depressed Characters in Alice McDermott's Novels*

Gail Shanley Corso
Neumann University, Pennsylvania

Characters from literature who experience complications from love and loss often exhibit depression[1] in its many forms. Such is the case for characters in novels by Alice McDermott. These characters may resort to pretense and lies as a means to cope with loss, or silences to avoid shame for their family or themselves, as in *Charming Billy* (1998); they may become unable to respond appropriately in situations, or they may have a sense of confused identity about their self-worth or relationships to others, as in *A Bigamist's Daughter* (1982). Some underlying guilt or unresolved emotional pain often underscores narratives of such characters, as in *Child of My Heart* (2002). While some might experience memory loss of cultural identity, as in *Charming Billy*, others experience a heightened remembrance of specific incidents in their life or in the life of someone whose memory they cherish. In such reminiscences, a character as a first-person narrator, or a community of narrators returns to a specific incident or two, or *peak moments*[2] through which they frame their beliefs and values. In *That Night* (1987), *Someone* (2013), and *The Ninth Hour* (2017a), peak moments surface in the cyclical structure of the stories, in those significant memories that the narrators select to retell. Through these moments, the readers recognize a character's moment of awakening about self, and the storytellers' understanding of the emotional pain and depression that their parents, neighbors from childhood, and ancestors experienced in their struggles to survive loss and trauma.

Telling the story matters as a way for the storyteller to reveal that which is less transparent to the reader—it may work toward healing relationships, removing the stigma of mental illness, or of mirroring self-insights for the narrator himself/herself/themselves to understand how a family's past influences its present. In other stories, characters remain impervious to their depressive symptoms, their reduced ability to experience pleasure (anhedonia), their absence of will power to act decisively (abulia), their ongoing loss of and their deep sorrow at the loss of love and absence of significant relationships (tristasia), or their ongoing feelings of hopelessness, guilt, sadness, or depression that last for at least two years (dysthymia). Others may recognize such problems, but some who suffer never will. As an antidote to their troubles, they resort to fantasy and dreams; delusions and lies may plague their lives; they may drown in *the curse*; they may choose suicide.

Shame and Silence

In Alice McDermott's novels, *Child of My Heart*, *A Bigamist's Daughter*, and *That Night*, adolescent girls, while provided for by their parents, experience silence about their parents' lives, an absence of the father caused by his job away from home, or his actual death, and an emotional distance from the mother, especially when the girl transgresses boundaries of propriety during decades of the early part of the 20th century through the 1960s; these girls experience a benign kind of neglect about which scholars have come to identify its effects on mental health.[3]

In *Child of My Heart*, the middle-aged narrator, Theresa, explains, in this memoir-like fiction, what happened one summer when she was 16. Petey Moran, her young, neglected neighbor, she explains, is destined to experience a lifetime fraught with conflicts, of highs and lows on the emotional continuum:

> [He] would be plagued all his life by anger and affection, by gifts gone awry, by the irreconcilable difference between what he got and what he longed for–by the inevitable, insufferable loss buried like a dark jewel at the heart of every act of love. (McDermott 2002, 242)

Theresa reminisces about her life, also characterized by love and "inevitable, insufferable loss." She portrays herself as a youth who retreats into her world by immersing herself into characters from her favorite classic books. As the oldest young resident in the East Hampton community on Long Island, she serves as the nurturing caregiver to children whose families may neglect their offspring, as does Petey Moran's mother and absent father, and to others whose parents need child and animal-care, while they work or socialize. That summer, Theresa also cares for an infant child of a famous, elderly abstract-expressionist artist to whom she is attracted, and with whom she, the virgin, engages in one-time only sex. Theresa's more mature narrative voice chronicles her movement toward crisis in the story; however, there seem to be two trajectories for the storylines: Theresa describes her growing desire during the 1960s to rebel against her elderly Irish-American parents and their values and beliefs, so she can align with the artist's life and beliefs without boundaries for propriety or rigid codes of conduct. Theresa interjects into this storyline her intensifying need to care for those who seem to be left behind in this community, and to advocate for social justice for all who experience social injustice in the culture at that time, the era of social protests against the Vietnam War, against sexism, against racism. Several incidents in the plot point to the counter-cultural movement, the generation gap, and the Civil Rights Movement, but they serve as a backdrop to the story's major focus that centers on Theresa's daily routines during this one summer early in the 1960s. Throughout, Theresa, a seemingly caring teenager with a growing social conscience, slides into the story's movement through incidents in the plot how she neglects to respond to the growingly urgent medical needs of her younger cousin, Daisy, the relative in her care. While the reader delights in Theresa's care and concern for others, her neglect to respond to the child's health issues signals some of Theresa's emotional and possibly psychological problems.

When this child arrives for a brief sojourn that summer from her life in Queens, New York, her life with many siblings, even one closer in age to Theresa, a peer, the narrator details her love and preference for Daisy. She describes her generosity toward her younger cousin, and she emphasizes her joy in sharing time only with this younger cousin. In the narrative, though, Theresa drops details about the young cousin's ever-present low-grade fever, and body bruises that surface on her feet, shoulder, and back, yet she neglects to respond appropriately. They keep it a secret. Suzanne Mayer (2018a) explains Theresa's failure to secure needed assistance for Daisy's dark bruises "despite her own presentiment of what the bruises and fevers signal" as a form of denial that combines her adolescent self-centeredness and her inability to see consequences of her neglect; such behavior researchers of trauma identify as "constriction." (qtd. in Corso 2018, 124) Theresa denies the reality, and in what the narrator describes as her own "flash of black anger," she rails against the shadow ["death of children"] as she wishes to banish it, and she wants all parables, songs, and narratives altered:

> Start over again. Draw a world where it simply doesn't happen, a world of only color, no form. Out of my head and more to my liking: a kingdom by the sea, eternal summer, a brush of fairy wing and all dark things banished, age, cruelty, pain, poor dogs, dead cats, harried parents, lonely children, all the coming

> griefs, all the sentimental, maudlin tales fashioned out of the death of children. (McDermott 2002, 179–180)

Mayer explains how not only does Theresa wish to change the traumatic narratives to which she alludes, but also she shows an Irish-American trait—denial through silence and secret-keeping (see 2018a, 124). Theresa's mother neglects to talk with her about any of her feelings or experiences from that summer. Busy with her own goal—to provide for her daughter a life filled with hope for happiness and economic stability, she separates her daughter from her working-class cousins in New York City and any of her ethnic and cultural ties to the Republic of Ireland. This silence between mother and daughter and Theresa's isolation from peers who live nearby set her up for what occurs—her neglect to respond to Daisy's physical illness, and her complicity as an underage sexual victim. As a servant in this community—one who works toward making others feel entertained—Theresa becomes enamored of and victimized by the globally-renowned elderly artist, known for his interest in young girls, his inspirational sacrificial virgins.

This silence between mothers and daughters in second and third-generation Irish-American families seems to be an accepted trait. McGoldrick et al. (1991, 173) explain how mothers in Irish-American families "raise their daughters … to take responsibility … [They are] more like sisters." As such, this kind of communication strips the daughter of being a child. Maureen Dezell (2002, 132) distinguishes two kinds of silences in the mother and daughter communication patterns within such an Irish-American family dynamic—the mother's emotional silence "which is defensive," seeming to avoid shame, and a punitive silence, characterized by omitting the truth. McGoldrick et al. (1991, 177) explain how the Irish tendency, in general, "use[s] denial, mystification, exaggeration, confabulation, and numerous other techniques to avoid facing painful emotions" to the "extreme." While this emotional pain in Theresa's family remains nonspecific, perhaps it is caused by the loss at the birth of their first child, a son, Robert Emmet, named after a famous Irish nationalist patriot who led an abortive rebellion against British rule in 1803. Theresa in *Child* fathoms a quiet resentment by her parents for her presence as she describes her sense of being a stranger at the breakfast table with them. She feels as if she intrudes upon their time together. She is an outsider, even within her own home.

Monica McGoldrick (2011, 13) emphasizes the importance of persons understanding "to whom we belong." While her book is intended for family therapists and counselors, she also acknowledges its value for those who wish to understand better their family to resolve relationship problems. McGoldrick cautions that without understanding those to whom we belong, "We are at risk of losing our center if we do not appreciate how much we are all linked in our journey through life and how much we need to find ways to hold on to our connections." (2011, 13) In literature, many characters like Theresa exhibit symptoms of long-term depression, or dysthymia;[4] however, the narrator or character may neglect to identify this form of psychological distress. In *Child*, the reader may see how the narrator years later from her lonely bed, experiences some pain from her guilt over her delayed response to Daisy's needs. Theresa reminisces about her side of the story to justify her choices and inactions, and perhaps to seek understanding and forgiveness. Her seeking understanding may be part of her psychological healing process. Characters in other McDermott's stories may refer to another's depression in passing without conveying its lifetime debilitating effects on one's well-being and self-identity.

Corso (2017) explains how the benign neglect that Theresa, the teenager, experiences in the absence of meaningful communication with her parents contributes to her conflicted identity. Isolated from peers and relatives of her age, Theresa lives in fantasy worlds that she creates and shares with the younger children in the community. McDermott envelops this narrative at the beginning and end with an image of broken nurturance, a metonymic device that signifies how a well-intentioned gesture of love and nurturance that due to ignorance and an impulse to love and to be loved is fraught with impending loss and death. Through Petey's gift to Theresa of wild bunnies, now separated from their mother, he attempts to show her his nurturance. The reader knows that this fairytale image will end only in Petey's grief for the impending death of the animals. The older Theresa, now alone in her bed, reminisces about these significant moments, years after her coming of age and her coming into sincere regret for her failure to respond to Daisy's physical needs. Theresa now is awakened to her skewed notion of nurturance. Just as Petey usurped the nurturant role of the mother rabbit, all with intentions to love and to care for the bunnies, Theresa, too, imagined a role of caretaker in this community, but her choice suggests neglect; in the absence of any model of nurturance in her own family or life, she engages in what she knows—benign neglect. While Theresa succeeds in spending more time with Daisy, ultimately, after the summer ends, "[Daisy] left us. She left me," Theresa states in an Irish-American turn of a phrase to indicate loss caused by death (McDermott 2002, 141).

Broken Relationships and Their Effects

In *That Night*, through the voice of a more mature female who can be characterized as "an unreliably reliable narrator," this unnamed narrator muses on what she witnessed and experienced during the 1960s as she blends "half-forgotten memories from her own life, her imaginative recounting of what she observed and overheard in the neighborhood, and her iterative, poetic recreation of the critical events of 'that night'." (Kovach, qtd. in Corso 2018, 146) Throughout the story, this narrator/witness remains unnamed, a detail of significance in this novel since even insignificant characters' names are known. This absence of detail represents a more expansive view of women's human condition—of her struggle with insecurities, doubts, desires, and needs to love and to be loved.

The narrative voice recalls incidents in the life of her childhood during the early 1960s when she witnessed the cruelty of an East Coast-hometown-suburban community toward two teenaged lovers whose romance is forced to be broken. The girl in this shattered relationship is the teenager, Sherry, who after her father died suddenly of a heart attack, feels compelled to experience the love that was lost by turning to a leader of a gang, Rick. She becomes sexually involved with Rick, whose love for her seems authentic, but whose projected identity and family in the community place him on the fringes of acceptance; they are outcasts. While Rick's father is a medical doctor, he is known to practice family medicine in an unconventional home practice. Aside from this anomaly, Rick's mother suffers from severe depression and schizophrenia, as explained by the narrator. His mother had a history of running away from home, and as quickly as an advertisement to find her was published in the community newspaper, she would be found in some obscure motel in other towns and states, for she "had decided on a fairly regular basis throughout his childhood that she would prefer not to live." (McDermott 1987, 37) When Rick and Sherry were dating, Rick's mother was in a treatment program at a state hospital that allowed her weekend visitations. Despite Rick's dysfunctional family, Sherry sees him for his charisma among his gang, for his presence as their leader, an influential paternal figure for the other guys while Rick is drawn to Sherry for her stability and nurturance that he does not receive at home; Rick idolizes Sherry. For at least one year, Sherry's mother welcomes Rick, this young rebel, into her home to see her daughter. However, after Sherry told her mother that she thought she was pregnant, the mother's hospitality toward Rick turned to ostracization and outright animosity.

This mother's sudden change in her interaction with Rick shows her depressed state and repressed anger over her newfound role as a widow in a community of married couples with their young children. Sherry's mother immediately has a doctor confirm this pregnancy, and the girl then is shuffled off to a cousin's home in Ohio, where after some time, she gives up her child to an adoption agency. Before she decides upon this adoption, Sherry runs away from her cousin's home and slit her wrists in an attempt to kill herself as she is desperate without her love, Rick. Without Sherry's being able to talk to Rick, she feels emotionally isolated and distraught; suicide seems to be her only option. Within days of Sherry's removal to Ohio, Rick tries to see her at her family home, as he had done every day for the prior year, but his telephone calls and visits to the house go unanswered until one night, *that night*, he returns with his friends in muscle cars, and frantically attempts to see Sherry, or to find out her whereabouts. In this world, before cell phones, such a removal made contact between the lovers impossible. Added to this abrupt end to a relationship, Rick is met with hostility, silence, and complete rejection by Sherry's mother. In the community, no one except the little girl, Sherry's unnamed neighbor, the now mature narrator, recognizes in Rick his authentic love for, and emotional pain from losing Sherry. Rick, at that time, remains unaware of this lone champion for his love, the child, who, as a mature woman, still holds onto her memory of that night, and of Rick's interior life, and his plea for the one he loved. The community remains unable to see beyond the stereotype of Rick as a rebel without a cause, or as a kid from the other side of the tracks, one who just does not belong.

The narrative circles back to that peak moment of *that night* when Rick explodes all of his desperate emotion in his appeal to Sherry's mother to be heard, but as a result, he becomes the scapegoat of all in the community except one—the narrator who believed in Sherry and Rick's relationship, and their love. The fathers in the community misunderstand Rick's intentions and lash out at him; Sherry's mother, grieving for her deceased husband and also caring for her elderly mother, responds with deep resentment and anger, probably frustrated and ashamed by this new complication of her unwed and pregnant-teenage daughter; the police laugh at Rick's devotion as a *Romeo* to this girl; the mothers gossip about him and Sherry and their indiscretion; and tragically, the two lovers totally disconnect. As an effect, both experience what might be perceived as an anaclitic depression[5] that often follows the disruption of a relationship when persons feel helpless.

At one point, though, we are told that Sherry recognizes how she longs for love in her life: "She wants to love someone else. This emptiness left like an impression by the way she loved her father must be filled or else it will be as though he had never lived." (McDermott 1987, 183) The unnamed narrator at yet another community gathering years later explains that she had been told how Sherry moved on; she met another guy and had two children and a house. Sherry got what she wanted, but the narrator wonders about what though of love remains, or what was lost after the lovers experienced this forced separation and total lack of understanding.

In one of the final chapters of the novel, the reader sees the stereotyped bad boy, the pariah of the community, Rick, now a man with a family, returning to the house that is for sale, and which is across the street from the house of memory's fame, the traumascape of *that night*. Years later now, with his wife, children, and an elderly woman, possibly a grandmother, he visits the narrator's family home from which she had observed his and Sherry's romance and raw passion, and his ultimate breakdown when Sherry had disappeared from his life. Though this house seems out of his price range, he schedules to visit it in a clear view of that traumascape, that landscape at which he experienced severe grief at the loss of his love, and severe shame caused by the community's cruelty. His children and the elderly woman, possibly his mother, who had experienced severe mental illness when he was a child, remain in the car. This place allows a bit of distance emotionally from the site of Rick's pain, but it places him close to where he once felt that he belonged, to the place where perhaps someday Sherry might return. It is the place where ultimately the community judged him to be worthless and guilty, as not being part of it. Living across the street from that site of his love and loss, he possibly imagines, would vindicate him, and prove them all wrong. He has returned as a family man, even though the narrator describes what she perceives as a heartless relationship between him and his wife, unlike that of passion, which she had witnessed between him and Sherry. It is the site where Rick had battled with other men when he had pleaded with Sherry's mother to know where his love had gone, and it is the site where he was defeated:

> That night when he came to claim her, he stood on the short lawn before her house, his knees bent, his fists driven into his thighs, and bellowed her name with such passion that even the friends who surrounded him, who had come to support him, to drag her from the house, to murder her family if they had to, let the chains they carried go limp in their hands. (McDermott 1987, 13)

The narrator's father, during events of that night, we are told, thinks: "This is *insane*." (1987, 13) After several attempts of shrieking her name, "He [Rick] called [Sherry] again, [and] doubled over now, crying." (1987, 4) Then the men in the community started swinging their bats at Rick and his friends. The nameless narrator remembers, "in the growing darkness, a hundred dumb, unrhythmical movements, only blow after artless blow." (1987, 5) The child, though, was enamored by this display of raw passion by Rick: "I remember only that my ten-year-old heart was stopped by the beauty of it all." (1987, 3) To her, Rick epitomizes a knight in shining armor.

This narrator acknowledges the "cowardly incompetence of memory, how it can be pushed around by time, bullied by desire, worked over by our intractable ability to see what we want to see." (1987, 164) Now a mature woman, the narrator sees Rick when he returns to this battlefield of sorts, and they talk. She reflects upon what he knows as his story of true love, loss, and its ensuing emotional pain, and associates it to her denial of signs of lost love in her marriage:

> No less than those stubborn and curious people who build and rebuild their homes on fault lines or slippery mountain slopes or at the edges of ever-eroding rivers and lakes, we seemed to live from day to day resigned or indifferent to what we knew was coming. (1987, 165)

The narrator reveals how Rick has become a family man despite the community's savage response to his situation, but he is one who always will remember his lost idealized love. Through his presence at the end and by what he says in response to the narrator's question, "Do you know why she moved away?" (1987, 172), we can empathize with him for the community's dismissal of his love, his awareness of his loss, and his public shaming in his understated response:

> 'Oh yeah', he said, and what sadness was in his voice was not private, or even personal, but only an acknowledgment of what he knew we all had once shared. 'I remember', he said, and nothing more. (1987, 172)

While Rick restores our understanding of his credibility, and we understand his shame and his pain of loss, there is hope and promise for him as he seems responsible for his family. However, his lack of affect in this response suggests some unresolved feelings for Sherry, his regrets, and his unrealistic wish to reconnect with his past. Mark Widdowson (2011, 258) characterizes a kind of depression that Rick may be experiencing—anaclitic depression, especially as he may be longing for replication of Sherry's feelings for him, for "intense wishes to be cared for, protected, and loved." The narrator, who tells the story, also reveals to the reader that at one point, she had an abortion when she, as a married woman, felt unprepared for parenthood. She, too, has suffered losses—her parents now retired to Florida, her unhappy marriage, the unwanted child, her displaced presence, too, in this community. She reflects about love and loss: "I could not quiet the thud of this old longing not merely to stop time and bring the dead back to life but to discover forever what part of love remains." (McDermott 1987, 127)

This story about *that night* is as much about the narrator's feelings and her losses, as it is about Rick and Sherry and their losses. The novel is told by the neighbor child now a grown woman; while not a memoir, this novel reads like the unnamed narrator's memoir. Katie Rose Guest Pryal (2010,

482) describes the memoirist as one "embrac[ing] her illness as not just a disability, but also a gift, building an *ethos* based on links between mood disorders and creativity." The neighbor narrator tells this story about love and loss and provides some hope that all can only connect,[6] and belong in reciprocal relationships—to love and to be loved. It becomes essential to retell such stories "for generating and recovering ethos in the face of mental illness or psychiatric disability." (Reynolds 2018, 10)

In yet another McDermott novel, *A Bigamist's Daughter*, the omniscient narrator reveals complications that the main character, Elizabeth Connelly, an editor at a vanity press in New York, has with her relationships. We get a sense of her lost identity. For all the time her father spent away from home when she was a child, she imagines his infidelity, possibly his having lived another life with another family elsewhere. Elizabeth's relationships with males, her relationships with her mother and her father, whose job outside of the home she never entirely understood, lead her to question her own identity within a family. As an adult woman and only child, she was unaware of her father's occupation, and even more troubling, later in her life, of her mother's deadly cancer. Her relationship with her mother is almost nonexistent. She had been disconnected from her mother for years, uninformed about her mother's move to Maine with her lover, Ward, and her impending death. Typical family ties hang by a slender thread for this mother and daughter relationship. After her mother's death, Ward intimates Elizabeth's father's sin of bigamy without precisely stating the word. Colleen McDonough explains that Elizabeth learns a bit of the truth through the voice of the adulterer, Ward, about her parents and their "carnal sins of the Catholic church." (qtd. in Corso 2018, 20)

In Irish-American families from this timeframe, talk excludes any details that might humiliate the family. Maureen Dezell (2002) describes stoic, genteel relationships between mothers and daughters in Irish-American families, as a way to avoid the harsh truth of the matter on otherwise taboo subjects, such as sex, religion, and any resulting shame. McGoldrick, Anderson, and Walsh (1991, 177) state that there was a tendency toward "denial and avoidance" in Irish-Catholic American families "facing painful emotions." Such silence, as a form of communication, was intended to avoid talking about shameful incidents in the family in the here and now, as well as in the past. McDonough identifies the effects of Elizabeth's being insecurely attached to her parents with her mother's surface words with her, and stretches of silences about anything significant, and her father's physical absence for many days at a time as a traveling businessman:

> Of the many end results of insecure attachment, such as low self-esteem, poor attachment motivation, inability to lead, poor self efficacy and many others,

> perhaps the most obvious for Elizabeth could be identified as her lack of identity and unstable relationships in adulthood. (qtd. in Corso 2018, 28)

One such unfulfilling romantic relationship she has with an author, Tupper, whose novel is being published by the vanity press where Elizabeth works as his editor. This new lover shows interest in her mysterious family. Tupper wants to discover the truth about Elizabeth's father, yet he wants her to deny and sever any connection to her Irish ancestry that he perceives as low class. He intends to discover an ending to his evolving novel. Tupper exploits her family history to profit from her pain. This situation, while farcical, sadly portrays Elizabeth's inability to bond with a caring partner. Displaced from any home and disconnected from the immediate family that had denied her any emotional ties, unknowing of her Irish-American ancestry, Elizabeth is lost. She tells Tupper that her father "had traveled a lot. Some kind of intelligence … He died when I was fourteen … In some kind of car accident … alone." (McDermott 1982, 76) To compensate for mysteries surrounding his death and for unsatisfying attachments to both her mother and her father, by the end of the novel, Elizabeth chooses to become a traveling editor, like her Irish ancestry, displaced from any identity within a normative group. The narrative voice tells us what she imagines in her new role, free of domestic life and any long-term relationship: "If she likes him, she'll say she is an artist, a mistress of her art. A hall of mirrors and secrets. A mystery. If she likes him, she knows she'll lie." (1982, 290) Elizabeth breaks from her life as the editor at the vanity press and commits to living like a gypsy of sorts, free from roots, but willing to embrace pretense and lies.

As Elizabeth uproots and decides to live even more promiscuously, detached from any real relationships, she seems to have accepted her life as already fated. According to Al Qahtani and Al Qahtani (2017), major life events have solid relationships to depression. The setting, biological, cognitive, and social factors, traumatic events, and childhood adversity become strong predictors of major depression as one ages. Elizabeth's genetics, her low self-esteem, pessimism about domestic life, her unsatisfying relationships with her parents and with those in romantic relationships, and her unhappiness in her job at a vanity press that lies to authors about the quality of their books, all point to a troubled person. She might even be experiencing dysthymia, a chronic form of depression that lasts for at least two years (Jidhun and Chitra 2016). Katie Hurley (2018) adds to the causes of dysthymia, a first-degree relationship with a relative with a depressive disorder and life events, such as the loss of a parent. Elizabeth's father's death may have been a suicide, which could account for the silences in her home. Elizabeth's mother seems to have been depressed about her ever-absent husband, and his sudden death when Elizabeth is a teenager. Elizabeth's feelings of hopelessness, pessimism, worthlessness, guilt, self-criticism, along with her inability to focus on any one job, and her choice to be uprooted from any home or any one place, and to travel as a loner, seem to identify her as a person experiencing dysthymia, and she like her father seems at risk for self-harm, or even suicide while on the road.

Peak Moments

While written as novels, several of these stories read as memoirs or family histories in which the narrator reveals much about herself or themselves, especially concerning specific incidents or words that inspire or sharpen one's awareness. The repetitive or cyclical return to significant events or treasured words in the narration can be explained through neuro-rhetorics as an awakening or epiphany like that experienced by the narrator in the mood memoir: "the description of the moment of the awakening reveals a memoirist's desire to establish an ethos of a reliable narrator—of a reliable observer of experiences" (Pryal 2010, 499) despite the character's having suffered some disabling mental illness or setbacks. For this analysis I identify how certain of McDermott's characters break from their lifestyle, and begin a journey of self-discovery that disconnects from their past (*A Bigamist's Daughter*); they create a narrative that seeks understanding and forgiveness for them or their family members (*Child of My Heart*; *Charming Billy*, *The Ninth Hour*); they need to have one listen to their side of the story (*Child of My Heart*; *That Night*); or they hold onto their hope that someone will be there to redeem or *catch* them (*Someone*) despite a world that seems increasingly indifferent to the needs of the vulnerable, the needs of those who are marginalized.

Such is the case in *Someone* (2013), when the narrator, Marie, an octogenarian, retells her family's story of loss, rejection, shame, and misunderstanding. The story, however, is not revealed through a chronological sequence of events. Edward Hagan (2018) identifies three broader frameworks of this narrative. Marie's early childhood, from approximately 1928 to 1949, when, as a child of Irish-American immigrants, she gives birth to her first child as she turns 30, and moves from Brooklyn to Rego Park in Queens. In this first segment of the novel, the deaths of her young neighbor Pegeen Chehab and Marie's father occur. Marie frames this story of her life—its mishaps and providence—with a childhood memory of Pegeen, whose kindness and hopefulness instill a lifelong positive influence upon her. Marie remembers her first loss of a loved one when she was a child in Brooklyn—Pegeen, a first-generation, Syrian-Irish-American neighbor. This early incident of love and loss resurfaces throughout Marie's memoir of her life from approximately the 1920s to the beginning of the 21st century. The second major segment of the novel relates to other significant incidents of love and loss—her work as a receptionist at a funeral home, her marriage to Tom Commerford, and the birth of her four children. The third segment shows Marie's sensitivity to her brother Gabe's psychotic break after he leaves the seminary. When he returns to her home, she disposes of sleeping pills that she thinks he might use to overdose as he moves away from his religious vocation and grapples with the secret that Marie's children joke about—Gabe is gay. Marie, perceptive of people and their emotional pain, remains tolerant.

The seven-year-old Marie, a child from an ordinary, working-class Irish-American family, idolizes Pegeen, who, she observes, treks back and forth to Manhattan each day for what the older Marie now understands as her menial job. Pegeen seems somewhat disabled, as she confides to the child how she falls frequently, and she loses or misplaces items, such as her library book and gloves on her daily commute from one borough to another. Pegeen also self-identifies as an *amadan*, Irish Gaelic, for a fairy fool or trickster found in Irish folklore as she tries to make light of her foolish physical instability, especially when she falls. She finds comfort in her fantasy of some Prince Charming, whom she believes will rescue her the next time that she falls. Pegeen's hopeful optimism, her faith, inspires Marie throughout her own complicated life.

Pegeen tells the child Marie, "But there's always someone nice … Someone always helps me up." (McDermott 2013, 5) She talks about planning to fall when she sees a specific young man, a stranger, someone nice who once before had helped her get up. Pegeen, whose father is an immigrant from Syria, and her mother from the Republic of Ireland, represents for Marie the promise of hope and love—though, sadly, the next time Pegeen falls on the steps at her home, no one rescues her, and she dies. Marie, who has experienced all kinds of emotional pain throughout her life, recalls those comforting words that Pegeen had told her when she was a little girl, how someone would always be there for her; she clings to this belief in the care and concern by an indefinite someone.

Edward Hagan (2018) identifies Marie's trauma throughout her life as very personal—a breakup in an earlier relationship, the early death of her father, her family's shame at her brother's having left the seminary, and then of his psychotic break and subsequent time at a mental health facility, the traumatic birth of her first child and caution to prevent further pregnancies, and finally, surgery on her wrong eye, a medical error or malfeasance that left her visually impaired for her entire life. Hagan explains how Marie's way of telling her story breaks from what is known as a male master narrative with an emphasis on chronology of events by having Marie start her life story with memory of Pegeen, by interspersing her presence throughout it, and finally, by concluding with reference to Pegeen: "McDermott is intent on revealing a simultaneity inherent in human remembrance … which Marie's perspective renders synchronous." (qtd. in Corso 2018, 75) The novel concludes with Marie's reflection about her lifetime of severe personal losses, yet she affirms what Pegeen and the mixed-marriage couple symbolize for her:

> I thought of Pegeen Chehab and her last fall. And then of the distance her parents had traveled to bring her to her brief life, sands of Syria and Mount Lebanon and the sick floor of the pitching ships, and then that brief flame in the parlor floor window. She told me, poor sparrow, poor fool. We'll see what happens then. (McDermott 2013, 232)

Marie holds onto her faith, hope, and love despite having witnessed and experienced personal trauma, grief, and pain of loss. When compared to the Chehabs' struggles and losses, especially in the loss of their only child, her pain from loss pales.

Often it is difficult to recognize the narrator or the age of the storyteller, as in *Someone*. Alice McDermott, in each of her eight novels, often creates what Beatrice Jacobson (2008) terms *the stealth narrator*, the teller of the story who reveals how and why certain characters, including themselves, suffer. Through the prose and narrative structure, we can identify a character's suffering as depression and other manifestations of emotional pain caused by loss, the presence of dark secrets in one's family story, shame caused by a character's having transgressed acceptable behavior or the silent presence of intergenerational trauma that the characters may experience, but about which they understand very little.

Telling Family Stories: Therapeutic Agency against Intergenerational Trauma

Cathryn Molloy (2015, 160) explains how retelling narratives of the family to introduce rhetorical *ethos* shows "how stigmatized persons attempt to reclaim their places in the world and how they use displays of their unique attributes to resist those who would leave them behind." Alice McDermott's characters in several stories reveal intergenerational pain even more explicitly than in those already analyzed. In *Charming Billy* and *The Ninth Hour*, family members reconstruct their family's story of being descendants of Irish immigrants. Edward Hagan, in "The American Wake," describes the traumatized alienation of such Irish Americans, brought on by their encounters with questionable American values, especially, as evidenced in *Child of My Heart* and *Charming Billy*. In each, Hagan explains how the narrators "lack Irish identity, although they are plagued by an aching consciousness of loss" and "the more [they] assimilate, the more they become traumatized." (2010a, 191–192) Suzanne Mayer (2018) adds insights about intergenerational trauma as a "wound that never completely heals, depriving the traumatized person of vital interpersonal abilities and hindering his/her function in life engagements, sometimes to extreme degrees." (qtd. in Corso 2018, 117) Mayer explains how descendants of those who experienced the famine in the 19th century, of those who survived impoverished conditions and prejudice against their social group as immigrants in the early 20th century, often were denied knowledge of these injustices; talk of the past was suppressed, as was a memory of the Irish struggle for freedom. Mayer identifies the result of such silence about past trauma:

> And the outcome is that their children and their children's children have been bound with a silence to death and an inclination to denial—of drink, of the drinkers, of the dearth of money, of the stifling of emotions, and of the crushing of hope for the future—all heritage of the Irish spirit reborn. (Mayer 2014, 197)

The aftermath of such trauma is passed on to the next generation. These wounds, Mayer (2018a, 117) argues, can become places of great healing.

In *Charming Billy*, much detail is provided about the extended family of Billy Lynch, the deceased, for whom his kinship group of immigrants and first-and second-generation Irish Americans join in a pub after his funeral in 1983. This interaction of the group comprises the introduction to the novel, as told to us by the daughter of Billy's best friend and cousin, Dennis Lynch. While we readers realize by the end of the novel that this narrator is middle-aged, we try to follow the story's movement over four decades and in different places to understand why she—Dennis's daughter, Matt's wife, or Mrs. Matthew West, but most significantly, the narrator without a first name—is compelled to tell her and Matt's inter-related family stories. It becomes a tale of Billy's loss of his first love, Eva, from Ireland, who, when she returns there, supposedly dies. The narrator's father, Dennis, however, is told by Eva's sister, Mary, the truth of the matter that Eva has married a fellow Irishman and purchased a petrol station in Clonmel (the largest settlement in County Tipperary, the Republic of Ireland) with funds that Billy sends her to buy passage tickets for her and her mother to emigrate from Ireland to the United States of America. In the late 1940s, Dennis tells Billy the lie that Eva has died. Dennis remains complicit with the lie even though Billy, decades later in 1975 while on a retreat for alcoholics on a trip to Ireland, seeks out Eva's grave, but unexpectedly meets her at the petrol station nearby. Despite Billy's knowing the truth, he sustains the lie to all in his social group that she is dead, and he avoids confronting Dennis about his role in perpetuating the lie. This *pledge* or cure for his *curse* has minimal effect, especially after Billy learns first-hand the truth about Eva. His vision of idealized innocence and the beauty of Ireland is believed to have been crushed, so he is perceived by members of the Irish-American clan as having wallowed in self-pity, and as having drunk himself to death.

Throughout the novel, pubs are perceived as part of the fabric of the Irish-American lifestyle. It is at the pub that men talk. Dennis, the propagator and keeper of the lie about Eva's death, rescues Billy regularly when Maeve calls him away from his home with his wife, Claire, and children to help Maeve carry the sodden Billy to his bed. It is Dennis, too, who identifies Billy at the morgue in the Veterans Administration Hospital. The novel is as much about Billy's deep sorrow as it is about the narrator's more in-depth understanding of her own father's lifelong sorrow and guilt as the perpetrator of the lie that almost gives Billy permission to drown his sorrows in liquor. The narrator describes her own father's [Dennis's] depression after the death of his father, Dan, and first wife, Claire:

> He thought of his father, as he did so often in those days when his father was first and foremost of those he missed, the very thought of him a prayer of sorts (one that said, I'm weary, Dad, and discouraged; I've lost all sense of delight), although truth be told, it struck him that night at that lonely hour, that his father in death was no more present to him, no more real, no more vivid than Eva was to Billy, in her just-over-the Atlantic afterlife, pumping gas on the convent road in Clonmel … Who can trace such things, he said, but it was perhaps the first tremor of the devastation that would strike him, knock him off his feet, in the weeks and months after my mother [Claire] died. Billy's thirty years of misdirected prayer, Billy's tenacious, life-changing belief. His [Dennis's] own lie. (McDermott 1998, 238–239)

At this social gathering in the pub after his burial, those in the kinship group whisper about Billy's love and loss of Eva despite Billy's having married another woman—Maeve, who is Irish American, and is silently present at the function. Maeve lives in the shadow of Eva and experiences the distress of caring for a person whose drunken oblivion often left her helpless, even vulnerable to physical assaults by him. Maeve, who was known to care for her elderly, alcoholic father, assumes a similar role in her care for Billy, whose life, described as *charming*, traumatizes all in the family circle. Dennis, the perpetrator of the lie, we learn marries Maeve ten years after Billy's death. While they delayed marrying, Dennis Lynch is the person to whom Maeve turns for help throughout her marriage when Billy Lynch, depressed for his losses, binges, and returns home intoxicated.

The narrator, Mrs. West, who moved far from her kinship group on the East Coast in New York to the West Coast, returns home each summer with her children but without her husband. Hagan (2010b, 216) identifies the husband's ongoing absence in contrast to her need to connect with her/their shared kinship group about which she knows very little as an "undiscussed psychic as well as geographic distance … that may actually threaten their marriage." She is driven to tell this story of her father's guilt and her connections to Matt's family in a previous generation almost as a way to understand not only her father's need to lie to Billy, but also to understand possible complications in her marriage that relate to their inter-related family history. She attempts to understand and to forgive her father for his role in Billy's sorrow, and to show how events of the past work toward shaping "each person's memory." (Mayer 2018b, qtd. in Corso 2018, 48) McGoldrick identifies an Irish pattern for dealing with those who are perceived as deceptive—how Eva's sisters who know the truth of her manipulation of Billy and her deceit refuse to communicate with her for 20 years (qtd. in Corso 2018, xii). Irish-American characters, in contrast, McGoldrick explains, avoid acting directly in Billy's case:

> [They] convey time and again a sense of past trauma that has closed them down. But often it seems that the history is not clearly known or remembered, so that what we see in them is the silence, the shutdown, the inhibition to risk. Underlying McDermott's characters seems to be that indistinct pain for traumatic history which they don't even know. (qtd. in Corso 2018, xii)

In the unfolding of this history of not just the family but its ties to emigration from Ireland, lies a pathway for breaking the silence as "the cure for the shame and the potential renewal of family members involved." (Mayer 2018b, qtd. in Corso 2018, 52) The narrator, like the Angel of History, as Mayer (2018a) points out, identifies something other than a "chain of events" in their family stories, but rather "one single catastrophe which keeps piling wreckage upon wreckage." (qtd. in Corso 2018, 249) Through the narrator's attempt to tell the truth of her father's initial deceit, of his bouts with depression and ongoing denials, a process of healing has begun.

In the most recent of McDermott's novels, *The Ninth Hour*, the story of family origins across 19 chapters is narrated by the unnamed *we* in the multi-vocal third person plural. The narrators through collective memory reveal their family story of their maternal grandfather's [Jim's] suicide in the early 20th century before the birth of their mother, Sally [Sr. St. Savior] Mc *Whatever*; their maternal grandmother's [Annie's] subsequent secret affair with the milkman, Mr. Costello; the late-in-life marriage of Annie to Mr. Costello, and the birth of her second child, Grace, the narrators' aunt; of their paternal great-grandfather Patrick Tierney whose family paid $300 to Red Whelan to substitute his presence for military service in the Union army during the Civil War in 1863 otherwise to be performed by schoolteacher Patrick; of their great-grandfather Patrick's estrangement from his only son, Michael, when he married an Irish immigrant who served as a housemaid in homes of the wealthy in Poughkeepsie, NY; of their father Patrick Tierney who marries their mother Sally, the child known as the *convent child*, who later in life becomes estranged from her own mother, Annie. The narrators remind the readers throughout the novel how their mother Sally experienced a life of melancholy, often disappearing from family spaces in the home to sleep in her bedroom. Patrick outlived Sally, and as a result, details somewhat scandalous stories that she must have confided to him, which then are retold by him to their children, and by them to us in this narrative: "Growing old ourselves, we indulged him. We listened to the same stories told again and kept silent about the truth: that our mother's midlife melancholy was clinical depression, unspoken of in those days." (McDermott 2017a, 241) Throughout the novel, the narrators interject how frequently Sally had been cared for by the Little Nursing Sisters of the Sick Poor. They reminisce: "We thought of the hushed afternoons of our childhood, our mother sleeping off her melancholy … keeping her in the world. Keeping her for us." (2017a, 243) The children begin to allude to what their father said, as "OUR FATHER SAID, 'After that [the untimely death of Mrs. Costello], your mother's life went from black-and-white to color'." (2017a, 239) In other words, Sally experiences happiness once her mother can remove the shame of her sin as the mistress to Mr. Costello by finally having all impediments removed to marry him. To remove the only obstacle to her mother's marriage to her lover, Sally had added to the disabled Mrs. Costello's tea, a spoonful of alum to poison her. Sr. Jeanne, too, as told by Sally's children, had served Mrs. Costello thick applesauce, a possible contributing factor to her choking to death. Sally, though, knows that she intended to harm this woman. Added to these troubling admissions, when she was older, Sally had learned the truth about her father—the child of an Irish immigrant, who drank, frequently arrived to work late, one so unhappy with his life that he commits suicide; he lost hope for achieving the American dream. Annie, too, lied to her daughter for years about her daily break each afternoon when she would rendezvous with the Milkman, Mr. Costello. When Sally finally learns the truth, she feels somewhat betrayed, and she imagines "looking out at all with what might have been her father's own eyes: envious, lonesome, buried, bereft." (2017a, 164)

The narrators' father, Patrick, also suffered. He had in the course of his life lived in *a dozen different tenements* until finally he inherited wealth from Red Whelan, the substitute for their grandfather during the Civil War, and assets from his Aunt Rose, their maiden aunt who cared for Red all of her life, to then buy an elegant brownstone in downtown Brooklyn. Since Michael's father had disowned him for marrying an Irish immigrant outside of his class structure, Patrick and his son Michael never again spoke after the marriage. Silence, that troubling response that McGoldrick (2018) identifies for dealing with differences among Irish-American family members, surfaces in this novel again. Michael Tierney, though generous to others, loans to Annie and Mr. Costello, the Milkman, money for them to buy a brownstone, too, a home that signals how they have achieved part of the American dream. Michael has learned the moral lesson of service to others, a trait that he has inherited from Red Whelan and his Aunt Rose.

In this novel, the descendants of Irish immigrants tell somewhat of a filtered story with the association of their grandmother with the good sisters as a way of diminishing her questionable behaviors. However, in the story, intergenerational trauma is chronicled, and severe punitive silences are portrayed, which begin to explain why the characters, especially Sally, experience severe clinical depression[7] that her children explain away as their mother's retiring to her bedroom.

Conclusion

In Alice McDermott's contemporary fiction, characters from many of her stories exhibit a range of responses to love and loss—sorrow, pretense and lies, delusions, loss of interest in pleasure, alcoholism, and even attempts at suicide. While in many of McDermott's novels, characters portray their self-conflict or distress, their little understood depression is evidenced here in six of her stories—for Elizabeth Connelly in *A Bigamist's Daughter*, the conflicted young professional who serves as an editor at a vanity press in New York and whose parents seem to have lived secret lives from which they excluded her; to the unnamed narrator who as a 10-year old in the early 1960s witnessed the love relationship between two teenagers end suddenly in *That Night* when the girl's recently-widowed mother demands that her unwed pregnant daughter leave her child with a Catholic adoption agency in another state, and sever her relationship with her young lover, Rick; to the deceased alcoholic, Billy, in *Charming Billy* who feeds his sorrow about the loss of his young love in the years following World War II, and wallows in the lifetime effects of a lie about the death of this loved one as told by his best friend-cousin, Dennis; to the more mature narrator, Theresa, who in *Child of My Heart* in a memoir-like narrative tells of her coming of age during a summer in the 1960s when she grows to rebel against her elderly, genteel Irish-American parents, and to neglect to act responsibly when she observes her younger cousin's signs of physical distress; to the memoir like story, *Someone* told by an octogenarian female narrator who identifies significant traumatic incidents in her life, the life of an ordinary person, an *Every[wo]man* type narrative, yet she frames her story with a relentless hope despite her experiences with love and loss; and finally, to the grandchildren narrators in McDermott's most recent novel, *The Ninth Hour*, who tell the life stories of their mother who is depressed, their grandmother, who is the widow of a young Irish immigrant who had commit suicide as a response to his depression, and of their Tierney ancestor who during the Civil War paid for another to serve in his place as a soldier in the Union army. In each of these stories, depression seems to be characterized as intergenerational that is complicated by environmental factors, including embodied shame, loss of the father, female characters' difficulties communicating honestly with their mothers, and best friends being unable to find words to discuss harsh realities. It is through persons like the characters in these novels telling their story, Swiss systems analyst Rosemarie Welter-Enderlin (1993, 53) identifies how "breaking the silence and putting events into language" can work toward healing wounds caused by family secrets and lies, and a past filled with trauma that they have forgotten to remember.

Notes

1. Eugene S. Paykel (2008), in "Basic Concepts of Depression," identifies core symptoms of depression among which DSM-5 requires one: depressed mood, and/or loss of interest or pleasure (anhedonia). ICD-10 identifies other eligible symptoms, such as decreased energy or fatigability. Beyond these symptoms, others contribute to a diagnosis of depression: appetite or weight loss or gain; insomnia or hyperinsomnia; agitation or retardation; loss of energy or fatigue (DSM-5); loss of confidence or self esteem (ICD-10); worthlessness or guilt; reduced concentration or indecisiveness; thoughts of suicide or suicide attempt.
2. Claudia M. Kovach (2018) identifies how in *That Night* the narrative circles back to the peak moment, for the novel starts with the climax to the story, that night when the fathers, who otherwise seemed detached from any personal connections in the community, rallied against Rick Slater and his gang's members. Kovach explains how McDermott returns to this incident throughout the novel, for it has become for the narrator as a witness to the violent response by the fathers "a moment of growth and

maturation for the pre-pubescent girl." (qtd. in Corso 2018, 132) Kovach portrays a psychological reality "that exposes and connects to the innermost heart, the core of relationships." (2018, 132)

3. Carol Gilligan (1982, 127) in *In a Different Voice* identifies the importance of connection in relationships, especially as a woman confronts a dilemma or crisis. When one realizes that "self and other are interdependent and that life, however valuable in itself, can only be sustained by care in relationships," truth in relationships is cultivated. Carol Gilligan and Grant Wiggins (1994, 135) in "The Origins of Morality in Early Childhood Relationships" identify how "the vulnerable child, due to the physical or psychological loss of intimacy, experiences a 'disordered mourning' resulting in 'compulsive caregiving' or 'independence of affective ties'." Many of these "victims of loss of intimacy are subject to intermittent discontinuities in parental affection and profound mixed messages from parents about their love for the child." (1994, 135) Such ambivalence of feelings between parents and child relate to psychological difficulties with relationships.
4. Dysthymia, a chronic form of depression, lasts for at least two years for adults. Jidhun and Chitra (2016) identify nine symptoms of dysthymia: feelings of hopelessness, sadness, or pessimism; sleep issues including oversleeping or difficulties with sleeping; high level of fatigue that causes a person to delay completing tasks; feelings of worthlessness, guilt, or constant self-criticism; being unable to focus; being irritable or frustrated; being indecisive; showing changes in appetite; being at risk for self-harm or suicide. Katie Hurley (2018) identifies five possible causes for dysthymia: brain chemistry; genetics with first degree relatives having depressive disorder increasing one's risk of it; environmental or life events including traumatic events and high levels of stress; personality traits that include negativity, including low self-esteem, pessimism; self-criticism; history of other mental disorders.
5. Anaclitic depression is explained by Mark Widdowson in "Depression: A Literature Review on Diagnosis, Subtypes, Patterns of Recovery, and Psychotherapeutic Models." (2011) He distinguishes it from another kind: introjective depression. Anaclitic depression is explained as occurring after some disrupted relationship. The person may feel weak and helpless, and Widdowson explains, they have "intense wishes to be cared for, protected, and loved." (2011, 358) That person often is preoccupied with disruptions from the past and present, and they anticipate problems with future relationships, as they relate to "issues of abandonment, rejection and aloneness." (2011, 358) To deal with this kind of depression, the person tends toward trying to please others and attempting to avoid conflict to calm their fears of being abandoned and rejected (2011, 359).
6. "Only Connect" is one of Alice McDermott's essays in which she analyzes the importance of writers reading and rereading their novels in progress to identify the significance of details in the evolution of the story's plot and development of characters. This retrospective process allows for creative insights upon connecting details. McDermott comments on the incredible craft of Shakespeare and Forster, and poses a question to contemporary fiction writers: "Why wouldn't we want to go over what we've already set down again and again, just as a scholar would, looking for consequence, for pattern, sowing the psychological seeds in one scene that will blossom in another, as well as culling those seeds that fail to bloom?" (2017b, 447)

7. Clinical depression is understood through nomenclature, such as "major depression," "dysthymia," or "depression not otherwise specified" that is diagnosed on a continuum for "intensity, duration, and impact on daily functioning." (Williams et al. 2002)

References

Al Qahtani, A., and N. Al Qahtani. 2017. "Prevention of Depression: A Review of Literature." *Journal of Depression and Anxiety* 6: 292. https://doi.org/10.4172/2167-1044.1000292.

Corso, G. S. 2017. "Psychoanalyzing Theresa: Telling It Slant in Alice McDermott's *Child of My Heart.*" *Studies in Arts and Humanities* 3 (1): 20–33. http://dx.doi.org/10.18193/sah.v3i1. 88.

Corso, G. S. 2018. *Alice McDermott's Fiction: Voice, Memory, Trauma, and Lies.* New York, NY: Peter Lang Publishing.

Dezell, M. 2002. *Irish America: Coming into Clover.* New York, NY: Anchor.

Gilligan, C. 1982. *In a Different Voice: Psychological Theory and Women's Development.* Cambridge, MA: Harvard University Press.

Gilligan, C., and G. Wiggins. 1994. "The Origins of Morality in Early Childhood Relationships." In *Mapping the Moral Domain*, edited by C. Gilligan, J. V. Ward, and J. M. Taylor, 111–138. Cambridge, MA: Harvard University Press.

Hagan, E. A. 2010a. "The American Wake: Alice McDermott, *Child of my Heart.*" In *Goodbye Yeats and O'Neill: Farce in Contemporary Irish and Irish-American Narratives*, 191–203. Amsterdam/New York, NY: Rodopi.

Hagan, E. A. 2010b. "Being Irish and Being Nothing: The Abyss of Identity in Alice McDermott's *Charming Billy* and Edward J. Delaney's Fiction." In *Goodbye Yeats and O'Neill: Farce in Contemporary Irish and Irish-American Narratives*, 206–231. Amsterdam/New York, NY: Rodopi.

Hagan, E. A. 2018. "Narration as Experience of Simultaneity in Alice McDermott's *Someone.*" In *Alice McDermott's Fiction: Voice, Memory, Trauma, and Lies*, edited by G. S. Corso, 73–82. New York, NY: Peter Lang Publishing.

Hurley, K. 2018. "Persistent Depressive Disorder (Dysthymia)." *Psycom.* Accessed May 24, 2019. https://www.psycom.net/depression.central.dysthymia.html.

Jacobson, B. 2008. "Alice McDermott's Narrators." In *Too Smart to Be Sentimental: Contemporary Irish American Women Writers*, edited by S. B. Ebest and K. McInerney, 116–135. Notre Dame, IN: University of Notre Dame Press.

Jidhun, P., and P. Chitra. 2016. "A Case on Childhood Dysthymia-Low Mood Triggers the End." *International Journal of Nursing Education* 8 (2): 219–222. https://doi.org/10.5958/0974-9357.2016.00079.9.

Kovach, C. 2018. "Love and Grief: Recollection, Reiteration, and Replication in Alice McDermott's *That Night.*" In *Alice McDermott's Fiction: Voice, Memory, Trauma, and Lies*, edited by G. S. Corso, 127–148. New York, NY: Peter Lang Publishing.

Mayer, S. 2014. "Tell the Story: Intergenerational Trauma and Healing." In *Clinician's Guide to Self-Renewal*, edited by R. J. Wicks and E. A. Maynard, 189–203. Hoboken, NJ: John Wiley & Sons, Inc.

Mayer, S. 2018a. "Celibate Bride, Shrewish Sage, and Fey Cousins: Intergenerational Trauma among the Women of McDermott's Novels, *Charming Billy* and *Child of My Heart*." In *Alice McDermott's Fiction: Voice, Memory, Trauma, and Lies*, edited by G. S. Corso, 115–126. New York, NY: Peter Lang Publishing.

Mayer, S. 2018b. "The Narrator as Angelus Novus: Collective Memory, Truth, and Lies in *Charming Billy*." In *Alice McDermott's Fiction: Voice, Memory, Trauma, and Lies*, edited by G. S. Corso, 45–53. New York, NY: Peter Lang Publishing.

McDermott, A. 1982. *A Bigamist's Daughter*. New York, NY: Random House/Dell.

McDermott, A. 1987. *That Night*. New York, NY: Farrar, Straus & Giroux.

McDermott, A. 1998. *Charming Billy*. New York, NY: Farrar, Straus & Giroux.

McDermott, A. 2002. *Child of My Heart*. New York, NY: Farrar, Straus & Giroux.

McDermott, A. 2006. *After This*. New York, NY: Farrar, Straus & Giroux.

McDermott, A. 2013. *Someone*. New York, NY: Farrar, Straus & Giroux.

McDermott, A. 2017a. *The Ninth Hour*. New York, NY: Farrar, Straus & Giroux.

McDermott, A. 2017b. "Only Connect." *Sewanee Review* 125 (2): 420–443. https://doi.org/10.1353/sew.2017.0033.

McDonough, C. 2018. "'Not What It Seemed': Pretense and Identity in *A Bigamist's Daughter*." In *Alice McDermott's Fiction: Voice, Memory, Trauma, and Lies*, edited by G. S. Corso, 17–43. New York, NY: Peter Lang Publishing.

McGoldrick, M. 2008. "Finding a Place Called Home." In *Revisioning Family Therapy: Race, Culture and Gender in Clinical Practice*, edited by M. McGoldrick and K. V. Hardy, 97–113. New York, NY: The Guilford Press.

McGoldrick, M. 2011. *The Genogram Journey: Reconnecting with Your Family*. New York, NY: W. W. Norton & Company, Inc.

McGoldrick, M., N. Garcia-Preto, P. M. Hines, and E. Lee. 1991. "Ethnicity and Women." In *Women in Families: A Framework for Family Therapy*, edited by M. McGoldrick, C. M. Anderson, and F. Walsh, 169–199. New York, NY: W. W. Norton & Company, Inc.

Molloy, C. 2015. "Recuperative Ethos and Agile Epistemologies: Toward a Vernacular Engagement with Mental Illness Ontologies." *Rhetoric Society Quarterly* 45 (2): 138–163. https://doi.org/ 10.1080/02773945.2015.1010125.

Paykel, E. S. 2008. "Basic Concepts of Depression." *Dialogues in Clinical Neuroscience* 10 (3): 279–289. https:// doi.org/10.1017/bec.2019.4.

Pryal, K. R. G. 2010. "The Genre of the Mood Memoir and the Ethos of Psychiatric Disability." *Rhetoric Society Quarterly* 40 (5): 479–501. https://doi.org/10.1080/02773945.2010.516304.

Reynolds, F. J. 2018. "A Short History of Mental Health Rhetoric Research (MHRR)." *Rhetoric of Health & Medicine* 1 (1–2): 1–18. https://doi.org/10.1080/02773945.2010.516304.

Welter-Enderlin, R. 1993. "Secrets of Couples and Couples Therapy." In *Secrets in Families and Family Therapy*, edited by E. Imber-Black, 47–65. New York, NY: Norton.

Widdowson, M. 2011. "Depression: A Literature Review on Diagnosis, Subtypes, Patterns of Recovery, and Psychotherapeutic Models." *Transactional Analysis Journal* 41 (4): 351–364. https://doi.org/10.1177/ 036215371104100411.

Williams, J., N. P. Hitchcock, J. A. Cordes, G. Ramirez, and M. Pignone. 2002. "Is This Patient Clinically Depressed?" *The Journal of the American Medical Association* 287 (9): 1160–1170.

8 *Broken Promise: Depression as Ex-Gifted Girl Identity in Elizabeth Wurtzel's* Prozac Nation

NORA AUGUSTINE
The University of North Carolina at Chapel Hill

Few scholars of either depression or literature can long abide in those pursuits without encountering some form of *Mad Genius* mythology (as I call it). This mythology comprises a broad set of cultural and theoretical discourses positing an essential link between various states of mental disorder and various mental gifts. Definitions of both *madness* and *genius* vary widely, thus Mad Genius investigators never lack for new adaptations of this mythology to pursue. Nor has the increasing medicalization of American psychiatry weakened Mad Genius's credibility; science instead promises ever-new means for operationalizing mental traits and measuring their relationships. Is there a real connection between madness and genius? The allure of this hypothesis is evident in the multitude of studies that try to prove it, yet such research rarely delves deeply into why this should be so alluring (to whom) or what results from humans' attachments to Mad Genius. Moreover, no studies known to me have drawn from self-referential writing by persons diagnosed with mental illness to analyze the effects of Mad Genius mythology on their stories. The enduring popularity of Mad Genius indeed cannot be explained by science alone. To understand what this mythology means to real people who live with mental illness—as well as those who identify as gifted—we ought to listen for its echoes in their own words.

In this chapter, I read Elizabeth Wurtzel's 1994 memoir *Prozac Nation: Young and Depressed in America* for a critique of Mad Genius mythology in a post-feminist United States context.[1] As a bestselling work of creative non-fiction, *Prozac Nation* could be construed as evidence that depression does beget literary prowess (or vice versa)—but it might also complicate Mad Genius mythology by revealing social forces that govern its appropriation by this specific author in her specific place, time, and story. I examine how Wurtzel's portrayal of her depression borrows from one popular strain of Mad Genius mythology: the cliché that formerly "gifted" children grow into depressed, burned-out adults. In particular, I argue *Prozac Nation* enacts a series of archetypal "Gifted Girl" dilemmas—as indexed by feminist psychologists in the 1970s and beyond—in which a precocious girl is increasingly traumatized by her environment's ambivalence to her achievements. Insofar as mainstream American culture continues to value eminence and independence yet oppose these qualities to normative femininity, the Gifted Girl will be punished for displaying her talents even as she is also lightly rewarded. It is the impossibility of being both gifted *and* a girl that continually destroys Wurtzel's will to live in the world of *Prozac Nation*; thus, she comes to suspect she is "one of those people … who are just better off dead." (1994, 8)

I begin with an overview of *Prozac Nation*, consciously departing from existing scholarly analyses of this book and dwelling on popular press reviews that unintentionally highlight the Gifted Girl dilemmas at its center. Informed by my reading of these reviews as well as feminist psychology research from the same era, I read backward from Wurtzel's adulthood to her childhood and explore how the text connects her depression and giftedness across these life stages. Lastly, I sketch an interpretation of Wurtzel's recovery as a dissolution of the Gifted Girl's depression into unrestrained passions: fury towards the people who failed her, grief for the child she once was, and compassion for the adult she is becoming.

In the field of American life writing, Elizabeth Wurtzel was undoubtedly one of the most unpopular-popular people of the past 25 years. An accomplished journalist, memoirist, and attorney, Wurtzel was a subject of intermittent controversy from the publication of her first book, the 350-page memoir *Prozac Nation: Young and Depressed in America* (1994), up until her untimely death in 2020. *Prozac Nation* recounts Wurtzel's life story from birth to age 26 as organized around her chronic clinical depression and, eventually, her recovery through medication and therapy. Wurtzel's narrative voice is characterized by its "rock and roll aesthetic"—nearly every page of her memoir contains some reference to contemporary pop culture, sexual exploits, or illicit substances (Bullard 2002, 287). Given that two-thirds of *Prozac Nation* address Wurtzel's college years at Harvard University, her academic experiences and budding career in music journalism drive much of the plot. Also essential are her relationships with her parents, a "hysterical, exhausted, overwrought" mother and "deadbeat" father too preoccupied with "their own untrammeled, unfettered, unresolved, and unexamined emotional immaturity" to prioritize their daughter's needs (Wurtzel 1994, 5, 27, 77). But despite Wurtzel's descent into depression at "at ten or eleven or twelve" (1994, 41), we learn she was a remarkably accomplished adolescent: she recounts an internship at *New York* magazine while in high school, a prestigious college journalism award from *The Rolling Stone* (for her work with *The Harvard Crimson*), a summer reporting job with *The Dallas Morning News*, a semester of independent study in London, etcetera (Wurtzel 1994).

Considering the salience of Wurtzel's achievements throughout *Prozac Nation*, it is curious that most existing scholarship on this book overlooks its potential insights into female giftedness in favor of analyzing the author's relationship with Prozac. Scholars across the academy have taken *Prozac Nation* as a case study in the overall medicalization of mental illness in American psychiatry, wondering how scientific knowledge about the brain can be reconciled with humanist notions of self and identity. Thus sociologists Jette Westerbeek and Karen Mutsaers (2008, 26, 30) read Wurtzel's memoir alongside several other self-referential works about depression in the "age of Prozac," asking "to what extent and in what way do [authors] intentionally relate their identity to the disease?" Many argue Wurtzel blurs the line between illness and identity—by weaving each and every one of her experiences into the broader tapestry of illness, she arguably depicts depression "not as a hindrance to or a vehicle for realizing the self but rather as the self itself." (Cheever 2000, 350) Others suggest *Prozac Nation* nullifies its central debate—the question of whether depression is a biological illness or a personal identity—through Wurtzel's fairly positive response to Prozac at the end of her memoir. For instance, sociologist Dwight Fee argues her use of Prozac collapses the book's earlier complexity into "a straightforward recovery tale … a culturally dominant mode of story-telling." (2000, 85) In describing Prozac as a revolutionary technology that finally relieves her depression with no obvious obligation to make or use a therapeutic narrative, Wurtzel risks rendering the social causes of her depression (and *Prozac Nation* itself) irrelevant.

This de-contextualized vision of depression inevitably clashes with social constructionist theories of psychiatry, the most extreme of which would envision Prozac as a weapon of social control. Moreover, as Wurtzel is a woman writer, her views are also frequently compared against decades of feminists' arguments regarding the role of gender-based oppression in women's so-called *madness* (see Chesler 2018; Gilbert and Gubar 2000; Showalter 2009). To resist psychiatry's well-established history of violence against women, feminist scholars have worked to disentangle women's subjective experiences of distress from the broader cultural contexts in which they are assigned unfitting roles of passivity, domesticity, and heterosexuality. For example, feminist psychiatrist Jonathan Metzl attends to women's narratives that challenge Prozac as "a specifically gendered form of oppression"—yet his study intentionally excludes *Prozac Nation* and other "high-profile members of the Prozac literary family." (2003, 176, 177) According to Metzl, these texts paint Prozac problematically as "an agent that restores heterosexual normativity and stability … once cured, the women return to the men in their lives." (2003, 177) If *Prozac Nation* serves to reinforce the notion that "madness" means violating gender norms and "recovery" means fulfilling them, then this mega-popular memoir could indeed have dangerous implications for real women with depression.

Fortunately, *Prozac Nation* is not quite guilty of these charges. Revisited nearly 30 years after it was written, Wurtzel's portrayal of depression may not seem as medicalized as it once did; likewise, the environmental factors affecting her illness might seem more complicated. In truth, the first 12 (of 14) chapters of *Prozac Nation* contain no mention of Prozac whatsoever. When the drug finally appears in the text, it is praised not for its provision of quick-and-easy relief, but rather because its stabilizing effects help to integrate a decade's worth of incomplete solutions—"all the therapy, all the traveling, all the sleeping, all the drugs, all the crying, all the missed classes, all the lost time"—into one slow, vaguely perceptible "recovery process." (Wurtzel 1994, 329) At no point in this process does Wurtzel morph into an ideal daughter, girlfriend/wife, or mother; nor is it clear she expects such a transformation to occur. What *is* clear is her commitment to self-discovery through psychotherapy: dissatisfied with her life even after years of taking Prozac, she writes in the epilogue to *Prozac Nation*, "I needed therapy … I needed a good therapist … I needed a psychologist to teach me how to live." (1994, 346–347) Therapy without Prozac could not keep Wurtzel alive, but Prozac without therapy could not teach her "how to live"—she could not move forward with her future until she had constructed her narrative of the past. Thus Wurtzel affirms, "The secret I sometimes think that only I know is that Prozac really isn't that great … it is not the end but the beginning." (1994, 343–344) The present analysis of *Prozac Nation* also aims to end at the beginning. I seek to understand the environment that both fostered Wurtzel's depression in her childhood and (consequently) determined how she would relive, rewrite, and recover from her traumatic past in the writing of this memoir. Such therapeutic processes, like mental health itself, are "so much more complicated than any pill that any mortal could invent"—neither one's traumas nor the tools one has for narrating them can be extricated from one's contexts (Wurtzel 1994, 344). To begin historicizing Wurtzel's account of depression in *Prozac*

Nation, then, I pivot from scholarly perspectives on this text to dwell on popular press reviews.

American readers made *Prozac Nation* an instant bestseller in the early 1990s, but Wurtzel's writing—and indeed, Wurtzel herself—was eviscerated by critics. Two months before the book's release, *Kirkus Reviews* was the first of many publications to accuse Wurtzel of narcissism, concluding that "[e]ither she's a brat who won't shape up or she needs the drugs. Ultimately, you don't care which." (1994) In *The Boston Globe*, Jim Sullivan summed *Prozac Nation* as "one long whine, a tedious tome, a depresso-manifesto, a celebration of self-pity." (1994, 31) Likewise, Karen Schoemer of *Newsweek* compared it to "the self-absorbed rantings of an adolescent … so rife with hyperbole, so devoid of context, that it's virtually impossible to identify with her." (1994) Countless critics suggested *Prozac Nation* was as likely to induce depression as to relieve it (Goldberg 1994; Harris 1994; Kirkus 1994; Shrader 1994; Tucker 1994; Werner 1994; Marlan 1996). On the other hand, at least five reviews claimed Wurtzel would incite violence in her readers, for example, to "shake" her (Kakutani 1994, C19); throw her book across the room (Goldberg 1994; Harris 1994; Sullivan 1994); and even "hit her with a Nerf bat." (Udovitch 1994, 97)

Before long, reviewers of *Prozac Nation* began to invoke a critical consensus, agreeing that its "fingernails-on-the-blackboard tone … explain[ed] the astounding amount of negative press" it had received (Goldberg 1994, G3). In a 1995 interview with Wurtzel for *The Chicago Tribune*, Julie Deardorff simply included a supplementary inset (titled "Critics have their savage say"), citing five other critics' "scathing opinions" of *Prozac Nation* (1995, F1). In those excerpts, Wurtzel is charged with narcissism, self-pity, grandiosity, and blatant opportunism in appointing herself the "poster child" of Generation X depressives (Kirn 1994, 50). In particular, variations of the word "whine" ("whiny," "whining," etcetera) and "brat" seemed to be the most favored descriptors of her conduct (Corrigan 1994; Kakutani 1994; Moir 1995; Shrader 1994; Sullivan 1994; Werner 1994). The critics' repetitious use of insulting, infantilizing language like "whiny brat" certainly belies the fact that Wurtzel was 27 years old when *Prozac Nation* was published. To be sure, these reviews reified long-standing suspicions towards women's expressions of pain—not to mention women's writing—in patriarchal societies. Still, one cannot help but wonder why exactly Wurtzel's memoir provoked such a venomous response. What led so many seemingly credible reviewers to represent an adult woman's life-threatening depression as the mere whining of a narcissistic child?

A closer look at *Prozac Nation*'s reviews quickly points to Wurtzel's academic and professional accomplishments as a driving force behind many critics' animosity. As I mentioned above, *Prozac Nation* primarily takes place during Wurtzel's high-achieving college years at Harvard University. To Wurtzel's detractors, it seemed nigh impossible that a young woman who earned impressive grades, awards, and internships could have possibly been depressed—or at least, not as depressed as she claimed to be. Wurtzel's successes were cited as preface to copious amounts of sarcasm: one critic alleged her "series of triumphs … serve to remind us that no matter how low the author felt, she was still more successful than many of us" (Tucker 1994, BR 11); another asserted she was "inordinately fond of reminding her readers [she] pretty much had it all … even more determined to tell us, none of this ever brought her any joy" (Goldberg 1994, G3); a third pointedly observed that "None of this [depression] seems to affect her job performance, or her schoolwork" (Shrader 1994, A6); and so on. Interpreting *Prozac Nation* as an ode to the author's specialness, these reviewers all but accused Wurtzel of exaggerating her depression to make her achievements more extraordinary to her comparatively ordinary readers. Still other critics felt Wurtzel had understated her talents, claiming (for instance) that "through all the horror … she hasn't dropped a clue that she was all the while functioning, superachieving." (Harris 1994, 62) Wurtzel's nonchalance about her career was mocked as false modesty: "Gosh, Liz: No ambition? Just dumb luck?" (Sullivan 1994, 31) Regardless of how much *Prozac Nation* discusses the author's education and career—too much for some critics' taste, too little for others—the mere fact of Wurtzel's achievements seemed to preclude any expressions of unhappiness on her part. Her depression was dismissed not just because the critics felt her highs should counteract her lows, but also because her ability to reach such heights signified (to them) she was never really all that low in the first place.

In weaponizing Wurtzel's triumphs to silence her account of depression, these reviews alluded to a paradox quite familiar to gifted women: either neglect one's talents and suffer personal distress, or embrace one's talents and be rejected by one's environment. As a result, past media responses to *Prozac Nation* inadvertently identify this memoir as a source of valuable insights into women's giftedness in a post-feminist United States context. Spanning 1967 to 1994, the events of *Prozac Nation* represent an era in which second-wave feminism ostensibly liberated girls from Wurtzel's generation to seek educations and careers inaccessible to their mothers. But in 1986, feminist psychologist Linda K. Silverman contemplated "the Strange Case of the Disappearing Gifted Girl" (1986, 43), asking why—if IQ testing identifies equivalent numbers of gifted girls and boys—are there so many more eminent adult men than women? In other words, as her study is titled: "What Happens to the Gifted

Girl?" (1986, 43) Such analyses can be traced back to Leta Hollingworth; her research on giftedness in the early 20th century criticized societal norms for directing all of the women's energies towards child-rearing and housekeeping, "a field where eminence is impossible." (1914, 528) Six decades later, despite enormous victories for women's legal rights in the United States, Matina Horner nonetheless noted how "the new freedom for women" had failed to lift the "psychological barrier" to their success (1972, 171). A common question arose among late-20th-century feminist psychologists: who or what is to blame for "the disappearance of the gifted female," and what are the consequences of this loss? (Olshen and Mathews 1987, 251).

The answer for Silverman and her contemporaries was that, despite the expansion of women's professional opportunities, social norms continued to discourage girls from developing their talents by labeling successful women unfeminine, unlikeable, and abnormal. Indeed, Kathleen Noble indicted society's "long-standing history of ambivalence toward highly capable women" for fostering self-doubt and social dependence in the Gifted Girl (1987, 368). According to Noble, when caretakers claim to support all children's success yet subtly undermine, discourage, or ignore young girls, the Gifted Girl loses faith in her abilities. Forced to choose between cultivating her (uncertain) abilities and maintaining interpersonal relationships vital to her survival, she will fall into her socially prescribed role. Similarly, Silverman exhorted caretakers to protect the Gifted Girl's freedom, arguing that "[t]o the extent that independence is drummed out of little girls, these girls lose their giftedness." (1986, 67) Of course, feminists have long argued all girls and women—regardless of innate ability—can be driven "mad" by society's ambivalence to their success. Nevertheless, Silverman affirmed the highly Gifted Girl suffers more than non-gifted girls because she has "more to lose." (1986, 67)

When *Prozac Nation* is studied in its socio-historical context, the Gifted Girl dilemmas at its center are unmistakable. Though Wurtzel does not explicitly analyze her giftedness through the lens of gender, the text repeatedly incriminates her environment for simultaneously sabotaging and rewarding her achievements. In one especially relevant passage, she remembers fantasizing about the sympathetic press coverage she would receive if she should die by suicide. Desiring to drown herself in a swimming pool at Harvard, she writes:

> any death at my age would be considered a tragedy, surely worthy of a full-length feature in some publication, maybe the Boston Phoenix or New York ... I knew perfectly how the story would go: She was so full of potential, Harvard, a dancer, a writer, blah blah blah. And then the reporter would try to figure out what it says about our society when a promising young person with so many options

> chooses to do herself in. I could see it all: My life would suddenly be infused with all sorts of symbolism and meaning that it simply did not have as long as I was alive. As long as I was alive, I'd be staring into swimming pools at daybreak, empty and aching. (1994, 144–145)

Still an adolescent at this time, Wurtzel feels assured her untimely death "would be considered a tragedy" worthy of national publicity—wholly unlike the lackluster medical and familial attention she has secured for her depression before this moment. With obvious irony, she imagines a reporter who would lovingly document her gifts for posterity and ponder "what it says about our society" that even someone as exceptional as she could die by suicide. Though Wurtzel has shown symptoms of depression since she was a pre-teen, she realizes that those around her do not perceive any emotional depth ("symbolism and meaning") lurking beneath her seemingly "promising" demeanor—as long as she is alive and achieving, her talents have felt more like a liability than an asset. If she died a tragic premature death, however, the loss of her potential would suddenly be mourned by the very same people who failed to nurture her and her gifts when she was still alive.

This passage's disaffected tone ("blah blah blah") reverberates through nearly all those in *Prozac Nation* that discuss Wurtzel's suicidality; her frustration is directed at the notion that, instead of being commended for her ability to survive her depression, it is only by dying that she can win support from those around her. Whereas this reporter might profile the dead Wurtzel as inexplicably "choo[sing]" suicide over the "many options" available to her, the living Wurtzel has long suspected that suicide is the only possible outcome of her situation. As early as age 13, she recalls increasingly growing fixated with thoughts of threatening her life:

> I couldn't hope to end up in [a hospital] unless I made a suicide attempt serious enough to warrant oxygen or stitches or a stomach pump. Until then, I would remain woefully undertreated by a Manhattan psychiatrist who could offer only a little bit of help amid the chaos of my home life. I used to wish—to pray to God for the courage and strength—that I'd have the guts not to get better, but to slit my wrists and get a whole lot worse so that I could land in some mental ward, where real help might have been possible. (1994, 70)

Throughout Wurtzel's life, others have wrongfully perceived her above-average achievements as a mark of excellent mental health, but Wurtzel herself cannot fathom her depression getting better without serious familial support and medical interventions ("real help"). Her parents' constant fighting and mistreatment of their daughter ("chaos of my home life") merely exacerbates her mental state rather than relieving it, and her psychiatrist's intermittent talk therapy is "woefully" insufficient to relieve her despair. As far as she knows, only those who credibly threaten their lives are granted the type of medical attention she needs; thus, her depression will be invisible to those places unless and until she similarly externalizes her distress. Paralleling her later reasoning at the pool, she wishes for an outcome she believes to be both inevitable and absurd—for the ability to be unable to survive. But as both of the above passages suggest, Wurtzel's sense of obligatory suicidality poses abundant problems. First of all, she cannot possibly pinpoint the moment at which a suicide attempt becomes "serious enough" to secure necessary resources yet not so severe as to result in death (1994, 70). If she were to die, any subsequent recognition of either her misery or her gifts would certainly be useless to her then. Even worse, as she is well aware ("I knew perfectly … I could see it all"), such recognition would still hinge on others' gross misunderstandings of her death as a tragic mystery rather than the logical conclusion of her undertreated depression (1994, 144). She may dream of relinquishing her high-functioning status—and even risking her life—in order to get better, but it seems the only surefire way to elicit others' empathy is never to be gifted at all. Unfortunately for Wurtzel, she is faced with two impossible options: die by suicide, or else expunge her lifelong giftedness so others might see her depression. That she resigns herself to an "empty and aching" life (1994, 145), deferring suicide and planning to stare into pools or bewilder psychiatrists *ad infinitum*, hints that she is grasping for a third option in which her depression, giftedness, and environment could all be reconcilable.

Neither death nor dysfunction fundamentally appeals to Wurtzel; despite her misery throughout of *Prozac Nation*, she consistently resists the urge to self-destruct. While reflecting on her high level of functioning in college, she affirms she has "always been a coper" who could manage to "do what little must be done to scratch by" even at her lowest points (1994, 133–134). For instance, she responds to an especially acute depressive episode by resolving to work harder in her next semester at Harvard, asking herself, "Hadn't I always retreated to the splendid isolation of my studies?" (1994, 125) Indeed, the text frequently identifies Wurtzel's schoolwork as a means of escaping her depression: it is a welcome distraction in the short-term, and her educational achievements provide a flicker of long-term hope for her to "get out of this rut of a rotten life" and improve her situation "at some unspecified time in the future." (1994, 97) Moreover, her willingness to be a "perfect little Ivy League daughter" is positioned as a necessary condition of her (hypercritical) mother's affection and her (absentee) father's attention (1994, 137). Never having experienced "unconditional love" from her mother, Wurtzel muses that "if I'm not the girl who got into Harvard … she just doesn't love me the same way." (1994, 256) Thus Wurtzel describes Harvard as an "anchor" without which she would "disintegrate and float into the ozone layer"—her intense attachment to this institution is as much a symptom of her despair as it is a remedy for it (1994, 254). Whereas those around her can only interpret her achievements as a negation of depression, the text indicates that these two aspects of her identity are inextricably linked.

As illustrated by Wurtzel's memories of adolescence, the journalist who would romanticize her gifts and ponder the sociological symbolism of her suicide is scarcely better than the journalist who would attack her gifts as evidence of her narcissism and dishonesty. Both visions fail to capture the relationship between her depression and her achievements as understood by Wurtzel herself; they also overlook the significance of her environment as a determinant of the specific identity she constructs in *Prozac Nation*. My contention throughout this chapter is that Wurtzel's depressed persona resonates meaningfully with Gifted Girl discourse, linking her distress to her troubled giftedness. Such a reading entails that her environment's misrecognition of her achievements—viewing them either as unrelated or antithetical to her mental illness—exacerbates her depression by leading caretakers to withhold resources she has no power to access alone. Revisiting Wurtzel's reflections on her education and career, I have instead suggested her achievements can be read as symptomatic of her worsening depression throughout her adolescent years. What remains to be discovered, though, is the extent to which *Prozac Nation* also indicts environmental sexism as a *cause* of the author's mental illness. To delve more deeply into the influence of feminine gender norms on Wurtzel's depressed persona, we look no further than the earliest chapters of her memoir. Through their emphasis on the author's intrinsic potential versus her environment's hostility, these scenes from Wurtzel's childhood formulate a mythos of depression as thwarted Gifted Girl identity that follows her through the remainder of her memoir, albeit not (perhaps) the remainder of her life.

Long before *Prozac Nation* details the author's impressive education and career—before her clinical depression emerges within the timeline of this book—Wurtzel recalls her years as a highly precocious young girl. Aptly titled "Full of Promise," the first chapter of *Prozac Nation* stresses Wurtzel's nascent potential for greatness through lengthy lists of the talents, interests, and ambitions she exhibited in her childhood (1994, 16, 39, 79). Per Wurtzel's narration, there were no limits to her "overwhelming sense of invincibleness": she easily surpasses other children at school, winning school-wide competitions and placing into a particular class with two other students (1994, 40). Nonetheless, the text is quick to clarify her giftedness "wasn't just in academic achievements," for she spends her time at home immersed in "many odd projects" which range from science experiments and athletics to visual arts and creative writing (1994, 40, 39). It is productive to note that Wurtzel's memoir never refers to IQ testing, although this practice has been most common in the identification of gifted children in the United States since the early twentieth century. On the contrary, her specialness seems to have been evident since birth—she mentions playing elaborate games of make-believe with her pacifiers as a toddler and even appearing "in Pampers commercials at six months." (1994, 29, 16) In summary, Wurtzel's erstwhile "golden girl" persona is so central to her early childhood that she notes, "no one in her right mind would ever have believed I'd come to this: eleven and almost gone." (1994, 39, 16)

As *Prozac Nation* progresses into Wurtzel's pre-teen years, the author considers a plethora of explanations for her transformation from a precocious young girl into a depressed, suicidal adolescent. While doing so, she puts significant scrutiny on her relationships with her parents, who amicably "separated and divorced before [she] was two" but grow ever more adversarial as they struggle to raise their only child (1994, 29). Although Wurtzel locates herself within "a generation of children of divorce" (1994, 77), insisting her some of her experiences are so widespread as to be "common and trivial" (1994, 34), her narration also seems predicated on the unique anguish of growing up female and gifted in an unsupportive family. Through myriad allegations of parental neglect—primarily through her feelings of abandonment by her guardians in spaces of rigid conformity—*Prozac Nation* highlights Wurtzel's gradual victimization by a logic of (ab)normality that is transparently sexist. In this sense, Wurtzel's narrative once again offers crucial insights into its socio-historical environment, both elucidating the conditions that inspired her depressed Gifted Girl persona and gesturing at the process through which her depression might eventually be put to rest.

From an early age, Wurtzel remembers being absorbed with her mind: "my inner resources were so thorough and complete that I often had no idea what do with other children." (1994, 39) Despite the stress of her home life, the text underscores her perceptions of her innate self-sufficiency ("thorough and complete") as justification for retreating from potentially supportive peer relationships ("other children"). Young Wurtzel is "always perfectly content to be left alone," suggesting her projects are independently chosen and she neither needs nor wants others' encouragement in order to pursue them (1994, 39). However, as she approaches adolescence, the intensification of her past contentment into plaintive appeals for solitude—"By God, I was genuinely happy being alone"; "How bad would it be for me to just hang out ...? How bad?"—reveals her environment's decreasing tolerance for her mental life (1994, 79, 83). Whereas she had once unconsciously "compensated" for her familial distress by "being adorable and charming in the way of precocious little girls," her conscious attachment to her gifts seems to solidify in the same moment at which her ability to cultivate them is most endangered (1994, 39). In reading Wurtzel's preadolescence with an eye to Gifted Girl experience, then, it becomes clearer how her potential for achievement is undone by gender socialization that opposes feminine independence to a girl's ability to be normal.

In a manner wholly consistent with trends observed by Gifted Girl psychologists, Wurtzel's caretakers come to disregard her gifts, reject her autonomy, and pressure her to prioritize the formation of interpersonal relationships. Specifically, the narrative attends to Wurtzel "being left in a lot of different odd places" to limit her access to her inner life and push her to socialize (1994, 84). Over the course of her childhood, she is placed into nursery school, day camp, sleepaway summer camp, an after-school program, field trips on "days off from school," and so on (1994, 27, 39, 78, 84). Wurtzel identifies her parents' distaste for her solitude as "the exact reason" why she was persistently "forced to deal with other kids" despite her rapidly declining mental health in these years (1994, 79). For Wurtzel, there can be no illusion that her parents abandoned her in such spaces for the belief that she found it stimulating or even tolerable to interact with her peers; instead, she asserts, "I'm sure ... This was yet another bid at making me normal." (1994, 79) That Wurtzel's withdrawn personality is *not* normal for a pre-teen girl is a sentiment vaguely echoed by her friends, her rabbi, a teacher at her school, and one of her many camp directors (1994, 45, 48, 57, 85). Yet in emphasizing young Wurtzel's powerlessness against the constraints of her environment, *Prozac Nation* suggests it is depression—not normative femininity—that arises from the sacrifice of Wurtzel's giftedness.

In one noteworthy, under-analyzed section of *Prozac Nation*, Wurtzel reflects at length on her parents' decision to send her to camp for five summers of her youth (implicitly, from ages nine to 13). Designating summer camp as the place where "it all went wrong" and where her "spirit broke—and broke and broke and broke," Wurtzel's narration erupts into a moment of rage that is decidedly rare in this text (1994, 79). She writes:

> And what I feel as I think of summer camp is completely ugly: *I want to kill my parents for doing this to me! I want to hack them to death for this because I was the best little girl in the world and instead of making me feel good about all the things that were good about me, they sent me away and I never really found my way back*

> *home! I was special! I had promise! And instead they threw me away and tried to make me ordinary! They threw me away with a bunch of normal kids who thought I was strange and made me feel strange until I became strange! And after all these years, I still despise them for doing this to me!* The tears come down, not like rain, but like blows. (1994, 80)

This passage is one of several throughout *Prozac Nation* that subtly connects the origins of the author's depression to her thwarted childhood giftedness. Calling attention to her memoir's retrospective quality, the adult Wurtzel condemns her parents' preoccupation with her supposed (ab)normality as a young girl. As in most descriptions of her youth, she does not challenge the notion that she deviated from the norm; the childlike exaggeration of her specialness ("the best little girl in the world") instead serves to highlight the absurdity of her parents' ambivalence towards her gifts and thus the legitimacy of her anger. Now conscious of the extraordinary child she once was, Wurtzel alludes to the sense of belonging, acceptance, and "home" she felt in her childhood freedom—not just in the freedom she had to pursue her interests, but also in her freedom *from* the social rejection of "normal kids." The text's repeated affirmations of her "promise" suggest that, if her environment had only made her "feel good" about her uniqueness instead of making her feel bad ("strange" and abnormal), Wurtzel would have claimed the bright and happy future rightfully owed to her. However, according to this passage, Wurtzel's parents have done something far worse than merely overlooking her abilities and failing to nurture her properly. Her bitter exclamations that "they threw *me* away …! They threw *me* away …!" instead accuse them of actively discarding her potential and, along with it, her entire life and livelihood. It is Wurtzel herself, not just her giftedness, that has been permanently lost.

Critics of *Prozac Nation* might cite the above passage as proof of Wurtzel's *whiny* outlook—on the surface, she seems to blame summer camp for triggering her depression—but doing so would forfeit a valuable opportunity to bear witness to her childhood pain and her means of coping (or not) in the intervening years. The emotion in this passage stems not from Wurtzel's hatred of the "ordinary" per se, but rather from her estimation of the extraordinary future she may have lost. Judging that her parents made choices based on predetermined social norms at the cost of her own best interests, Wurtzel feels she "never really found [her] way back" to her authentically gifted self and the triumphant life she might have lived. Mounting pressures on her individuality brought her to a breaking point in her pre-teen years ("my spirit broke"), but she never did become normal—instead, she "became strange." That Wurtzel omits a clear definition of "strange" here is significant, as is the lack of a clear antecedent for the pronoun "this" across her testimony ("for doing *this* to me," "for *this*," "for doing *this* to me"). Contextually, she seems to refer to her depression, but the ambiguity of her language also hints at the futility of seeking justice for a Gifted Girl. That is, Wurtzel cannot clarify what her parents did to her, because she does not know what she has lost—she can never know who she would have been if they had nurtured her differently. Not only "strange" to others, but she has also become strange to herself, and perhaps she always will be. For all of "this," she unapologetically hates her parents. Yet even their violent death at her own hands will never restore her lost potential, and so her furious ruminations can only collapse into speechless, almost involuntary grief ("the tears come down").

Read through the lens of Mad Genius mythology, *Prozac Nation* presents a disquieting conflict between the author's giftedness and her environment's perverse attempts to mold her into a "normal" girl. That popular press reviewers implicitly reinforced this conflict—failing to realize the irony of their attacks—suggests to me that the portrayal of Gifted Girl identity in this book calls for new scholarly inquiry. Hence, my analysis resists prevailing responses to Wurtzel's narrative and reclaims its significance as a case study in the complicated relationship between madness, genius, and gender in a post-feminist United States context. I find that she provides a deceptively pessimistic response to the question of "What Happens to the Gifted Girl?" According to Wurtzel, the Gifted Girl becomes depressed. Yet *Prozac Nation*'s story culminates in the writing of a bestselling memoir rather than the Gifted Girl's demise. Indeed, the refraction of Wurtzel's past through the perspective of her adult self suggests her (Ex-)Gifted Girl persona is itself a coping mechanism for childhood trauma, and its uses may be limited. Like all variants of Mad Genius mythology, Gifted Girl discourse rests on controversial assumptions: it assumes some children's minds hold exceptional intrinsic potential for achievement in adulthood, and it also assumes such potential can be wasted, damaged, or even permanently lost. As *Prozac Nation* reinforces these assumptions, then, readers are invited to attribute Wurtzel's perceived faults to extrinsic factors beyond her control while nonetheless believing in the unique intrinsic "promise" she may yet fulfill someday. Steeped in radical self-compassion, such a narrative holds obvious appeal for any young woman struggling to survive suicidal depression and prove (to herself and others) her life is one worth living. Moving forward with that life, however, requires her to reckon with the present: the mixture of hard work and random luck still essential to extraordinary achievement. Or perhaps she will decide her self-worth need not rely on her ability to achieve at all. One way or another, the Gifted Girl must grow up.

Note

1. This study employs the phrase "post-feminist" solely to refer to a historical era following the rise of second-wave feminism in the United States and (accordingly) the American social imaginary. I do not mean to suggest an era in which feminisms are being critiqued and/or judged irrelevant.

References

Bullard, A. 2002. "From Vastation to Prozac Nation." *Transcultural Psychiatry* 39 (3): 267–294. https://doi.org/10.1177/136346150203900301.

Cheever, A. 2000. "Prozac Americans: Depression, Identity, and Selfhood." *Twentieth Century Literature* 46 (3): 346–368. https://doi.org/10.1215/0041462X-2000-4005.

Chesler, P. 2018. *Women and Madness.* Chicago, IL: Lawrence Hill Books.

Corrigan, M. 1994. "Unhappy All the Time." *Washington Post*, October 2, 1994. https://www.washingtonpost.com/archive/entertainment/books/1994/10/02/unhappy-all-the-time/d473012a-79df-4a7e-9824-c2a02ee54635/?utm_term=.21f22f193945.

Deardorff, J. 1995. "Totally Bummed." *Chicago Tribune*, February 10, 1995. https://www.chicagotribune.com/news/ct-xpm-1995-02-10-9502100065-story.html.

Fee, D. 2000. "The Project of Pathology: Reflexivity and Depression in Elizabeth Wurtzel's Prozac Nation." In *Pathology and the Postmodern: Mental Illness as Discourse and Experience*, edited by D. Fee, 74–99. London: SAGE.

Gilbert, S. M., and S. Gubar. 2000. *The Madwoman in the Attic: The Woman Writer and the Nineteenth-Century Literary Imagination.* New Haven, CT: Yale University Press.

Goldberg, C. 1994. "'Prozac Nation': Downer of the Year, Maybe Decade." *Hartford Courant*, October 23, 1994. https://www.courant.com/news/connecticut/hc-xpm-1994-10-23-9410190107-story.html.

Harris, M. 1994. "A View to a Pill." *Entertainment Weekly* 241: 62.

Hollingworth, L. S. 1914. "Variability as Related to Sex Differences in Achievement: A Critique." *American Journal of Sociology* 19 (4): 510–530. https://doi.org/10.1086/212287.

Horner, M. S. 1972. "Toward an Understanding of Achievement-Related Conflicts in Women." *Journal of Social Issues* 28 (2): 157–175. http://dx.doi.org/10.1111/j.1540-4560.1972.tb00023.x.

Kakutani, M. 1994. "The Examined Life Is Not Worth Living Either." *New York Times*, September 20, 1994. https://www.nytimes.com/1994/09/20/books/books-of-the-times-the-examined-life-is-not-worth-living-either.html.

Kirkus. 1994. "Prozac Nation: Young and Depressed in America." *Kirkus Reviews*, July 1, 1994. https://www.kirkusreviews.com/book-reviews/elizabeth-wurtzel/prozac-nation/.

Kirn, W. 1994. "For White Girls who Have Considered Suicide." *New York Magazine* 27 (35): 50.

Marlan, D. 1996. "Prozac Nation: Young and Depressed in America by Elizabeth Wurtzel; Girl, Interrupted by Susanna Kaysen." *The Chicago Review* 42 (1): 93–102. https://doi.org/10.2307/25306033.

Metzl, J. 2003. *Prozac on the Couch: Prescribing Gender in the Era of Wonder Drugs.* Durham, NC: Duke University Press.

Moir, J. 1995. "Top of the Poppers." *The Guardian*, April 19, 1995.

Noble, K. D. 1987. "The Dilemma of the Gifted Woman." *Psychology of Women Quarterly* 11 (3): 367–378. https://doi.org/10.1111/j.1471-6402.1987.tb00911.x.

Olshen, S. R., and D. J. Matthews. 1987. "The Disappearance of Giftedness in Girls: An Intervention Strategy." *Roeper Review* 9 (4): 251–254. http://dx.doi.org/10.1080/02783198709553066.

Schoemer, K. 1994. "To Be Young, Gifted, and Blue." *Newsweek* 124 (9): 58.

Showalter, E. 2009. *The Female Malady: Women, Madness, and English Culture, 1830–1980.* London: Virago.

Shrader, J. 1994. "The Vintage Whine of Generation X." *The Wall Street Journal*, November 25, 1994.

Silverman, L. K. 1986. "What Happens to the Gifted Girl?" In *Defensible Programs for the Gifted*, edited by C. J. Maker and D. C. Berliner, 43–89. Rockville, MD: Aspen.

Sullivan, J. 1994. "Prozac's Poster Girl and Her Alien Nation." *The Boston Globe*, September 20, 1994.

Tucker, K. 1994. "Rambunctious with Tears: A Memoir by a Depressive Who was One of Prozac's First Customers." *New York Times Book Review*, September 25, 1994. https://www.nytimes.com/1994/09/25/books/rambunctious-with-tears.html.

Udovitch, M. 1994. "Endless Bummer." *The Village Voice*, September 27, 1994, 96–98.

Werner, E. L. 1994. "Prozac Nation: Elizabeth Wurtzel's Unofficial Guide to Whining." *Harvard Crimson*, September 29, 1994. https://www.thecrimson.com/article/1994/9/29/prozac-nation-elizabeth-wurtzels-unofficial-guide/.

Westerbeek, J., and K. Mutsaers. 2008. "Depression Narratives: How the Self Became a Problem." *Literature and Medicine* 27 (1): 25–55. https://doi.org/10.1353/lm.0.0017.

Wurtzel, E. 1994. *Prozac Nation: Young and Depressed in America.* New York, NY: Riverhead Books.

9 *Unclean Subject(s) of Depression within the Singaporean State*

HANNAH MING YIT HO
University of Brunei Darussalam

Introduction

In Singapore, any threat to the family structure is taken seriously. With its well-documented moral crises (Kuah 2018, 63), the government has taken to systematically administering its interventionist approaches to counteract any damage to the nation's carefully constructed image as a "clean state." (Trocki 2006, 137) This cleanliness translates across domains that are not limited to physical environs, but also bureaucracy, health, family and personal life. As one of Asia's "Four Tigers," (Chia et al. 2007) Singapore enjoys great economic wealth that supports a world-class health care system. To instantiate, the Institute of Mental Health offers a broad range of clinical services, including treating depression ("Clinical Services"). With the nation's industry at preserving cleanliness through its committed focus on first-rate services for the family, it is no wonder that its reputation has preceded it. Praise has been heaped on the Singaporean state for its "miracle [systems]" (Klein 2017; Zarina 2015) that ensure effective politics, economics, and health services. Ultimately, the nation's focus on sustaining cleanliness is aimed at fully supporting the unit of the happy family—"an anchor [that is firmly] situated in the nation's development narrative." (Teo 2010, 329)

However, a social crisis has recently begun to reveal itself through the city-state's increased rates of depression and suicide, thus upsetting the public narrative of a clean state. Between two national studies conducted in 2010 and 2016 (Choo 2018), Singaporeans' lifetime prevalence of depression rose from 12% to 13.9%. Within these studies, depression was also reported as the most common mental disorder. Moreover, Singapore's suicide rate soared by 10% in 2018 compared to the previous year ("Suicides in Singapore" 2019). Such escalating rates correlate to familial dysfunctions due to extreme levels of stress, which may trigger a cyclic trend of depression in surviving family members (Wong 2018). With such an alarming rise in numbers, it is timely to assess the discourse of depression and the ways that the nation-state and citizen-subjects respond to each other within this discourse.

Considering Youyenn Teo's statement that "The story of the state and family in Singapore unfolds in two directions that do not gel," (2010, 337) it is evident that at least two theoretical positions underpin the state's discourse on the family. Firstly, some segments of Singaporean society view the state's interventions as necessary for the mitigation of negative influences due to modernization and globalization processes (Saw 2005). In contrast, a second camp has expressed a distaste for the state's authoritarian hand (Kurlantzick 2001) as its policies are deemed mechanistic and too aggressive. In aims to produce "socially responsible individuals and deepen the bond Singaporeans have with our country," (Ministry of Community Development 2003) the public discourse of the family has been articulated loudly over the years. Instead of focusing on an individual's resistance to the state, my position aligns with YouYenn Teo's conceptualization of "collective productions of meanings and practices" (2010, 354) at the site of the family. I argue that collective responses to official discourses of Singaporean identity are, significantly, production of a new social order within counter-narratives that go beyond their resistive function forge society anew.

To this end, this chapter examines Singaporean writer Amanda Lee Koe's *Ministry of Moral Panic* (2013), a debut collection of fourteen short stories foregrounding characters whose cases of depression manifest themselves through various symptoms. Suicide, self-isolation, and self-injury are a few indications of the psychic illness of depression. In their unhappy dispositions, depressed characters present an opportunity to interrogate "alternative truth," (Cheang 2018) to use the author's own words, which essentially scrutinizes "the characteristics of state rule and society-state dynamics." (Teo 2010, 338) This other world-view works in dialogue with, rather than separate from, the official narrative of the Singaporean state and its ideological positioning of its citizen-subjects. In three short stories that will be discussed, characters suffering from psychic and social depression provide insights into their social disconnections with the nation-state. In my analysis, I argue that depression is an elicited response to a social dis-ease, in which individuals struggle to align themselves seamlessly with national standards of success. Depression, eventually, becomes the social disease that consumes their identities, to an extent where familial ties are severed and responses to the nation-state are fragmented. In this way, they beget a new social norm.

Subsequently, an inability to internalize the nation's gendered prescription of citizens as "sons and daughters" (Chew 2004, 6) creates fissures in the local production of Singaporean subjects. By examining *Ministry of Moral Panic*, I contend that characters' non-conformity to prescriptive gender roles (Teo 2009, 533) deems them as unclean subjects, thus punishable by the state. In Amanda Lee Koe's anthologized short stories, disobedience when not subscribing dutifully to the status quo is not punished legislatively, but rather rebuked by their loved ones within the family and society. Bad husbands, bad wives, and bad daughters are a few examples of aberrant male and female citizenship within the nation. In effect, a failure to meet models of masculinity and femininity set by the government's narrative of good sons and daughters is prefigured in these stories.

Singapore: A Clean Nation-State with Obedient Citizens

Singapore holds a reputation for being a clean city-state because of strict punitive measures set by the government for littering offenses (Theseira and Tan 2011, 179). Within the nation, a subscription to a high standard of physical cleanliness is indicative of citizens' obedience to its set of laws too. Furthermore, national campaigns such as "Keep Singapore Clean" have run since the 1960s and have received wide support from the public. "The Keep Singapore Clean Movement" continues to mobilize citizens around the collective cause of advancing from a "cleaned city to a truly clean city" ("Keep SG"). In effect, such campaigns advocate for an internalization of cleanliness. More significantly, such efforts reflect governmental standards to establish obedience as normative amongst its nationals.

Consequently, such disciplinary attitudes to cleanliness are a commentary on the state's interventionist measures to eliminate acts of disobedience that disconnect with an official discourse and disrupt the state's narrativization of a clean Singapore. As a "nanny state" (Ng 2015; Tay 2001, 24), the state's hegemony governs the conventional rules of living within the nation. Aiming for high levels of productivity in every aspect of life, the government has insisted that sanitization is not only necessary for the city-state's physical environments (Tan et al. 2009), but also applies to each citizen-subject who is called upon to serve the nation responsibly. Just as legislative enforcement against anti-corruption punishes unclean financiers (Thong and Albakri 2016), the government also dispenses prescriptive advice and promulgate the notion of clean subjects through media campaigns. One area in which this is evident is the reinforcement of gender roles within families in the nation. A few examples are baby bonuses and romance campaigns, which also carry the message of a "powerful [and] interventionist state." (Teo 2010, 338) Such gendered impositions are driven by the primary objective of forging intimate connections, to rule out disconnections, with the state.

Along this line, the state ideology of "Asian Values" or "Shared Values" is a significant means by which a clean Singapore is promoted, framed and centralized. Here, the values disseminated are premised on Eastern moral principles to mitigate the encroachment of Western values, such as individualism (Chua and Kuo 2014, 61) perceived to threaten the cohesive unit of the family. With Singapore's quick rise to a first-world nation (Furlund 2008), Singaporeans have been seen to embrace Western values increasingly (Chua 2000) or at least merging Western and Eastern cultures into their identities (Ho 2006). By strategically dichotomizing these dual cultural worlds, Asian Values serves as a nation-state's response to eliminate undesirable Western influences that stand to disintegrate the family unit. Using the lens of Asian Values, cleanliness is reconfigured as an inherent state ideology. It is aligned with a centrality placed on age-old Eastern ideas of an intact family (Tamaki 2007, 289), where social roles and responsibilities are reiterated over individual goals and ambitions.

Ascribing Gender Roles: Sons and Daughters of a Singaporean Nation

Gendered roles are encouraged by the Singaporean government, who often publicly refer to their citizens as sons and daughters of the nation. In his recent national day rally speech, Prime Minister Lee prides citizens for their "achievements" based on their "solid instincts as sons and daughters of Singapore." (Lee 2019) Such language casts citizens within a narrative of a successful and, by extension, happy family. It also designates and imposes a gender hierarchy, in which the authoritarian government identifies itself as their authoritative, albeit nurturing, father. By praising collective feats such as "our unity and harmony," (Lee 2019) Prime Minister Lee lauds the excellent obedience of citizens who have measured up to the nation-state's definition of success. In this vein, solid instincts point to a stable, indissoluble and resilient commitment to the nation demanded from all male and female citizens. However, they also carry a less innocuous inference: "solid instincts" (Lee 2019) pathologize those struggling to establish a firm sense of belonging within the nation's family. Should Singaporeans dispense with their gendered roles, they become lacking sons and daughters.

The People Action Party's leader, who has been informally referred to as PAPa (Heng and Devas 1995; Lyons 2005), underscores citizens' duty to subscribe respectfully to state-established goals. In fact, PM Lee implores "all Singaporeans" (Lee 2019) to contribute wholeheartedly to the common agenda of nation-building. To this end, there is an overwhelming emphasis placed on "family as the basic building block of society." (Singapore Parliament 1991) As the cornerstone of the nation, the cohesive family unit has been established as one of five "Asian Values" or "Shared Values," (Tan 2012) which provide key tenets for Singaporeans to uphold to beget a successful nation. On the celebratory occasion of Chinese New Year in 2020, PAPa (PM) Lee reiterated this point by asserting, "Strong families make for a strong nation. Singapore should be a society where families are celebrated and supported." (Lee 2020) It is this narrative of the family that consolidates the people as one nation. In this way, coherent identities are simultaneously ascribed to citizens by the government who, in turn, serves as the patriarch by offering provisions of a social infrastructure that primarily starts with citizens' gendered roles within the family.

Unclean Depression: Debunking the Myth of a Happy Family

Depression that manifests itself through suicidal attempts, social detachment and self-injury is a divisive condition that disrupts the unity of the happy family. While depressive patients are traditionally diagnosed by detecting chemical imbalances in the brain (Burton 2015, 80; Lawlor 2012), depressive moods or low spirits are also triggered by external stimuli, including social and cultural factors. For instance, behavioral expressions of individual desires may cause a severing of social relations within the family, whose attunement to the national society and its collective needs are then attenuated. Breakdowns in marital relationships due to gambling addictions, extra-marital affairs, heavily prescriptive gendered roles such as the perfect "Asian wife" (Koe 2013, 95) also contravenes the nation-state's demands for Singaporeans to ascribe dutifully to the harmonious unit of the family.

Social fragmentation may, in turn, initiate psychic depression—a form that may now be defined as both mad (individual) and bad (unclean). The social stigma attached to mental illness (Lai et al. 2001; Ng 2018) is perpetuated by censures against shameful acts of social discord, which deem perpetrators unclean within their dysfunctional families. By the nation-state's prescriptive standards, suicide was punishable by a term of imprisonment under Section 309 of the Penal Code, until repealed on 1st January 2020 (Singapore Statues). The punitive hand of the government, until recently, reflects the disciplinary measures taken on a suicidal citizen, whose lack of obedience is closely scrutinized. Rather than attending to a remedy for the citizen's psychic depressive state, the nation-state aggressively chastises the suicidal subject and simultaneously marks suicide as a form of uncleanliness. This process of punishment also displays recognition that depression presents itself as a social problem.

Unclean subjects of depression disrupt the seamless myth of harmonious social relations existing within a nation, whose people are closely guided by a status quo established by the state. Not just an individual health problem, depression is also a social problem—in the sense that it is endemic and symptomatic of a social disconnect with national aims. By shifting from the personal to the sociocultural lens, depression presents itself not as an individual illness, but a social dis-ease that underlines society's struggles and enormous pressures to fit into the nation-state. In this perspective, the gendered roles of a good son (a husband leader, financially secure, emotionally stable) and a good daughter (sacrificing wife, chaste, educated) hold up established ideals of the happy family, which citizens wrestle with daily.

Ministry of Moral Panic: Reading Depression as a Social Disease

Philip Holden elucidates that *Ministry of Moral Panic* sets up a "tension between the instrumental developmental goals of public institutions and the demands of autonomous self-expressions." (2017, 102) The discrepancy between an individual's articulation of Singaporean subjectivity and the state's requests to conform to prescriptive gender roles is delineated in three stories discussed in this section: *The King of Caldecott Hill*, *Love is No Big Truth*, and *Chick*. In focusing on the roles of the bad gambler, failed wife and unhinged schoolgirl, I will demonstrate that their depression is a social disease that is endemic, therefore not localized, and points to their disconnections with the state.

But, I pause first for a brief overview of this anthology. Initiating a second wave of Singaporean short stories, *Ministry of Moral Panic* (2013) was written in a time when the nation-state had begun to attenuate its authoritarian rule, at least ostensibly. With PM Lee Kuan Yew's resignation, his authoritarian father leadership (Low 2006, 89) was replaced with a self-claimed "nurturing parent" (Chew 2004, 6) in PM Goh Chok Tong. The newly instated Singaporean PAPa leader and his successor, PM Lee Hsien Loong, mark a move towards a new narrative of the caring father figure. Informed by this historical change in leadership, Amanda Lee Koe reflects on a social milieu that suggests a "greater autonomy from the state." (Holden 2017, 102) In her stories, the author foregrounds struggles with living up to impossibly high standards of the "ideal Singaporean." (Teo 2009, 533) Just as the nation's leader identifies himself as the nurturing father, his citizens are cast as sons and daughters, whose obedience is a reflection of the father's success as a patriarchal nurturer.

In this vein, characters face a host of difficulties in adhering to gendered roles prescribed by the nation-state. The internal conflict that is experienced because of their failure to live up to hegemonic masculinity and selfless femininity takes a toll on them. If their depressive symptoms are indicative of a rupture with the public discourse of the nation's leader, then it is no surprise that his heavy hand is not palpable in these stories. In fact, the father leader is altogether absent from these stories. In *King of Caldecott Hill*, a Chinese television actor's suicidal attempt and his gambling addiction jeopardize his duties as a Singaporean son and husband. In *Love is No Big Truth*, the female protagonist is persistently disillusioned as she chides herself for failing to be the perfect wife. In *Chick*, a self-injuring schoolgirl is sent to a psychiatrist as a corrective procedure, but he too is afflicted and initiates an extra-marital affair. These are instantiations of failed family units. Their acts of disobedience by not complying with good citizenship—defined in the family that, in turn, produces a clean nation—reflect their social disconnections and suggest a new social norm.

Suicide: Bad Gambler in The King of Caldecott Hill

Even as Philip Holden stresses that "psychic infrastructure" (2017, 102) is troped in Amanda Lee Koe's stories, depression is much more than just the internal workings of the mind (Ho 2019). In *The King of Caldecott Hill*, I argue that the male protagonist instantiates that depression signals a dissonance between society (citizens) and state (the government). Despite, and precisely because of, his local fame as a television actor, this eponymous anti-hero struggles to keep up with expectations of hegemonic masculinity as dictated by the nation-state. When away from the limelight, he is depressed and suicidal. His "depression" (Koe 2013, 52) is caused by pressures that he faces to replicate ideal models of masculinity when he is off the screen. In Singapore, given that the media is used to promote messages about the value of an intact family (Teo 2009, 539), then the king's role on the screen is to serve as a mouthpiece for the nation-state's imposition of gendered roles within the family. In front of the camera, the king aligns himself seamlessly with state-sanctioned models of masculinity. He plays the male lead in the Mediacorp sitcom "The King of Caldecott Hill," in which he waxes lyrical about authority, leadership, and control required within the family and society. His other personae are "the patient surgeon [and] the stoic husband,"

(Koe 2013, 58) which conform to hegemonic standards affiliated with the state's discourse of masculinity. His on-screen roles are starkly contrasted to his actual turbulent disposition. In his suicidal meltdown, he attenuates any coherent ties with the nation and its discourse of successful men. Beneath his veneer of quiet masculinity, he is ambivalent about measuring up to the state's hyper-masculine but also family-oriented ideals. To this end, prototypes of male success established by the nation-state are exposed as damaging as they break citizens, including the local celebrity. Hence, social pressures to conform to gendered roles that have been heavily "naturaliz[ed]" (Teo 2009, 537) by the state leads to his depressive and suicidal condition.

Given that the family is a fundamental unit in Singapore's nation-building, the king's failure to build his own family glaringly contravenes the state dictates on this matter. Considering that Youyenn Teo states that "The Singaporean state's gendered policies around the family, somewhat counterintuitively, produce a political discourse in which gender is consequential and yet ultimately disarmed," (2009, 545) it is understandable then that the king is not seen to articulate his displeasure with the state's gendered policies through his gendered orientation. Instead, he internalizes it. Thus, he uses depression as a gender-neutral response to voice his dissatisfaction with state interventions into the family. Nowhere is the internalization of failed male citizenship more evident than in his acts of self-harm—his routines of self-laceration that culminate in a failed suicide. In this vein, suicide attests to his seeking for an expressive outlet to displace and disavow his discontentment with the nation-state. The state's impositions of male leadership within the family, such as in "Eat with your family day" campaigns, simultaneously promotes familial cohesion as normative. But, for this king, he fails to be domestically enthroned, as he cannot speak of reproductive ties with his queen since he is unable to brag about the existence of any children. In this fruitless marriage, there is a lack of communication, including physical intimacy with his wife that suggests that state imperatives, such as "Romancing Singapore" campaigns, go unheeded and unattended.

Another significant factor contributing to his suicidal tendencies is his financial blunders—a fault that is magnified by the nation-state's expectations that men are ultimate breadwinners in the family. Even as dual-income households are growing in the economically competitive and increasingly expensive city-state, "the public discourse and institutional environment still uphold a bifurcation of gender roles." (Teo 2009, 533–534) As Phyllis Chew further explains, "Fathers and sons bring in the grain, mothers and daughters raise the family." (2004, 7) Away from the cameras, the king is a bad gambler—"fingers burnt on the stock market, bad investment, lost his life savings at the casino." (Koe 2013, 52) Departing from his on-screen role as "the skilled gambler," (Koe 2013, 28) he is in fact financially incompetent. While PM Lee Kuan Yew was known as a "shrewd" (Kraar 2015; Gu 2013) man for successfully transforming Singapore into a first-world economy, this king fails to emulate the father leader as exemplar model. As a Singaporean son, he thus disappoints in his inability to uphold the public discourse of the shrewd man modeled after the national leader.

Loneliness: Failed Wife in Love Is No Big Truth

In addition to their male counterparts, women face great pressures in the production of citizenship. As Youyenn Teo plainly states, "Being an ideal Singaporean is hard." (2009, 533) However, for women, several more state policies intervene directly in their efforts to belong within the nation. An instance is the government's call for daughters of the nation to assist in Singapore's growth as an economic powerhouse through their high levels of education (Kho 2015, 67). Another instance is Singapore's pro-natalist policies, which were made through explicit calls by the government for women to have more babies. These put a tremendous strain on educated Chinese women to set up a family (Heng and Devan 1995; Wong and Yeoh 2003). On the other end of the spectrum, women have also been scrutinized much more closely than their male counterparts for ostensibly serving as the source of moral crises, such as the threat posed by sarong party girls in their licentiousness and penchant to marry non-Singaporean Caucasian men (Ho and Ho 2019, 146; Kuah 2018, 63). Feminist organizations, such as "The Association of Women for Action and Research" (AWARE), have also responded to policies affecting women while advocating for their collective causes.

In view of the state's decisive positioning of female citizens within the familial context, women's choice of loneliness poses itself in conflict with state demands. In *Love is No Big Truth*, the female protagonist initially invests considerable effort to meet the expectations of the nation. Married for a number of years, she has successfully heeded the state's call to produce babies; she has a daughter who passes university and is now married. Subscribing to a neo-Confucian view of femininity in the "Asian wife" model (Koe 2013, 95), she has also responded positively to the nation's Asian Values ideology. However, on both a personal and familial level, these same subscriptions have significantly failed her. Due to her husband's and daughter's physical abandonment of her, she is left dejected and lonely. Her mood is highly despondent, as she displays clinical symptoms of depression: "There was a point

I was lying down so much, I forgot to bathe. I forgot to eat." (Koe 2013, 100) Significantly, her deep-seated disconnection with the family and surrender to loneliness are evident when declaring that being "set free" exposes her to a self-revelatory "truth." (Koe 2013, 102) Thus, she quits the state's measurements of success through its cohesive family.

The female protagonist exhibits her negative reactions to the external pressures imposed on her to keep intact her family unit. Representative of Singaporean wives suffering from a similar plight, she remains nameless throughout. She complains of "deadweight tiredness," (Koe 2013, 100) in which she bemoans her helplessness and increasing reluctance to correct her strained familial relations. Throughout the story, she is at odds with her husband and lacks communication with her daughter (Koe 2013, 100). When she declares, "*loneliness is freedom*," (Koe 2013, 101; italics in original) she betrays a resignation of her (faded) efforts to re-connect with her loved ones. Even if tinged with slight delusions about her new-found independence from social roles and responsibilities (Koe 2013, 102), she severs herself vehemently from her family and nation-state by relating to profound loneliness instead. Despite her husband abandoning her first, their failed marriage reflects not so much on him, as it does her. She has forsaken him, as she under-performs her "duties" (Koe 2013, 102) and thus has not kept up her part of the bargain in their marriage. She explains, "As an Asian wife you learn to hold your tongue. Your husband is always right—it isn't worth the fight." (Koe 2013, 95) Suggestive of her subscription to Singapore's "Asian values," her gendered responses to the nation's designs of a good wife appear in her quiet obedience. Recalling a female silence tied to Confucian patriarchy from which Asian Values are appropriated (Zhang 2002), she displays conformity with female (self-) sacrifice in the family of the nation. This point comes across clearly in her first-person narration. In her account, she reveals that her husband blames her entirely for a bus accident that leads to her facial misalignment, which causes him to leave her for a mainland Chinese woman. If her husband is in any way to be faulted for their failed marriage, she shows no signs of this cognizance. At the end of the day, she is plagued by overwhelmingly negative thoughts that drain her physically and mentally. As she bluntly states, "A relationship means exhaustion. Entrapment. I haven't the energy for the eventuality of it. Love is no big truth." (Koe 2013, 100) By calling out social connections as a form of "entrapment," she exposes that she now fails to deliver on her gendered role just as much as the rest of her family has failed her. Love—used as a metaphor for the family—is, therefore, no big truth, as claimed by the nation-state who dispenses this truth as a grand concept for all its good citizens to apply.

Manifesting itself through clinical symptoms, it would be rather easy to read off her depression as an individual experience that is solely indicative of her madness. Along this line, there is an inclination to reduce her depression to a condition that reflects her personal failings only. However, such a reading overlooks the more potent causes that are found in her sociocultural environment. Kamalini Ramdas states that the "global city vision" of Singapore has meant that "from the late 1980s onwards, [the government's] strategic use of Asian Family Values as the panacea for the threat of Westernisation ha[s] resulted in a more divided movement that distances sexuality from gender." (2015, 109) Belonging to the older and disciplined Chinese generation, the protagonist has hitherto forged good connections with the nation-state in her daughterly role, as both a good wife (Koe 2013, 94) and sexless mother (Koe 2013, 95). However, she eventually surrenders the single pursuit of a happy family by forsaking state demands of a "singular production of a gendered subject." (Peake and Rieker 2013, 9) Even as the severity of her depression is evident in her physical symptoms, they are simultaneously indicative of her disconnections with the younger generation and larger nation. While her clinical symptoms include diminished functioning of daily activities, such as neglecting her personal hygiene (Koe 2013, 100) and poor appetite (Koe 2013, 100), her social depression is signaled through her visible dissonance with her biological daughter. Suggesting a gulf between them, she explains, "But your generation—the thing you are best at is placing yourselves first." (Koe 2013, 102) Even while the protagonist is unready to embrace more liberal values as evident in her criticism of her daughter's non-traditional and Western ideas of self-importance, she is not altogether to be faulted. In fact, the state is complicit in the conflict it has created through its aggressive impositions on citizens to prioritize the family first. While younger generations tend to indulge in Western "decadence," (Mahbubani 1993, 10) the protagonist often acquiesces to an authoritarian pragmatism. PM Lee Kuan Yew is the "Confucian patriarch" (Chew 2004, 7) who sets the tone for the state's directorial control over citizen-subjects. He is "a critical parent – very disciplined, very demanding," according to PM Goh Chok Tong. By "engineering" (Kuah 2018, 5) gendered roles in the "imagined community," (Anderson 1983, 25) the government pursues a vision of familial cohesion and social harmony that serves as a source of tension and conflict instead.

The protagonist's decoupling from the nation-state is most evident when she completely stops sleeping in the marital bed: "I threw my bed away. Depression is easy when you have a bed." (Koe 2013, 100) At this point, she refuses to have intercourse with the state over its Asian Values. The action of throwing out her bed also suggests her move from passivity to activity. She has been a sleeping partner to the state in her entire marriage. In confessing that sex was "always for someone" (Koe 2013, 95) and a "wife's duty to her husband," (Koe 2013, 94) she acknowledges the sacrificial efforts of the female citizen to comply unbendingly with male (state) authority who binds her into a set of contractual obligations. But, as she begins to illustrate, her position is now asserted through opting for disentanglements from the state. When explaining, "I was independent of being a wife, a mother, even, a woman," (Koe 2013, 102) she refers to the way she has been constricted to gender stereotypes in the family and nation. The gender restrictions placed on her as a woman in the nation are subsequently resisted by re-claiming "I" – "I was simply, me." (Koe 2013, 102) Phyllis Chew contends that "the political woman is regarded as an apolitical creature." (2004, 7) Placed outside the norms of the state, women are ranked below men and their patriarchal and patrilineal interests. The gender hierarchy of the state is resoundingly loud; in her final moments of articulated self-liberation, her voice of freedom is tinged with inner thoughts that "someone had left me a note under the door" (Koe 2013, 101)—which, on a subliminal level, suggests the state's continuous role as an intervening force telling her who she needs to be. However, unintimidated by social backlash, she declares that "Finally, for once, I can do whatever I want." (Koe 2013, 101) Thus, she severs her disconnections with the state by asserting a counter-narrative of femininity.

Self-Injury: Unhinged Schoolgirl in Chick

As a form of social dis-ease with the nation-state's ascribing of prescriptions of gendered roles, depression becomes a social, rather than a merely individual, disease. In *Chick*, a profuse propensity for self-injury appears across different social segments and the gender divide. While the unhinged daughter in this short story is a recognizable stereotype, she is not alone in her depression. A male psychiatrist to whom her parents send her for professional treatment is, likewise, self-harming. His reproach to her, "That's no way to treat yourself," (Koe 2013, 155) belies his own injurious self-treatment. Even as he admonishes her for her unwholesome behavior, he is just as guilty of self-neglect. The female protagonist suffers from chronic depression—ten years of experiencing an "internal landscape [that] was burning." (Koe 2013, 149) As a straight "A" student, she clearly meets familial and state discourses of a bright young citizenry, in terms of educational success. However, the constant pressure of academic success takes its toll on her. Caveats include void parental communication, sexual licentiousness (Koe 2013, 158), and being devoid of empathy, which betrays her social disconnections. With the economically successful psychiatrist estranged from his wife (Koe 2013, 156), both of them fall short of meeting restrictive gender roles.

I proceed by first examining the unhinged schoolgirl before moving on to analyze the psychiatrist, who enters into the frame of the narrative precisely because he has been called on to treat this seemingly anomalous case of (female) rebellion. Insofar as this schoolgirl has trouble forging meaningful connections with others, such as family, friends, and lovers, she remains deeply isolated in these non-relationships. An endemic inability to connect with others affects her and leads to her depression. As denoted in the title *Chick*, a biology experiment gone wrong exposes her lacking compassion when killing a live bird specimen. As she already self-harms, she fails to show any ability to understand that differential treatment should be offered to others. As a result, she harms the baby bird too. Holding the "dead chick in [her] hand," (Koe 2013, 148) she demonstrates neither sympathy nor regret for her destructive action. This incident where she takes away a life shows her propensity to smother another living creature, as the chick dies from asphyxiation. By extension, this suffocation reflects the stifling conditions she faces when inhabiting Singapore's "Orwellian state," (Edidin 2004, 47) where PAPa's regime looms large in life to affect Singaporeans as a whole. In this vein, her unhinged behavior can be seen as attributed to the nation-state's strict policing and immense interventionist measures. Even as her depression is a response to her boredom or "emptiness," (Koe 2013, 155) it thus speaks of her social dissatisfaction with the state's narrow set of ideological prescriptions handed to her.

The psychiatrist is a minor character whose clinic is visited by the schoolgirl because her parents have summoned her to him. However, his character is extremely telling because he provides an antidote to the state narrative of women as needing more correction than men (Kuah 2018). Along the gender binary, women are highly likely to be regarded as unclean as they "hold the shorter end of the stick." (Teo 2009, 534) Unable to bring themselves to speak to her, the schoolgirl's parents have chosen to seek out professional intervention to help their daughter align herself back with an accepted behavioral norm. During his clinic, the psychiatrist serves as a pseudo-state actor who intervenes as part of a corrective mechanism to repair selected individuals. Yet, he is just as "off the far edge" (Koe 2013, 160) and in need of correction. Confiding in her, he reveals his sexual estrangement from his wife: "I can't even look at her anymore." (Koe 2013, 156) This lack of communication with his wife denotes a breakdown in his leadership role in the family. Through his further sexual liaison with the schoolgirl, he betrays his wife and acts against accepted behavioral norms for men. Knowing that the family should be upheld at all times and having flouted terms of patient-doctor agreement, he asks her to make a secret of his "broke[nness]" (Koe 2013, 160)—"It'll be over for me, I worked so hard to have this clinic." (Koe 2013, 156) If his depression is anything to go by, this doctor who is meant to provide a remedy is ironically exposed as suffering from the ailment in which he has been trained. He appears pathetically depressed: "He rolled up the sleeves carefully and showed you his arms. They were way shallower than the incisions you used to make. Try harder, you said. He began crying …, and you shushed him." (Koe 2013, 158) Here, a role reversal occurs as the female patient admonishes her doctor. An alternative truth is thus presented to counteract and tarnish the state's "official narrativization" (Cheang 2018) of men and women in the nation. In interactions with the psychiatrist, the unhinged schoolgirl consequently reveals the pervasiveness of self-injury. Self-harm is a response to severed social relations and, significantly, the crushing weight of a state's absolute image of cleanliness that is shouldered by gendered citizen-subjects.

Conclusion

Since depression is a product of a personal struggle, it is rather easy then to isolate it as a mere psychological condition. However, an inclination to individualize depression as a self-triggered illness overlooks serious social determinants, such as a gambling social culture, marital disintegration and other forms of failed interpersonal communication that fracture the family unit. By shifting away from depression as an individual's failure at achieving a mental equilibrium, *Ministry of Moral Panic* introduces a sociocultural discourse of depression. By addressing social and cultural catalysts, these stories illustrate that depression may manifest itself as a social disease. In this perspective, depression illuminates a wide-ranging and extensive social disconnection with the family and nation-state, who establishes the gender status quo. In other words, failing to meet with a state's normative obedience to gendered roles results in depression, which reflects on the larger society. Thus, depression as a social disease serves as a tacit indictment of a hierarchical Singaporean state, including its promulgation of a gender binary.

The critique of the nation-state offered by *Ministry of Moral Panic* suggests that the unclean subject of depression is not only reduced to a personal level. Just as the nation-state is ready to censure its citizen-subjects for civil disobedience, characters who suffer from a failed suicide, self-injury, and depressive mood are also afflicted by the state's informal decision to punish them for their mad, but also bad, acts. They have behaved disobediently and not adhered to demands for safeguarding the family unit as the building block of the nation. Their failed capacity to serve as sons and daughters of the nation is subsequently reflected in their poor performances as a husband, wife, and daughter within their families. A gambling husband in *The King of Caldecott Hill*, a disillusioned wife in *Love is No Big Truth*, and a self-orientated daughter, as well as a cheating husband in *Chick*, undermine normative ideals of unstinting obedience to gendered roles within the family and, by extension, nation.

As these stories demonstrate, the narrative of a clean Singapore is dismantled through their depressive symptoms. Rather than individual cases that appear in isolation, depression is a social disease that is evident through their collective infringements of the gender norms dictated within the nation. In *Ministry of Moral Panic*, depression is not an anomaly. It is set up as the new social order that disaffirms, and shifts, normative standards of subjectivity established by the Singaporean state. Using the metaphor of uncleanliness, depression is re-framed as a mechanism that offsets the Singaporean state's gendered formation of citizen-subjects. Through this lens, depression presents itself as social dis-ease with prescriptive identities demanded by the nation-state. Ultimately, depression's common symptoms include familial disconnections that are suggestive of conflicted state-society relations, as citizen-subjects become altogether disillusioned by excessively high ideals of the Singaporean state.

References

Anderson, B. 1983. *Imagined Communities: Reflections on the Origins and Spread of Nationalism*. London/New York, NY: Verso.

Burton, N. 2015. *The Meaning of Madness*. Oxford: Acheron Press.

Cheang, K. L. 2018. "Amanda Lee Koe Wants to Be Super Serious but Super Frivolous." *Yale Daily News*, April 20, 2018. https://yaledailynews.com/blog/2018/04/20/amanda-lee-koe-wants-to-be-super-serious-but-super-frivolous/.

Chew, P. G. L. 2004. "Sons and Daughters: Benevolent Patriarchy." *NIASNytt* 1: 6–7.

Chia, H. B., C. P. Egri, D. A. Ralston, P. P. Fu, and M. H. C. Kuo. 2007. "Four Tigers and the Dragons: Values Differences, Similarities, and Consensus." *Asia Pacific Journal of Management* 24: 305–320. https://doi.org/10.1007/s10490-006-9033-0.

Choo, C. 2018. "More People in Singapore Have Experienced a Mental Disorder in Their Lifetime, Study Finds." *Today*, December 11, 2018. https://www.todayonline.com/singapore/more-people-singapore-have-experienced-mental-disorder-their-lifetime-study-finds.

Chua, B. H. 2000. "Singaporeans Ingesting McDonald's." In *Consumption in Asia: Lifestyles and Identities*, edited by B. H. Chua, 183–201. New York, NY: Routledge.

Chua, B. H., and E. Kuo. 2014. "The Making of a New Nation: Cultural Construction and National Identity in Singapore." In *From Beijing to Port Moresby: The Politics of National Identity in Cultural Policies*, edited by V. Domingues and D. Wu, 35–74 London: Routledge.

Edidin, P. 2004. "Word for Word/Singapore Swingers: Romance, the Patriotic Duty of Procreation and the Fate of Nations." *The New York Times*, February 8, 2004. https://www.nytimes.com/2004/02/08/weekinreview/word-for-word-singapore-swingers-romance-patriotic-duty-procreation-fate-nations.html.

Furlund, E. B. 2008. "Singapore, from First to Third World Country: The Effect of Development in Little India and Chinatown." Master Diss., Norges teknisk-naturvitenskapelige universitet, Top of Form Norway.

Gu, W. 2013. "Too shrewd?" *Business Standard*, January 20, 2013. https://www.business-standard.com/article/opinion/too-shrewd-111083100032_1.html.

Heng, G., and J. Devan. 1995. "State Fatherhood: The Politics of Nationalism, Sexuality, and Race in Singapore." In *Bewitching Women, Pious Men: Gender and Body Politics in Southeast Asia*, edited by A. Ong and M. G. Peletz, 195–205. Berkeley, CA/Los Angeles, CA/London: University of California Press.

Ho, D. G. E. 2006. "I'm Not West. I'm Not East. So How Leh?" *English Today* 22 (3): 17–24. https://doi.org/10.1017/S026607840600304X.

Ho, H. M. Y. 2019. "Personal Narratives of Illness: Redressing Madness in Singaporean Literature." *Humanities* 8 (2): 70. https://doi.org/10.3390/h8020070

Ho, H. M. Y., and D. G. E. Ho. 2019. "Sarong Party Girl: The Pursuit of a 'Good Life'." *Asiatic: IIUM Journal of Language and Literature* 13 (2): 146–166.

Holden, P. 2017. "The Social Life of Genres: Short Stories as a Singapore Form." In *Singapore Literature and Culture: Current Directions in Local and Global*, edited by A. M. C Poon and A. Whitehead, 97–113. New York, NY: Taylor & Francis.

Kho, E. M. 2015. "Economic Pragmatism and the 'Schooling' of Girls in Singapore." *HSSE Online* 4 (2): 62–77.

Klein, E. 2017. "Is Singapore's 'Miracle' Health Care System the Answer for America?" *Vox*, April 25, 2017. https://www.vox.com/policy-and-politics/2017/4/25/15356118/singapore-health-care-system-explained.

Koe, A. L. 2013. *Ministry of Moral Panic*. Singapore: Epigram.

Kraar, L. 2015. "Singapore, the Country Run Like a Corporation (1974)." *Fortune*, March 23, 2015. https://fortune.com/2015/03/23/singapore-leekuanyew-corporation-1974/.

Kuah. K. E. 2018. *Social Cultural Engineering and the Singaporean State*. Singapore: Springer.

Kurlantzick, J. 2001. "Love, Singaporean Style." *The Atlantic Monthly* 288 (July/August): 42–43.

Lai, Y. M., C. P. H. Hong., and C. Y. I. Chee. 2001. "Stigma of Mental Illness." *Singapore Medical Journal* 42 (3): 111–114.

Lawlor, C. 2012. *From Melancholia to Prozac: A History of Depression*. Oxford: Oxford University Press.

Lee, H. L. 2019. *National Day Rally 2019*. Singapore: Prime Minister's Office. Accessed April 8, 2020. https://www.pmo.gov.sg/Newsroom/National-Day-Rally-2019.

Lee, H. L. 2020. *Chinese New Year Message 2020*. Singapore: Prime Minister's Office. Accessed April 8, 2020. https://www.pmo.gov.sg/Newsroom/Chinese-New-Year-Message-2020-by-PM-Lee-Hsien-Loong.

Low, P. K. C. 2006. "Father Leadership: The Singapore Case Study." *Management Decision* 44 (1): 89–104. https://doi.org/10.1108/00251740610641481.

Lyons, L. 2005. *Making Citizen Babies for Papa: Feminist Responses to Reproductive Policy in Singapore*. Frederiksberg: Asia Research Centre. Copenhagen Business School.

Mahbubani, K. 1993. "The Dangers of Decadence: What the Rest Can Teach the West." *Foreign Affairs* 72 (4): 10–14.

Ministry of Community Development and Sports. 2003. *Official website*. Accessed April 8, 2020. https://www.mcys.gov.sg.

National Environment Agency. n.d. "Keep SG Clean Movement." *National Environment Agency*. Accessed April 8, 2020. https://www.nea.gov.sg/programmes-grants/campaigns/keep-sg-clean-movement.

Ng, C. 2018. "Many Still Steer Clear of People with Mental Illness: Poll." *The Straits Times*, September 8, 2018. https://www.straitstimes.com/singapore/many-still-steer-clear-of-people-with-mental-illness-poll.

Ng, I. Y. H. 2015. "Being Poor in a Rich 'Nanny State': Developments in Singapore Social Welfare." *The Singapore Economic Review* 60 (3): 1550038. https://doi.org/10.1142/s0217590815500381.

Peake, L., and M. Rieker. 2013. "Rethinking Feminist Interventions into the Urban." In *Rethinking Feminist Interventions into the Urban*, edited by L. Peake and M. Rieker, 1–22. London: Routledge.

Ramdas, K. 2015. "Beyond 'Backwater' Island to Global City Vision? Rethinking Feminist Geographies for Singapore after Lee Kuan Yew." *Geoforum* 65: 108–111. https://doi.org/10.1016/j.geoforum.2015.07.016.

Saw, S. H. 2005. *Population Policies and Programmes in Singapore*. Singapore: Institute of Southeast Asian Studies.

Singapore Parliament. 1991. *White Paper on Shared Values*. Singapore: Prime Minister's Office.

Singapore Statutes Online. n.d. "Penal Code – 309." *Singapore Statutes Online*. Accessed April 8, 2020. https://sso.agc.gov.sg/Act/PC1871?ProvIds=pr309-.

Tamaki, T. 2007. "Confusing Confucius in Asian Values? A Constructivist Critique." *International Relations* 21 (3): 284–304. https://doi.org/10.1177/0047117807080197.

Tan, C. H. P. 2012. "'Our Shared Values' in Singapore: A Confucian Perspective." *Education Theory* 62 (4): 449–463. https://doi.org/10.1111/j.1741-5446.2012.00456.x.

Tan, Y. S., T. J. Lee, and K. Tan. 2009. *Clean, Green and Blue: Singapore's Journey towards Environmental and Water Sustainability*. Singapore: Institute of Asian Studies.

Tay, S. 2001. "Commentary/Analysis: What Do Singaporeans Want? Nanny States and Markets." *The Straits Times*, April 7, 2001.

Teo, Y. 2009. "Gender Disarmed: How Gendered Policies Produce Gender-Neutral Politics in Singapore." *Signs: Journal of Women in Culture and Society* 34 (3): 533–558. https://doi.org/10.1086/593332.

Teo, Y. 2010. "Shaping the Singapore Family, Producing the State and Society." *Economy and Society* 39 (3): 337–359. https://doi.org/10.1080/03085147.2010.486215.

Theseira, W., and D. S. Tan. 2011. "Are Fines Compatible with Building a Truly Fine Country?" *Crisis Management and Public Policy*: 179–196. https://doi.org/10.1142/9789814340908_0011.

Thong, C. K., and M. Albakri. 2016. "14 Anti-Corruption Enforcement in Singapore." In *Finance, Rule of Law and Development in Asia: Perspectives from Singapore, Hong Kong and Mainland China*, edited by J. Hu, M. Vanhullebusch, and A. Harding, 409–435. Leiden: Brill.

Trocki, C. A. 2006. *Singapore: Wealth, Power and the Culture of Control*. London: Psychology Press.

Wong, K. K. 2018. "It Changed My Life: How a Mother Lost Her 11-Year-Old Son to Depression." *The Straits Times*, February 4, 2018. https://www.straitstimes.com/singapore/itchangedmylife-help-me-mommy-im-very-lonely.

Wong, T., and B. S. A. Yeoh. 2003. *Fertility and the Family: An Overview of Pro-natalist Population Policies in Singapore*. Singapore: Asian MetaCentre for Population and Sustainable Development Analysis.

Zarina H. 2015. "How Lee Kuan Yew Engineered Singapore's Economic Miracle." *BBC News*, March 24, 2015. https://www.bbc.com/news/business-32028693.

Zhang, W. B. 2002. *Singapore's Modernization: Westernization and Modernizing Confucian Manifestations*. New York, NY: Nova Science Publishers.

Part III Narrations and Metaphors on Depression from and for the Clinical Practice

10 *Inner Voices: Literary Realism and Psychoanalysis*

Josie Billington
University of Liverpool

The synergy of Freudian psychoanalytic thinking and modernist experimentation is well-documented (Abel 1989; Stonebridge 1998; Ffytche 2010; Spitzer 2014). So, too, is the relation of the formation of psychology as a discipline to the orientation of certain 19th-century literary (poetic and fictional) cultural forms or modes (Block 1982; Faas 1988; Taylor 1997; Rylance 2000; Tate 2012) and to the development of particular novelists (Shuttleworth 1996), one of which, George Eliot, is the focus of this chapter (Shuttleworth 1984; Davis 2006). However, the realist novel and the development of psychoanalysis are usually regarded as two historically distinct and consecutive responses to the loss of religious explanations for mental suffering (Lucáks 1971), rather than intrinsically connected (Matus 2010; Ryan 2012).

I argue that the realist novel and psychoanalytic theory and practice, as propounded by Freud and thence developed by Wilfred Bion in particular, might be regarded as analogous projects, connected mainly via the realist novel's employment of free indirect discourse. I concentrate on George Eliot for these purposes for three chief reasons: first, as the virtual founder of the literary realist tradition, her use of free indirect discourse is technically virtuoso and thus its relation to psychoanalytic practice is at its most visible; second, the relation of George Eliot's role as writer to that of healer or therapist has been adumbrated by scholars from a range of disciplines, a distinction which, to my knowledge, is unique among 19th-century novelists (Bennett 1990; Rotenberg 1999); third, her fiction offers compelling fictional case demonstrations of Freud's understanding of melancholia or *depression.*

Freud's Melancholia: A Case Study from 19th-Century Realist Fiction

Let me try to make good that last claim first of all, by turning to George Eliot's very first work of fiction, arguably the foundational beginning of literary realism (Noble and Billington 2015, xxvi).

"Janet's Repentance" (1857)—the final tale in George Eliot's *Scenes of Clerical Life* (Noble and Billington 2015)—tells the story of Janet Dempster, a desperately unhappy wife, who, long the victim of her brute drunken husband's violence, and, childless and often alone, has herself been driven to the consolation of drink and is now an alcoholic. The climax of Janet's story is the moment when she defies her husband, almost daring him to kill her. Instead, in the dead of a bitter winter's night, Janet is thrust out into the night by him, and forced to take refuge at a neighbor's, where she awakes the following day:

> That moment of intensest depression was come to Janet, when the daylight which showed her the walls, and chairs, and tables, and all the commonplace reality that surrounded her, seemed to lay bare the future too, and bring out into oppressive distinctness all the details of a weary life to be lived from day to day, with no hope to strengthen her against that evil habit, which she loathed in retrospect and yet was powerless to resist. Her husband would never consent to her living away from him: she was become necessary to his tyranny; he would never willingly loosen his grasp on her … She felt too crushed, too faulty, too liable to reproach, to have the courage, even if she had had the wish to put herself openly in the position of a wronged woman seeking redress. She had no strength to sustain her in a course of self-defence and independence: there was a darker shadow over her life than the dread of her husband—it was the shadow of self-despair. (Noble and Billington 2015, 277–278)

Janet has left her husband and marriage only to find that she cannot get out of her own story of internalized punishment and pain. Even now, as day follows night, Janet finds only unending, day on day, repetition of her "weary life"—"bare," "oppressive," hopeless. In *Mourning and Melancholia,* Freud asserts that melancholia shares the same traits as mourning, namely, "profoundly painful dejection, cessation of interest in the outside world, inhibition of all activity." (Freud 1984, 252) It is that kind of terrible dead stop and yawning blankness which Janet exhibits here. However, Janet also offers a case illustration of the one key mental feature, which, Freud claimed, distinguished melancholia from mourning: that is, "an extraordinary diminution in self-regard … that finds utterance in self-reproaches and self-revilings." (1984, 252, 254) So Janet, "loath[ing] in retrospect" a mode of life which she is "powerless to resist" in the "future" (Noble and Billington 2015, 277), blames *herself* for her helplessness: she is "too crushed, too faulty, too liable to reproach" (2015, 278):

> If one listens patiently to a melancholic's many and various self-accusations, one cannot in the end avoid the impression that often the most violent of them are hardly applicable to the patient himself, but that with significant modifications they do fit someone else, someone whom the patient loves or has loved or should love … The woman who loudly pities her husband for being tied to such an incapable wife as herself is really accusing her *husband* of being incapable, in whatever sense she may mean this. (Freud 1984, 257)

"The key to the clinical picture," Freud concludes, is that "the self-reproaches are reproaches against a loved object shifted away from it onto the patient's own ego." (1984, 257) Where mourning is the reaction to the loss of a loved person and the work of mourning is achieved when the ego is freed from its attachment to the lost object and can turn to a new one, in melancholia, the loss is occasioned by being "slighted, neglected or disappointed" (1984, 260) by the loved one and the attachment is not displaced onto another object, but withdrawn into and identified with the ego. The hostility the ego feels for the loved object by which it has been rejected is turned back upon the ego itself. "The patient represents his ego as worthless, incapable of any achievement and morally despicable; he reproaches himself, vilifies himself and expects to be cast out and punished." (1984, 254)

At the risk of over-literalizing, and more by way of mutual illumination, let me put Freud's picture of melancholia, and his terms of understanding, side by side with George Eliot's depiction (immediately below) of Janet's situation:

> The future took shape after shape of misery before her, always ending in her being dragged back again to her old life of terror, and stupor, and fevered despair. Her husband had so long overshadowed her life that her imagination could not keep hold of a condition in which that great dread was absent; and even his absence—what was it? only a dreary vacant flat, where there was nothing to strive after, nothing to long for. (Noble and Billington 2015, 276)
>
> The shadow of the [lost or rejecting] object fell upon the ego and the latter is henceforth judged as though *it* were an object, the *forsaken* object. Object-loss is transformed into ego loss … Melancholia behaves like an open wound, drawing to itself energies from all directions and emptying the ego until it is totally impoverished … In mourning, it is the world which has become poor and empty: in melancholia it is the ego itself. (Freud 1984, 254, 258, 262; author's emphasis)

Freud's powerful analytic language of explanation helps us to understand the dynamic by which Janet, even though she has just escaped the wrong story, must be "dragged back again" into it, the only prospect "before her" a continual destructive return of her old life and self. The shadow of her husband *is* the condition of Janet's mentality here, such that she will turn to drink again all the more certainly now to replace or evade the very absence of the dread which had driven her to drink in the first place. Where Freud's language explains, George Eliot's novelistic language operates here not for fictional invention, but to register the inner aftermath which cannot fit into a straightforward narrative of escape or which is imprisoningly and damagingly left behind by it. It gives substance to that terrible vacancy—"nothing … nothing," what Freud calls "ego loss," a self "poor and empty"—as Janet, by suffering from its existential reality, cannot possibly do. It is as if George Eliot's language is summoned at such moments to give tangible reality and articulate presence to thoughts and feelings which belong to individual humans, which often cannot be acknowledged or are inexpressible by humans themselves.

This use of literary language, thus, to express the inexpressible does not merely complement psychoanalysis; instead, it seems to perform, in advance of the invention of psychoanalysis, the latter's very function. The realist novelist, in her role of finding the inner life, is an anticipatory equivalent of the psychoanalyst. Moreover, free indirect mode, I wish to argue, is the realist novelist's precision linguistic-analytical tool.

The Realist Novelist and the Psychoanalytic Task

To get to the heart of what the realist novelist and the psychoanalyst share as practitioners, as it were, here is Freud's late summary of what he felt his life's work in psychoanalysis had primarily set out to do. In Freud's last book, *An Outline of Psychoanalysis*—first published in 1940 and arguably the finest exposition of his theory and therapy (2003, xvii)—Freud sought to give, as he put it, "a dogmatic conspectus of psychoanalysis by bringing together all its doctrines in the most concentrated and clear-cut form." (2003, 175) Part two, entitled "The Practical Task," begins by summarizing the central premise of the psychoanalytic situation. In health, the *Ich* (or ego) is charged with simultaneously satisfying the demands of reality, of the *Es* (Id), and of the *Über-ich* (Super-ego), while maintaining its organization and independence. Illness is produced by a weakening of the *Ich* or ego such that it finds it impossible to fulfill these tasks. Freud goes on to describe the psychoanalytical "task" as follows.

> The *Ich* is weakened by the internal conflict: we have to come to its aid. It is like being in a civil war that is to be decided by the assistance of an ally from outside. The analyst and the patient's weakened *Ich* are, basing themselves on the objective external world, supposed to form a team against the enemies, namely the drive-demands of the *Es* and the conscience-demands of the *Über-ich*. We make a deal with each other. The ailing *Ich* promises to be fully honest with us, that is,

> to put at our disposal all the material that its self-deception offers it; in return, we promise it the utmost discretion, and we put at its service our experience in interpreting the material influenced by the unconscious. Our knowledge is supposed to compensate for its *lack* of knowledge: it is supposed to return to the *Ich* its dominance over the lost zones of the psyche. This deal constitutes the analytical situation. (2003, 201)

Freud's description of how the analyst's possession and use of knowledge compensates for a "*lack*" on the part of the patient, and is deployed by the analyst on the patient's behalf, precisely expresses, analogously, the position of the writer in relation to her character in George Eliot's most famous novel, *Middlemarch*. I use the following example as one of the starkest instances in all 19th-century literature of the novelist-narrator *returning* to a character the knowledge which his "self-deception" (Freud's term) has evasively dislodged and disowned. As will become apparent, this moment also offers a telling illustration of how the realist novel, as a 19th-century cultural phenomenon, occupies the boundary between religion and psychoanalysis in understanding and alleviating the burdens of the inner life (a concern to which I return later in this chapter).

The passage quoted here concerns Mr. Bulstrode, the most formidably controlling personage in the town of Middlemarch. Though he can by no means be described as "depressed," he arguably displays the novel's most diseased mentality. A powerful banker, his fiercely dogmatic religious devotion and judgmental morality nonetheless mask a criminal past, by which, late in the novel, he is dogged and pursued. In this passage, he finds himself in the position of nursing the sick Raffles (Bulstrode's former accomplice in his dubious business practices, who is now blackmailing him), with strict instructions from the doctor (Lydgate) as to his treatment. In the dead of night, Bulstrode is keeping watch over his patient.

> Whatever prayers he might lift up, whatever statements he might inwardly make of this man's wretched spiritual condition, and the duty he himself was under to submit to the punishment divinely appointed for him rather than to wish for evil to another—through all this effort to condense words into a solid mental state, there pierced and spread with irresistible vividness the images of the events he desired. And in the train of those images came their apology. He could not but see the death of Raffles, and see in it his own deliverance. What was the removal of this wretched creature? He was impenitent—but were not public criminals impenitent?—yet the law decided on their fate. Should Providence in this case award death, there was no sin in contemplating death as the desirable issue—if he kept his hands from hastening it—if he scrupulously did what was prescribed. Even here there might be a mistake: human prescriptions were fallible things: Lydgate had said that treatment had hastened death—why not his own

> method of treatment? But of course intention was everything in the question of right and wrong. (Carroll 1997, 692–693)

What makes temptation so powerful for Bulstrode here is that desire is experienced not as thought, idea or word but as something more primary—as an image or perception: "there pierced and spread with irresistible vividness the *images* of the events he desired"; "he could not but *see* the death of Raffles, and *see* in it his own deliverance." (1997, 693) In this "civil war" (Freud 2003, 201), *Es* has the upper hand. The images of the desired events are irresistible to the point that neither *Ich* nor *Uber-ich* can put up a defense: on the contrary, "In the train of those images came their apology." (Carroll 1997, 693) The desired end dictates the decision and religious doctrine—the dominant manifestation of *Uber-ich* in Bulstrode—is now put *in the service* of *Es*!: "Should Providence in this case award death, there was no sin in contemplating death as the desirable issue"; "Even here there might be a mistake: human prescriptions were fallible things." (1997, 693) Yet as soon as that higher authority is thus used to justify Bulstrode's wrong-doings, and effectively jettisoned as a corrective force, *Uber-ich* comes retributively back in those "yet," "if," "but" clauses which ensue: "yet the law decided"; "if he scrupulously did what was prescribed"; "But of course intention was everything." (1997, 693)

As has been noted frequently, George Eliot's psychologically probing language and intelligence have their most persuasive analogy within the novel itself in the doctor Lydgate's pursuits in biology. Seeking the basis of all anatomical structure—"What was the primitive tissue?" he asks—Lydgate's aim is

> to reveal subtle actions inaccessible by any sort of lens ... to pierce the obscurity of those minute processes which prepare human misery and joy, those invisible thoroughfares which are the first lurking-places of anguish, mania, and crime, that delicate poise and transition which determine the growth of happy and unhappy consciousness. (Carroll 1997, 163)

The invisible lurking-place where Bulstrode sees his "deliverance" in Raffles' death is—in this self-consciously post-religious novel and in this man of professed Christian faith—the equivalent of the moment of the Fall. This is noteworthy for two reasons. First, the instance offers a compressed explanation and an image in miniature of the very inception of psychological realism, the seismic transition which converts the grand narrative of temptation and sin into the subterranean story of the individual inner life. Second, it is a clue that the thoughts articulated here, though they originate in Bulstode and are recognizably his, could not be fully admitted or expressed by him. "What was the removal of this wretched creature?" (1997, 693) is virtually an internalized version of the devil's own voice. When Bulstrode *sees* the death of Raffles, it is in part because he could not strictly *think* it in such explicit terms, even to himself.[1] Likewise, Bulstrode cannot fully admit into consciousness the second thoughts contained in those "yet," "if," "but" clauses and still go on with the course he contemplates. Thoughts banished by Bulstrode are re-captured in George Eliot's language as she articulates thoughts that originate with Bulstrode, and only with him, but which he refuses to own or embody. Thus, the whole paragraph's minute unfolding of the deep syntax of Bulstrode's inner life at this critical moment in his history—a kind of primary mental "tissue"—is his inner life as it authentically is and as he cannot experience it.

Free Indirect Mode: The Novelist's Precision Linguistic-Analytical Tool and the Literary Descendant of Religious Confession

This is the power of free indirect discourse. The most demonstrable examples in the two quoted passages—"What was the removal of this wretched creature?" (in Bulstrode's sequence) (Carroll 1997, 693) and "even his absence—what was it? Only a dreary vacant flat" (in Janet's) (Noble and Billington 2015, 276)—penetrate and pinpoint the instant of existential and psychic crisis ("sin," "ego loss"). Linguistically, free indirect discourse is marked by a suppression of the quotation, speech or dialogue which separates actual monologue from the narration, while the preservation of the authorial mode indicates, however unobtrusively, the continued presence of the narrator (Pascal 1977, 22, 55; Cohn 1978, 112). It is where "the thought-thread of the character is most tightly woven into the texture of the third-person narration" (Cohn 1978, 111), such that the two are "merged" (Genette 1983, 174) or undergo "fusing" (Pascal 1977, 22, 55; Lodge 1992, 54–55) to produce "the very special two-in-one effect" that is neither exclusively "dual" or "single." (Cohn 1978, 112) For this is a mode of narration which exists somewhere between narratorial interpretative comment (which George Eliot is famous for using liberally) and the explicit thoughts and direct speech of a protagonist (the mode of the epistolary novel) in order to "render inner movements, perceptions, reactions at the levels that precede thought and words, before they have found their way to consciousness and articulate utterance." (Pascal 1977, 59) Free indirect speech is the novel's great invention and instrument for translating the inner world. Piercing, probing, penetrating the hidden thoroughfares of the psyche, it is to the novel what the microscope was to Lydgate's biology in the 19th century, and what the analyst is to the patient in the 20th.

However, crucially, "Janet's Repentance" (Noble and Billington 2015) demonstrates how free indirect discourse is not so much a new invention as a continuation and translation of older expressive practices. This literary mode is closely tied to that specific moment of the novel's development, says Dorrit Cohn, when third-person fiction entered the domain reserved for first-person epistolary or confessional fiction and began to focus on the mental and emotional life—specifically the personal crises—of its characters (1978, 113). Twice at moments of deep and dangerous despair, Janet Dempster's trouble finds expressive relief in the form of confession to the minister, Mr. Tryan:

> She was unable to utter any words of mere politeness, or even of gratitude; her heart was too full of other words that had welled up the moment she met his pitying glance, and felt her doubts fall away … In this artificial life of ours, it is not often we see a human face with all a heart's agony in it, uncontrolled by self-consciousness; when we do see it, it startles us as if we had suddenly waked into the real world of which this everyday one is but a puppet-show copy. For some moments Mr. Tryan was too deeply moved to speak. (Noble and Billington 2015, 283–284)

Religious confession, substituting both for lonely silence on the one hand and the "mere politeness" of conversation on the other, is offered in this work as the only serious available language in which Janet can discharge the hidden burden of her hitherto unused "other words." Yet, as George Eliot's narrating voice explicitly recognizes at this moment, this deep heart-language, the essential register of reality amid artificiality, is simply not available under ordinary life conditions: "In our moments of spiritual need, the man to whom we have no tie but our common nature, seems nearer to us than mother, brother or friend." (2015, 279) Significantly, free indirect discourse occurs in the novel at precisely those crises when Janet's literal confessor, Tryan, is absent. So when, with Dempster now dead, and while she is still fighting her addiction, Janet inadvertently discovers a decanter of Dempster's brandy. Desire overwhelms her, and she dashes it to the ground and flees.

> Where should she go? In what place would this demon that had re-entered her be scared back again?… The temptation would come again—that rush of desire might master her the next time—she would slip back again into that deep slimy pit from which she had once been rescued, and there might be no deliverance for her more. (2015, 318–319)

In this interval between crisis and explicit confession, free indirect discourse—"Where should she go?" "The temptation would come again"—takes the place of the ancient religious practice of confession as an emotionally attuned verbal witness. At once a descendant and a secular, prosaic replacement for religious discourse, the free indirect mode was uniquely equipped to "listen in" to the kind of spiritual crisis which is now called "depression" (Dowrick 2009, 144–147), in anticipation of the secular listener we find in Freud's analyst.

In *An Outline of Psychoanalysis*, Freud acknowledged the similarity of the role of the confessor to that of the analyst. "[In the psychoanalytic situation] we make this deal: total honesty in return for complete discretion. This gives the impression that we were simply aiming to take the place of a secular father confessor." "But," Freud goes on to say "there is a great difference":

> [The patient] is not simply to tell us what he intends to say, what he is happy to say, the things that would give him the kind of relief he would get after a confession: he has to tell us everything that his self-observation yields to him; everything that comes into his mind, even if it is unpleasant to him to say it, even if it seems to him to be unimportant or even ridiculous … For we don't simply want to hear from the patient the things he knows and hides from others: he also has to tell us what he *doesn't* know. (2003, 202)

Analogously, free indirect discourse tells the experience of a person's life as he or she never entirely lives it (Miller 2003, 60) and offers an analytic interpretation of that experience that is inaccessible to the subject immersed in it. For Janet, at this moment, the only reality is her weakness, the overwhelming sense of all that she cannot be or do. Indeed, from any point of view other than that of the novelist, Janet's life is more or less a failure. Only the novel, by subvocally capturing the deeper reality of her hidden struggle, with its agonies *and* its brave resistances, can find in Janet's story a narrative of heroic achievement. This is what the patient seeks from the analyst. 'Tell me the true story about myself: the one I cannot see and most need to have.' As Ricoeur puts it in "Life: A Story in Search of a Narrator" (2012, 197): "the goal and outcome of analytic sessions" is that the person analyzed "presents the psychoanalyst with bits and pieces of lived histories" and "draws from these bits and pieces a narrative that is both more bearable and more intelligible." The burden of high Victorian realism was always thus analogous to that of psychoanalysis: finding means to release into expression the intimate human matter which is otherwise lost to the subterranean inwardness of private and more or less neurotic psychology.

Nevertheless, neither free indirect discourse nor the so-called omniscience of author-narrator are, of course, truly *there* for Janet herself in any sense. The character does not know of an author; she cannot see or hear her thoughts as the reader does; she cannot benefit from this understanding, as a patient would benefit from an analyst's, and as George Eliot surely wishes her character might benefit from her insight. This is not fictive naivety or simplistic realist convention. It is a belief in what is there even when—especially when—humans cannot realize it as characters in life. That is what Wilfred Bion called the "really real," and which he designated "0" (Bion 1970, 26) in recognition that no ordinary definition would serve for what exists before language and cannot be "contained" by it. Literary realism and psychoanalysis primarily intersect, I wish to argue, in the acceptance that humans do not have access to, and can barely hold, all that they contain. This is not a deficiency, but one of the rules.

Free Indirect Mode as the Technical Bridge between Novelistic and Psychanalytic Practice, Capturing "0" or the Moment of Reality

It is an axiom of Bion's theory that the inability "to 'think' with one's thoughts" is a catastrophic "deprivation of truth" where truth is "essential for psychic health." (1962, 56, 84) "Thoughts" in Bion's writings, are unmetabolized "beta" elements. "Thoughts" require the capacity to think, "alpha function," in order to be digested and converted for use as "alpha elements." (Bion 1967, 117) In the unhealthy psyche, thoughts are evaded, ejected, or stored as inert, undigested facts and symptoms: "Failure to eat, drink or breathe properly has disastrous consequences for life itself. Failure to use the emotional experience produces a comparable disaster in the development of the personality." (Bion 1962, 42) However, Bion also knew that thinking one's thoughts could be almost impossibly hard to achieve. In the first place, the truth that is the object of our thinking—the really real, "0"—proves intolerably frustrating precisely because it cannot be truly known except by experience or discovery. The ultimate reality "does not fall in the domain of knowledge or learning save incidentally"; it can "become" (its presence can be recognized or felt), but it cannot be "known" except in the moment or happening of experience (Bion 1970, 26). The really real is lived, experienced in absorption, it is not abstractly comprehended.

What is more, the thinking tools that are at our disposal—our mental or verbal *containers* for the experience of reality—are liable, in the very effort at containment, to falsify or misrepresent through over-definition or inadequate frameworks:

> The words I write are supposed to 'contain' a meaning. The verbal expression can be so formalized, so rigid, so filled with already existing ideas that the idea I want to express can have all the life squeezed out of it. (Bion 1967, 141)

In particular, this problem might apply to therapeutic containers: the term and concept of "depression," for example, says Christopher Dowrick, is driven by "a set of cultural perceptions in western societies, where our expectation that happiness is the natural way of being leads us to see negative emotional states as intrinsically deviant from normality." (2009, 101) The diagnosis might be valuable to a suffering person in externally *holding* his or her potentially explosive inner pain. Equally, there is the danger that this automatic language and default attitude blots out the suffering reality that it contains.

"On the other hand," Bion goes on, "the meaning I want to express may have such force and vitality, relative to the verbal formulation in which I would strive to contain it, that it destroys the verbal container." (1967, 141; 1970, 107) The problem of finding the right word "is analogous to that of the sculptor finding his form in the block of his material, of the musician finding the formula of musical notation within the sounds he hears, of the man of action finding the actions that represent his thoughts." (1962, 116) It is hard, struggling work; it is, Bion suggests, one of the most profoundly creative acts of being alive.

Literary realism and psychoanalysis, I have argued, share a commitment to finding and articulating the really real or "0," containing it, in lieu and on behalf of the suffering human, without thereby merely making it safe or diminishing or distorting it reductively. However, 19th-century realism does something else besides. For realism holds "0" while remaining bound to the limiting framework of common language and ordinary event. Realism, concluded Henry James, in his preface to *The American*, represents "the things we cannot possibly not know, sooner or later, in one way or another … our general sense of the way things happen." (Gard 1987, 473–475) Yet, realism, I am arguing, achieves a double loyalty: loyal to its subject matter of ostensibly mundane reality ("the way things happen") but loyal also to the truer reality often distortedly hidden within this one, confined inside people too small and compromised to see it (Billington and Davis 2011).

The final example from George Eliot's work is representative. It offers a demonstration of the central problem which, says Bion, psychoanalysis exists to address—the difficulty of adequately thinking one's own experience from within its struggling midst. However, it also gives the problem with all the common messiness and complicating determinants, and often surface invisibility and intractability, which it possesses in ordinary reality. I also choose this example—in which Dorothea Brooke, in *Middlemarch*, is on her honeymoon after her dreadfully innocent mistake of marrying the much older cleric scholar, Mr. Casaubon—because George Eliot explicitly offers it as an example of normal unhappiness, as nothing "very exceptional," by no means the "illness" which contemporary Western medicine might deem it. "Many souls in their young nudity are left to 'find their feet' in such circumstances," she says. "Some discouragement, some faintness of heart … is not unusual":

> However, Dorothea was crying, and if she had been required to state the cause, she could only have done so in some such general words as I have used: to have been driven to be more particular would have been like trying to give a history of the lights and shadows; for that new real future which was replacing the imaginary drew its material from the endless minutiae by which her view of Mr. Casaubon and her wifely relation, now that she was married to him, was gradually changing with the secret motion of a watch-hand from what it had been in her maiden dream. It was too early yet for her fully to recognise or at least admit the change, still more for her to have readjusted that devotedness which was so necessary a part of her mental life that she was almost sure sooner or later to recover it. Permanent rebellion, the disorder of a life without some loving reverent resolve, was not possible to her; but she was now in an interval when the very force of her nature heightened its confusion. (Carroll 1997, 192)

In melancholia, as in mourning, says Freud, a loss has occurred, but "loss of a more ideal kind": "one cannot see clearly what it is that has been lost, and it is all the more reasonable to suppose that the patient cannot consciously perceive what [she] has lost either." (1984, 253–254) Dorothea cannot identify the cause of her unhappiness in part because that cause is a hidden and continuing process ("secret" as "the motion of a watch-hand"), not the clear thing it might seem to be "now that she was married." (Carroll 1997, 192) This is not, for Dorothea, an "interval" in which progress is being made from one state to another. The shift from girlish ideal to married reality is happening so far inside the "endless minutiae" of mundane ordinariness, that the very fact of change is not "yet" clear for Dorothea, precisely because it is happening. Dorothea's crying—"the primary and natural expression of suffering and mental distress" (Darwin 1998, 157–158)—seems deeply primitive here for being a symptom of her radical inarticulacy.

The existence of something incontrovertibly wrong but not identifiably there ("to have been driven to be more particular would have been like trying to give a history of the lights and shadows") is where, says Bion, proto-thoughts begin. These inchoate, half-commenced thoughts originate in the sensation of need, lack, or that unnameable crisis when nothing outside clearly signals what it is that is wrong. If there is "no thing," then "no thing" is "a thought." (Bion 1962, 35) At such moments as this from *Middlemarch*, literary language shows human thought coming into being. What is so impressive here is that at no point does George Eliot specifically say what is wrong. Instead, she articulately inhabits the very indefiniteness from which Dorothea suffers, those painfully existent gaps which paradoxically generate thought's substance. George Eliot's language, in place of Dorothea's crying, occupies that barely experienceable "interval" where something is happening, some big thing is originating itself, secretly—before it can emerge in explicit formulation ("It was too early *yet* for her fully to recognise or at least admit the change"). Like the best ideal analyst, George Eliot takes seriously the human trouble which does not have a ready name or diagnosis and enters the indeterminate areas of individual experience, the inner life which is otherwise without an inner voice to think it. Dorothea, George Eliot tells us, lived on with

> no distinctly shapen grievance that she could state even to herself … and in the midst of her confused thought and passion, the mental act that was struggling forth into clearness was a self-accusing cry that her feeling of desolation was the fault of her own spiritual poverty. (Carroll 1997, 190)

"The mental act … struggling forth into clearness" demonstrates why we need George Eliot's language to release the meaning of Dorothea's predicament. The thought in Dorothea would shape itself as the characteristic melancholic self-denigration we saw in Janet: the "fault" would be "her own spiritual poverty." (1997, 190) George Eliot's emotionally attuned verbal witness recognizes instead that "the very force of her nature heightened its confusion" (1997, 190), that it is the very best of Dorothea that is making her situation worse! Depression, George Eliot's minutely responsive analysis suggests, might be the very opposite of loss of vital powers, or a deficiency in engaging with the experience.

It is the unique work of free indirect speech in George Eliot, however, not merely to articulate thoughts her characters need but cannot think for themselves, but to offer thoughts which perhaps no human would dare or could bear to have. It is much later in the novel, following a further cruel rejection from her husband, that Dorothea begins to admit the cause of her unhappiness:

> She was in the reaction of a rebellious anger stronger than any she had felt since her marriage. Instead of tears there came words:—'What have I done—what am I—that he should treat me so? He never knows what is in my mind—he never cares. What is the use of anything I do? He wishes he had never married me.' She began to hear herself, and was checked into stillness. Like one who has lost his way and is weary, she sat and saw as in one glance all the paths of her young hope which she should never find again. And just as clearly in the miserable light she saw her own and her husband's solitude—how they walked apart so that she was obliged to survey him. If he had drawn her towards him, she would never have surveyed him—never have said, 'Is he worth living for?' but would have felt him simply a part of her own life. (1997, 463)

Here is the explicit realization promised by that tiny *yet* in the earlier passage. However, Dorothea's own words chasten her into silence not only because they begin to say too much too bitterly and distortingly, but because they summon a partner thought too devastating to be borne. It is one that

George Eliot will later articulate on Lydgate's behalf concerning his wife, Rosamond. "In marriage, the certainty, 'She will never love me much', is easier to bear than the fear, 'I shall love her no more'." (1997, 702) The point at which the character cannot bear to "hear herself" is the point where George Eliot has to listen in more closely, to hear *for* Dorothea that terrible question which exists inchoately or resistedly *inside* her—"Is he worth living for?" Where in the previous examples offered, the author and reader might wish that the characters *could* "hear" the thoughts uttered on their behalf, and have access to their own true story, here it almost has to be the writer and not the character in whom intuition crystallizes into new recognition. For how could one ever be one's own witness to this and carry on? How is this deeply inconsolable recognition even possible as a thought, as a solid idea, for the person to whom it belongs? It is something barely thinkable except inside the book and an instance of realism's power to hold thoughts that humans feel it would almost kill them to contain in themselves.

Real thinking, says Bion, "is embryonic even in the adult and has yet to be developed fully by the race." (1962, 57) Indeed, the discovery of psychoanalysis, Bion claims, is itself a symptom of the fact that thinking and the tasks of self-knowledge have been forced upon a mentality ill-suited and underdeveloped for the purpose:

> An apparatus existed and had to undergo, still has to undergo, adaptation to the new tasks involved in meeting the demands of reality by developing a capacity for thought. The apparatus that has to undergo this adaptation is that which dealt originally with sense impressions relating to the alimentary canal. (1962, 57)

Alpha function, the human capacity to think our thoughts and ensure mental well-being, needs help. This chapter contends that literary realism both illustrates and helps amend that fundamental human difficulty by employing free indirect mode to think characters' half-thoughts for them. In so doing, literary realism has a role and power analogous to that of psychoanalysis in amending and aiding human thought function. It offers, that is to say, on behalf of its readers and of the species—on behalf of real people struggling for meaningful story and thought in the ordinary world which is realism's primary medium—a language for thoughts which humans customarily do not dare, or cannot bear, to think for themselves.

Note

1. Of Bulstrode's religious hypocrisy, George Eliot earlier stated that "[t]his was not what Mr. Bulstrode said to any man for the sake of deceiving him: it was what he said to himself—it was genuinely his mode of explaining events." (Carroll 1997, 513)

References

Abel, E. 1989. *Virginia Woolf and the Fictions of Psychoanalysis.* Chicago, IL: Chicago University Press.

Bennett, J. W. 1990. "The Apprenticeship of George Eliot: Characterisation as Case Study in 'Janet's Repentance'." *Literature and Medicine* 9 (1): 50–68. https://doi.org/10.1353/lm.2011.0136.

Bernstein, S. D. 2014. "In Treatment with George Eliot." *Romanticism and Victorianism on the Net*: 63. https://doi.org/10.7202/1025615ar.

Billington, J., and P. Davis. 2011. "Realism's Concealed Realities." *Synthesis: An Anglophone Journal of Comparative Literary Studies* 1 (3): 18–29. http://dx.doi.org/10.12681/syn.16871.

Bion, W. R. 1962. *Learning from Experience.* London: Maresfield Library.

Bion, W. R. 1965. *Transformations: Change from Learning to Growth.* London: Heinemann.

Bion, W. R. 1967. *Second Thoughts.* London: Maresfield Library.

Bion, W. R. 1970. *Attention and Interpretation.* London: Maresfield Library.

Bion, W. R. 1994. *Experiences in Groups.* London: Routledge.

Block, E. 1982. "Sully, Evolutionist Psychology, and Late Victorian Gothic Fiction." *Victorian Studies* 25 (4): 443–467.

Carrol, D. 1997. *George Eliot: Middlemarch.* Oxford: Oxford University Press.

Cohn, D. 1978. *Transparent Minds: Narrative Modes for Presenting Consciousness in Fiction.* Princeton, NJ: Princeton University Press.

Darwin, C. 1998. *The Expression of the Emotions in Man and Animals.* London: Harper Collins.

Davis, M. 2006. *George Eliot and Nineteenth-Century Psychology: Exploring the Unmapped Country.* Aldershot/Burlington: Ashgate.

Dowrick, C. 2009. *Beyond Depression.* Oxford: Oxford University Press.

Faas, E. 1988. *Victorian Poetry and the Rise of Psychiatry.* Princeton, NJ: Princeton University Press.

Ffytche, M. 2010. "The Modernist Road to the Unconscious." In *The Oxford Handbook of Modernisms*, edited by P. Brooker, A. Gąsiorek, D. Longworth, and A. Thacker, 410–428. Oxford: Oxford University Press.

Freud, S. 1984. "Mourning and Melancholia." In *On Metapsychology: The Theory of Psychoanalysis*, edited by A. Richards, 245–269. Harmondsworth: Penguin Books Ltd.

Freud, S. 2003. *An Outline of Psychoanalysis.* London: Penguin Books Ltd.

Gard, R. 1987. *Henry James, the Critical Muse: Selected Literary Criticism.* Harmondsworth: Penguin Books.

Genette, G. 1983. *Narrative Discourse.* Ithaca, NY: Cornell University Press.

Lucáks, G. 1971. *The Theory of the Novel.* London: Merlin Press.

Lodge, D. 1992. "*Middlemarch* and the Idea of the Classic Realist Text." In *Middlemarch*, edited by J. Peck, 45–64. Basingstoke: Macmillan.

Matus, J. 2010. *Shock, Memory, and the Unconscious in Victorian Fiction.* Cambridge: Cambridge University Press.

Miller, D. A. 2003. *Jane Austen, or, the Secret of Style.* Princeton, NJ: Princeton University Press.

Noble, T., and J. Billington. 2015. *George Eliot: Scenes of Clerical Life.* Oxford: Oxford University Press.

Pascal, R. 1977. *The Dual Voice: Free Indirect Speech and Its Functioning in the Nineteenth-Century European Novel.* Manchester: Manchester University Press.

Ricoeur, P. 2012. *On Psychoanalysis.* Cambridge: Polity Press.

Rotenberg, C. T. 1999. "George Eliot—Proto-Psychoanalyst." *American Journal of Psychoanalysis* 59 (3): 257–270. https://doi.org/10.1023/A:1021413526617.

Ryan, V. 2012. *Thinking without Thinking in the Victorian Novel.* Baltimore, MD: Johns Hopkins University Press.

Rylance, R. 2000. *Victorian Psychology and British Culture.* New York, NY: Oxford University Press.

Shuttleworth, S. 1984. *George Eliot and Nineteenth-Century Science.* Cambridge: Cambridge University Press.

Shuttleworth, S. 1996. *Charlotte Brontë and Victorian Psychology.* Cambridge: Cambridge University Press.

Spitzer, J. 2014. "On Not Reading Freud: Amateurism, Expertise, and the 'Pristine Unconscious' in D. H. Lawrence." *Modernism/Modernity* 21 (1): 89–105. https://doi.org/10.1353/mod.2014.0022.

Stonebridge, L. 1998. *The Destructive Element: British Psychoanalysis and Modernism.* New York, NY: Routledge.

Tate, G. 2012. *The Poet's Mind: The Psychology of Victorian Poetry: 1830–1870.* Oxford: Oxford University Press.

Taylor, J. B. 1997. "Obscure Recesses: Locating the Victorian Unconscious." In *Writing and Victorianism*, edited by J. B. Bullen, 137–179. London: Longman.

11 *Rewriting Mecca: Teaching about Late-Life Depression Using John Metcalf's "The Years in Exile"*

Lucia Gagliese
York University, Ontario

Although late-life depression is common, many mental health professionals do not receive adequate training in its assessment or management. Engagement with literary narratives to develop psycho-literary case studies may be an innovative approach to enhancing knowledge about aging and mental health. John Metcalf's short story, "The Years in Exile," is a subtle, sophisticated depiction of depression in a retired writer. This chapter illustrates the development of a psycho-literary case study of Metcalf's protagonist, including assessment, diagnosis, case formulation, and treatment planning consistent with lifespan developmental models and narrative frameworks. At each step, empirical and clinical research and theory are interwoven to highlight opportunities for evidence-based experiential learning.

Late-Life Depression

Depression is experienced by 10 to 38% of people over 60 years old (da Costa Lane Valiengo et al. 2016). Mild to moderate depression is most common, but over 10% report severe symptoms (da Costa Lane Valiengo et al. 2016). It is persistent and associated with decreased quality of life, increased physical, cognitive, and social impairment, as well as increased mortality, including suicide (da Costa Lane Valiengo et al. 2016; Casey 2018).

Depression may be more complicated in older than younger people due to comorbid illnesses and atypical presentation. Specifically, older people are less likely than younger people to experience overt sadness and guilt but more likely to experience anhedonia and somatic symptoms (Alexopoulos 2005). They also are more likely to present with irritability, anxiety, self-isolation, low energy, impaired activities of daily living, self-neglect, cognitive impairment, and psychomotor retardation (Alexopoulos et al. 2002; Casey 2018). Importantly, although the rate of attempted suicide does not differ, completed suicides are almost twice as frequent in older than younger people (Casey 2018). Given these complexities and the misconception that depression is a normal part of aging, it is not surprising that many healthcare professionals lack knowledge about its recognition and management (Davison et al. 2009). Therefore, innovative and practical approaches to improve assessment and management are needed.

Narrative as a Pedagogical Tool

Engagement with literary narratives may enhance learning about late-life depression. Narratives go beyond symptom lists, interweaving biological, social, and psychological factors to provide insight into lived experience and issues of identity and meaning (Charon 2006; Lewis 2011). They allow identification and deconstruction of stereotypes, fears, and stigma (Oró-Piqueras 2013). Additionally, they depict intersections and interactions among multiple simultaneous experiences such as depression, aging, and masculinity/femininity (Apesoa-Varano et al. 2015).

Tucker (1994) and Lewis (2011) developed an approach to training psychiatry residents that required them to imagine engaging in clinical assessment with fictional characters and reformulating literary works as case studies, an exercise similar to retrospective diagnosis (e.g. Hansen et al. 2018). Although engaging with literary depictions in this way is different than constructing illness narratives with patients, it is not a passive experience. Instead, an active reader processes the text through their own life experiences and health-related knowledge to produce meaning in collaboration with the author (McKie and Gass 2001; Metcalf 2018a). Thus, reading becomes a vicarious experience for trainees, enhancing their ability to comprehend and tolerate clinical ambiguities, adopt contradictory viewpoints, and embrace the metaphorical (McKie and Gass 2001; Charon 2006). In the end, this process enhances clinical confidence, competence, and empathy, by improving healthcare providers' engagement with patients' stories (Charon 2006), a primary goal of psychotherapy.

There are limitations and challenges to this approach. The trainee has less information than is available in a clinical encounter and cannot ask for elaboration or clarification. They must rely on a narrator who may or may not be the patient and who may have limited access to the patient's experience (Lewis 2011). Fiction may not accurately depict mental illnesses, as this may not be the writer's primary objective. However, few real patients are *textbook cases*; heterogeneity and idiosyncrasy abound. As such, fictional depictions may be valuable adjuncts to textbook case studies by stimulating consideration of alternative presentations and interpretations.

Although not as popular as novels or memoirs, short stories are a rich source of health and aging narratives (e.g. Lewis 2011; Tolan 2017; Defossez 2018). They may be more accessible than poems and less time consuming than novels or memoirs (Tucker 1994). Although they may include fewer details, their deep dive into characters' inner lives and emotions, compression, ambiguity, and lack of predetermined explanatory frameworks (Metcalf 2018a) may better approximate diagnostic interviews than do longer literary works.

The Process of Psycho-Literary Case Formulation

A standardized approach to psycho-literary case formulation is not yet available. In this chapter, I develop a formulation for the protagonist of John Metcalf's "The Years in Exile," extending Lewis' (2011) methodology. This approach integrates clinical psychology with narrative, literary, retrospective diagnostic, and linguistic analyses. Diagnosis is based on the *Diagnostic and Statistical Manual of Mental Disorders* (DSM-5) (American Psychiatric Association 2013) criteria.

The first step was selecting the story. "The Years in Exile" was chosen because it is by a Canadian author, written in English, and depicts depression in an older man but without explicit medicalization. Initially published in 1975, it is included in Metcalf's (2018b) recent selected works, *Finding Again the World*. The story is written from the first-person point of view. The protagonist is unnamed; he will be referred to as Mr. Tye (acronym of the title). Next, iterative close readings were undertaken. Pertinent information, such as demographics, history, current symptoms, and quality of life, was extracted to construct the case study. Symptoms were compared to DSM-5 diagnostic criteria for late-life depression (American Psychiatric Association 2013). Following diagnosis, narrative content analysis developed a case formulation consistent with lifespan developmental models. Throughout, the author's use of language at the word, image, and metaphor level was considered. While linguistic choices reflect rhetorical sophistication and craft (Metcalf 2018a), for our purposes, they connote the character's well-being and symptoms (Lewis 2011). This is consistent with the principals of linguistic analysis (Demjén 2014), Metcalf's (2018a, 422) suggestion that "*how* something is written is *what* is being written," and Charon's (2006) position that the meaning of an illness narrative emerges from the relationship between its structure and content. Finally, a treatment plan consistent with the case formulation was developed. Throughout, empirical and clinical research and theory about late-life depression were referenced to illustrate opportunities to interweave patient-centered and evidence-based approaches to understanding illness narratives.

The Years in Exile: Psycho-Literary Analysis

Plot Summary

The story takes place in one day, from mid-morning to late afternoon. For most of this time, Mr. Tye, a retired writer, sits alone in the garden, reminiscing about his past, commenting on his present, and engaging passively with nature (e.g. looking at flowers and trees). He is confronted with two challenges: (1) he must rest and prepare for an interview about his career that evening; and (2) he has been asked by his daughter, Mary, to organize his professional papers so they can be sent to Queen's University. He has been avoiding this, making it a source of contention between him and Mary. As the day passes, Mary cleans the house and brings Mr. Tye lemonade and lunch. She also moves his chair out of the shade back into the sun. Mr. Tye leaves his chair only once to go indoors to urinate. As the story closes, Mr. Tye anticipates the arrival of his son-in-law and grandson and being called indoors to dinner. He chides himself that he should prepare for the interview yet remains in the garden.

This simple plot is interwoven with Mr. Tye's precious reminiscences. "In my reveries the last half century fades, the books, the marriages, the children and the friends. I find myself dwelling more on my childhood years in England, the years when I was nine and ten." (Metcalf 2018b, 154) He also thinks about various people (grandfather, mother, ex-wives, children, colleagues, childhood playmates), his writing career, and lifestyle choices. Central to his reminiscences and his nightly dreams is Fortnell House, an 18th-century "spoiled mansion" (2018b, 155) on the outskirts of Christchurch. Mr. Tye reminisces about visiting the house as a boy, taking various abandoned objects, and finally being thrown out by a man cataloging the library.

Diagnostic Assessment

Demographics: Mr. Tye's age is not specified, but he is at least 80 years old as he emigrated from England to Canada as an adult 61 years ago. He is a retired writer and teacher. He is twice divorced. He previously lived alone independently but currently lives with his adult daughter, son-in-law, and grandson in their home. He has his own room and some personal belongings, primarily books and boxes of papers. Mr. Tye's age, marital status, retirement, and transition to dependent living are risk factors for late-life depression (Vasiliu and Vasile 2016).

Comment on gender is warranted. Depression is more common in older women than men, and symptom profiles and outcomes may differ (Burns et al. 2013; Price et al. 2018). Compared to older women, older men are less likely to express overt sadness but more likely to experience anger, irritability, anhedonia, and withdrawal (Price et al. 2018). They also are at higher risk for adverse outcomes, including inappropriate long-term care placement, pseudodementia, and suicide (Burns et al. 2013; Casey 2018). Concerningly, when symptoms are comparable, depression is less likely to be diagnosed or treated in older men than women (Lewis et al. 2006). Additionally, depression in older men is under-represented in narrative and psychological studies (Burns et al. 2013; Armengol 2018), an essential consideration in choosing this story for the current analysis.

Developmental History: It is unknown if Mr. Tye has/had siblings or how his parents died. There is evidence of a problematic relationship with his mother, "My mother's letters to me when I was young, how they amused yet rankled: *living like a gypsy, a man of your age, not a stick of furniture to your name.* My early books returned." (Metcalf 2018b, 156) His father is not mentioned. He describes his grandfather as remote, perhaps confused (2018b, 154). He had childhood friends of both sexes. He spent significant time alone, immersed in nature and fantasy worlds based on local history. There is no report of significant childhood trauma, abuse, or psychiatric history. Intellectual, physical, and psychosexual development were unremarkable.

Occupational History: Mr. Tye is a recently retired writer. His career success is suggested by the university's interest in his papers, the frequent interviews, and his self-description as "covered now with honours." (2018b, 154) Historical and epidemiological studies have shown that writers are at elevated risk for depression and suicide (Kaufman 2001; MacCabe et al. 2018). However, late-life depression has not been explicitly studied. Retirement from any occupation may precipitate depression, especially if it is involuntary or due to ill health, and conversely, people with depression are more likely to retire (Segel-Karpas et al. 2018). Physical comorbidities increase the risk of retirement-related depression (Byles et al. 2016). The circumstances precipitating Mr. Tye's retirement are unknown.

Presenting Symptoms: There is no overt report of sadness, but there is evidence of anhedonia ("I cannot abide this blandness," Metcalf 2018b,

163) and apathy (2018b, 153). These are not easily captured in direct quotes but are unmistakable within the text in contrasting descriptions of the past and present. His reminiscences are vivid, multisensory, and richly detailed, but the present is matter-of-fact, almost drab. Nonetheless, in the present, Mr. Tye expresses some pleasure when watching butterflies ("my beauties," 2018b, 181) and in response to particular words, "I hug the word to myself." (2018b, 161) He describes himself as "crotchety" and admonishes himself to "not get excited" (2018b, 153, 172), suggesting difficulties with emotion regulation and irritability. He says, "I lack the patience for reading" (2018b, 155), suggesting concentration difficulties. He also reports anorexia, fatigue, and sleep disturbance (2018b, 153–154). His affect is not flat; he laughs when thinking of his accountant (2018b, 166). He reports frequent withdrawals into silence: "I am lost in silence hours on end, dwelling on another time now more real to me than this chair." (2018b, 155)

There is evidence for diminished self-esteem and self-concept, mostly linked to aging and physical impairment. He describes himself as "an old circus lion with worn down teeth" and "a wounded thing," and wonders if he smells like other older people (2018b, 181–183). He also frequently describes erosion (e.g. carvings, 2018b, 157; dykes, 2018b, 158), perhaps connoting his self-concept.

He expresses regret about his younger adult years, especially his role as a father. He believes he failed his children because he did not provide the home or experiences he wished for them. "By the time I could have afforded land, the time and the children were gone … Once I felt bitter." (2018b, 184) Whether his current lack of bitterness reflects the resolution of negative emotions, apathy, or emotional flatness is unclear. Regret and loss are also suggested when he says, "one has learned how easily things break." (2018b, 170)

There is no current or remote self-harm or suicidal ideation, although the overt denial of suicidality is not available. This is important because older men often do not express frank suicidal ideation (Schmutte et al. 2009). Mr. Tye's risk factors for suicide include multi-morbidity, functional limitations, poor sleep, recent retirement, relocation, lack of a spouse, social isolation, and hopelessness about the future (Schmutte et al. 2009; Casey 2018). While he has access to means of self-harm, namely sedatives (Metcalf 2018b, 156), the quantity is unknown. Although his risk of self-harm may be low, the will to live, an essential correlate of depression (Carmel et al. 2018), may be compromised. Mr. Tye describes a recurrent dream of being thrown out of Fortnell House just as he begins to climb the stairs: "Nightly my hand grasps the great carved acorn of the newel post. But my dream does not continue." (Metcalf

2018b, 173) Concerningly, he hopes that he will not awaken in his room, but "perhaps one night soon—I have the feeling—I will round the dark oak acorn and reach the rooms above." (2018b, 173)

There is no evidence of substance use disorder, but polypharmacy cannot be ruled out. "Pills and bottles which crowd the [bedside] table-top, Milk of Magnesia, sedatives, digitalis, the inhaler, glycerine capsules." (2018b, 156) There is no evidence of psychosis, anxiety, personality disorders, organic brain disorder, or cognitive impairment.

Physical and Functional Status: Mr. Tye has several comorbid conditions: cardiovascular disease, gastrointestinal symptoms, respiratory disease (2018b, 156), and genitourinary dysfunction, specifically minor urinary incontinence and weak urinary flow (2018b, 161). He reports multiple somatic symptoms, including anorexia, fatigue, and tiring easily. It is difficult to disentangle overlapping symptoms of somatic and mental illness; misattribution leads to either over or under-diagnosis of depression (Alexopoulos et al. 2002).

Mr. Tye experiences significant limitations in activities of daily living, which led him to give up living independently. "Before moving here, life was becoming difficult; the long hill up to the shopping centre for supplies ... the silence broken only by the hum and shudder of the fridge." (Metcalf 2018b, 153) Functional decline is a common reason for older adults to transition from independent living to residing with an informal caregiver, most frequently an adult child (Ritchie et al. 2011). Mr. Tye remains able to walk; the use of an assistive mobility device is not mentioned. He can bathe and shave without assistance, although his daughter insists he leaves the door unlocked (Metcalf 2018b, 161), suggesting safety concerns, although falls are not mentioned.

Social Function: There is significant social withdrawal and isolation, which is common in older people and a known risk factor for depression (Vasiliu and Vasile 2016; Courtin and Knapp 2017). He has little interest in social relationships or interacting with his family. "I am content to sit in my aluminum chair and stare at the weeping willow tree." (Metcalf 2018b, 154, "weeping" may suggest his mood) He has no contact with one ex-wife and minimal contact with another, from whom he receives Christmas cards (2018b, 172). He refers to friends that have died but does not describe any recent bereavements (2018b, 154). Overall, he appears to have no social support beyond his family nor any involvement in activities for older people.

His living situation may play a role in his depression. As the population ages, multi-generational households will become increasingly common (Ritchie et al. 2011). These situations can be associated with stress, conflict, and depression in both the older adult and their adult-child caregiver (Ritchie et al. 2011). Areas of stress reported by Mr. Tye include differences in lifestyle and conflict with his grandson ("My youngest grandson … has called me fascist … It is, I suppose, natural to clash with those younger." Metcalf 2018b, 170) Although his daughter is home and goes to his chair at least three times, no meaningful interaction occurs. The opening sentence of the story "Although it is comfortable, I do not like this chair" (2018b, 153), and his statement that the butterflies "have disappeared in search of ground less disciplined" (2018b, 161), might be commentaries on his living situation. Nonetheless, he expresses gratitude towards his daughter and concludes, "I should not complain." (2018b, 153)

Diagnosis: The DSM-5 (American Psychiatric Association 2013) diagnostic criteria for major depressive episode are: at least one of anhedonia or depressed mood for most of the day for at least two weeks plus at least four of the following: changes in weight, changes in appetite, changes in sleep, fatigue, psychomotor agitation, or retardation; difficulties with concentration or decision making, feelings of worthlessness or guilt, and thoughts of death or suicide. Late-life depression is the diagnosis if the person is over 65 years old. Although the duration of symptoms is not clearly specified, Mr. Tye appears to meet the criteria for late-life depression with predominant anhedonia.

Case Formulation: Lifespan Developmental Framework

Erikson's (1982) lifespan developmental model proposes that different life stages require the resolution of specific challenges. Mr. Tye's current developmental challenge is consistent with Erikson's eighth stage, ego integrity vs. despair. In this stage, older people reminisce and grapple with questions about the meaning and legacy of their lives in preparation for accepting their mortality, leading to either satisfaction and pride (ego integrity) or failure and regret (despair) (Erikson 1982). When it ends in despair, with the belief that one's life has been wasted, depression may result (Dezutter et al. 2013).

Like many older people, Mr. Tye spontaneously engages in reminiscence and life review (Butler 1980). Although there is overlap, reminiscence is the deliberate or spontaneous recall of memories during activities like daydreaming, storytelling, and nostalgia, whereas life review involves systematic and deliberate evaluation and integration of memories around themes such as work or relationships (Butler 1980; Lo Gerfo 1980; Haber 2006). While reminiscence is mostly descriptive or informational, life review entails narrative construction, meaning-making, and dealing with difficult memories and emotions (Butler 1980; Lo Gerfo 1980; Haber 2006).

Usually, reminiscence and life review are adaptive, giving life unity and meaning and forming the basis of identity; however, they can become maladaptive, contributing to depression, if they include dysphoric rumination and obsessiveness (Lo Gerfo 1980; Pourjalali et al. 2009; Brinker 2013). In these maladaptive forms of reminiscence and life review, a person repeatedly thinks about only a few experiences and cannot integrate them with the rest of their life to arrive at a meaningful whole, thereby failing to achieve ego integrity (Brinker 2013). In writers with depression, maladaptive reminiscence may be challenging to control and may inhibit writing (Pourjalali et al. 2009). Mr. Tye reminisces almost exclusively and obsessively about his childhood, especially Fortnell House. Although he does think briefly about his wives and children, there is no real attempt to grapple with the meaning of these relationships or to integrate them with his earlier or later life. Such narrow, obsessive reminiscence may arise when older people are in stressful, unrewarding life situations and can function as an escape from the current situation, foreclosing present and future possibilities (Lo Gerfo 1980). The stress of not writing and of being dependent may underlie Mr. Tye's maladaptive reminiscence.

The seriousness of this is evident in his life-story metaphor: "I have thought myself a pilgrim, the books my milestones … not knowing all my life that the mecca of my pilgrimage had been reached so young and that all after was the homeward journey. Fortnell House." (Metcalf 2018b, 156) As Mr. Tye is a writer, it is not surprising that he spontaneously employs a literary device to give his life meaning (Keller-Cohen 2016). More important, his conclusion about the mecca of his life is a recent re-evaluation (Metcalf 2018b, 156). This revised life metaphor privileges a limited number of events (Fortnell House, book publications, emigration) while excluding or minimizing many others (fatherhood, marriages, career honors), some of which, like his books, he previously considered achievements. A reevaluation of this magnitude is destabilizing and may reflect a loss of coherence, identity, and meaning (Keller-Cohen 2016). It may be the core cognition underlying his current depression.

In summary, Mr. Tye's depression may be related to his decision to stop writing and to no longer live independently. These losses have triggered a negative re-evaluation of his life and the use of reminiscence as an avoidance strategy. Mr. Tye's destabilization and depression manifest in three interconnected ways: his struggle against the impulse to write, his unwillingness to organize his writing-related papers, and his reluctance to be interviewed.

It is unknown when Mr. Tye stopped writing. Although he says he is too old and tires too easily (Metcalf 2018b, 154), the impulse to write continues: "Were I younger, I would attempt to frame its insistence … A short story could not encompass it; it has the weight and feel about it of a novella. But the time for such considerations is past" (2018b, 155), and "[w]ere I younger, I would be making notes and outlines, drinking midnight coffee. But I will not write again." (2018b, 154) His insistence he is too old to write, despite having the desire, suggests narrative foreclosure. This is the decision that one's life story is complete and cannot be altered; therefore, it is *too late* to engage in meaningful activities (Bohlmeijer et al. 2011).

Mr. Tye's reluctance to organize his career-related papers may reflect difficulty accepting his decision to stop writing. He says, "I cannot bring myself to sort through years of manuscripts and letters from dead friends. Much of the order of things I cannot remember, and it is a task which smacks too much of some finality." (Metcalf 2018b, 154) However, he is aware that failure to do so will have negative consequences. "I do not want my papers abandoned … stored in the damp to rot. But if I don't put them in order perhaps they will be consigned to some air-conditioned but equal oblivion." (2018b, 167) Although his avoidance of this task may be exacerbated by fatigue and anhedonia, it is also a way to manage his grief over the end of his writing career.

Similarly, Mr. Tye is reluctant to be interviewed. He says, "it is difficult to talk to these young college men whose minds no longer move in pictures." (2018b, 171) The interview is an opportunity for intergenerational storytelling and life review, including generativity, through sharing experiences and lessons with younger writers (Haber 2006). By not engaging meaningfully with the interviewer, he avoids taking the full measure of his career and describing himself as a retired writer, a shift in his identity that he may not be able to tolerate.

It is important to note that Mr. Tye is not merely avoiding reminders of his mortality. He has successfully managed his other end-of-life preparations. "My will is drawn up, insurance policies in force, assigns of copyright assigned. I should not pretend any longer." (Metcalf 2018b, 467) This is consistent with recent evidence that individuals vary in ego integrity (vs. despair) and mortality acceptance across life domains (Westerhof et al. 2017). Also, it further supports the idea that Mr. Tye's depression is linked to a significant loss he cannot accept or integrate, that he *pretends* about, namely the end of his writing career. Sorting his papers and sending them to the university will be the final act of his writing career and an admission that it is over. Rather than weighing this profound loss and its implications for his identity and the meaning of his life, he focuses on minor losses (e.g. collectible plates) and escapes into reminiscences of an idealized boyhood, long before he became a writer.

Treatment Planning

There are several evidence-based pharmacological and nonpharmacological treatments for late-life depression (Niu and Arean 2015; Holvast et al. 2017). Mr. Tye's multimorbidity, especially cardiovascular disease and frailty, may increase the risks of pharmacotherapy (Niu and Arean 2015). Among non-pharmacological interventions, narrative therapy, in particular, reminiscence therapy with life story work, is consistent with the lifespan developmental formulation of Mr. Tye's depression. Reminiscence therapy developed within narrative gerontology as an intervention for people with dementia (Haber 2006). The goal is to help older people construct an integrated life story imbued with purpose and meaning through the exploration of their past, present, and future. Despite some contradictory research, many studies suggest reminiscence therapies improve psychological distress, self-esteem, sense of meaning, purpose, and connectedness in older people with depression (Hsieh and Wang 2003; Haber 2006; King 2018).

Reminiscence therapy is different from expressive writing interventions (Sexton and Pennebaker 2009). It does not focus primarily on writing about discrete traumatic events or negative emotions but on comprehensive life review (Haber 2006). It may not involve writing at all but instead can use oral or digital storytelling, visual arts, music, drama, and/or scrapbooking (Lo Gerfo 1980; Lyness and Thomas 1995; King 2018). However, adding writing improves outcomes (Haber 2006). Importantly, reminiscence therapy and expressive writing share the goal of meaning-making through narrative creation (Lyness and Thomas 1995; Kaufman and Sexton 2006), an activity familiar and acceptable to professional writers.

Opinions about the *writing cure* for professional writers are mixed. Pourjalali et al. (2009) suggest that writing and revision are in and of themselves exercises in rumination, and therefore, writing interventions have limited benefits for professional writers. Although most studies of expressive writing and reminiscence therapy do not focus on professional writers, there is evidence that writers do benefit, with prose writers showing greater improvements than poets (Kaufman and Sexton 2006). This may be because the construction of a narrative, which is absent in many poems, is essential for writing to benefit professional writers. Importantly, there is no evidence that therapeutic writing is contraindicated for retired prose writers.

Mr. Tye is a good candidate for reminiscence therapy. His spontaneous reminiscences include language associated with better outcomes such as metaphors, multisensory images ("I can smell the honeysuckle," Metcalf 2018b, 160; "I can feel it in my hands," 2018b, 167), and positive affective (e.g. liked, favorite) and cognitive-evaluative (e.g. knew, preferred) words

(Lo Gerfo 1980; Lyness and Thomas 1995; Alea et al. 2010). Importantly, despite depression, anhedonia, and multi-morbidity, Mr. Tye still experiences the impulse to write. If his depression was triggered, at least in part, by giving up writing, helping him resume writing could be beneficial.

The therapy will focus on reexamining his life story to collaboratively construct a narrative that integrates his childhood experiences, adult achievements, and relationships, including positive and negative experiences and emotions (Lyness and Thomas 1995). This *reauthoring*, by reconsidering his life metaphor and the larger narrative and meaning of his life, may reduce maladaptive reminiscence and improve his mood and overall well-being (Lo Gerfo 1980; Kaufman and Sexton 2006). There are three overlapping therapeutic goals: life story work and reduction of maladaptive reminiscence; preparation of his papers for the university; and reduction of social isolation.

The essential first step will be creating the therapeutic alliance necessary to engage Mr. Tye (Apesoa-Varano et al. 2010). Because he believes he is *too old* to write, therapy should begin with discussions rather than writing (Haber 2006; King 2018). Central to the therapy will be collaborative exploration and re-evaluation of Mr. Tye's pilgrimage/mecca life story metaphor (Lyness and Thomas 1995), including its relationship to stopping writing. It will be essential to address Mr. Tye's beliefs about writing, such as "I no longer have the strength to face the struggle with language, the loneliness, the certainty of failure." (Metcalf 2018b, 154) Eventually, short writing exercises that accommodate Mr. Tye's frailty could be introduced. These could include memoir, non-fiction, or fiction, whatever Mr. Tye's prefers, as each can be beneficial (Kaufman and Sexton 2006). Over time, the exercises should expand to challenge him to incorporate different roles, themes, and ages and to integrate his past and present with his hopes for the future. A week-by-week plan (King 2018) and creative writing exercises for older people in narrative therapy (Flood and Phillips 2007; Cantu and Fleuriet 2017), including exercises focused on retirement (Wright 2018), are available.

The second, complementary aspect of the therapy would be helping Mr. Tye organize his professional papers. This could be accomplished in a structured, paced manner consistent with behavioral activation, another effective treatment for late-life depression (Polenick and Flora 2013). However, unlike traditional behavioral activation, in this case, the manuscripts and old letters Mr. Tye identifies as particularly meaningful could serve as prompts for narrative work (Lyness and Thomas 1995; Haber 2006).

The third goal of therapy would be decreasing Mr. Tye's social isolation. Reminiscence therapy and life story work can be delivered individually or in groups, which has the advantage of ameliorating social isolation (Haber 2006). A group comprised of creative older people, as he has difficulty communicating with people who do not think in images, might be considered. There is evidence that group-based arts-engagement programs for older people improve mood and decrease isolation (Noice et al. 2014). Again, group-based intervention should wait until Mr. Tye is sufficiently engaged in individual work. A related part of therapy will be working with Mr. Tye's family to minimize conflict, maximize Mr. Tye's independence and activity, and plan for any further functional decline (Ritchie et al. 2011).

Admittedly, the therapy outlined is complex, and Mr. Tye, with his withdrawal, narrative foreclosure, avoidance, and frailty, may be unwilling to engage. However, untreated late-life depression usually does not resolve spontaneously and may exacerbate physical and cognitive decline (Alexopoulos et al. 2002). In the last paragraph of the story, Mr. Tye, who is still sitting in the garden, chooses reminiscence over interacting with family and preparing (shaving) for the interview. Note the ease with which Mr. Tye slips into reminiscence as an avoidant coping strategy (italics added to indicate reminiscence):

> The sun has long since passed over the house and I am sitting in the shade … I should go and shave. *But I will sit a little longer in the sunshine. Here between the moored houseboats where I can watch the turn of the quicksilver dace. Here by the piles of the bridge where in the refracted sunlight swim the golden-barred and red-finned perch.* (Metcalf 2018b, 173)

This ending implies that, without intervention, Mr. Tye will increasingly detach from the present using maladaptive reminiscence, thereby maintaining and possibly exacerbating his depression and isolation.

Conclusion

Engagement with literary short stories is an innovative adjunct to more traditional ways of learning about lifespan development and mental health. As shown, psycho-literary case formulation requires deep engagement with fictional characters and a thorough knowledge of clinical research and theoretical frameworks. John Metcalf's "The Years in Exile" is an outstanding story for this type of engagement. It presents a subtle and profoundly moving depiction of late-life depression, aging masculinity, frailty, and lifespan developmental challenges. This is not to suggest Metcalf's objective in writing this story was to educate or send a message, an approach to creative writing he has railed against (2018a).

Future directions for this work include identification and analysis of additional Canadian short stories that depict depression and other mental health challenges in older people, including those with cognitive impairments and disabilities. On a literary level, future work will consider stories told from a second or third-person point of view addressing challenges raised by narrator distance. Also fascinating would be an examination of concordance and discordance between authors' and characters' ages and genders. "The Years in Exile" demonstrates that literary fiction that is not overtly medicalized is a valuable resource for health humanities and that the short story is more than sufficiently rich for health narrative analysis, psycho-literary case formulation, and healthcare provider education.

References

Alea, N., S. C. Vick, and A. M. Hyatt. 2010. "The Content of Older Adults' Autobiographical Memories Predicts the Beneficial Outcomes of Reminiscence Group Participation." *Journal of Adult Development* 17 (3): 135–145. https://doi.org/10.1007/s10804-009-9079-6.

Alexopoulos, G. 2005. "Depression in the Elderly." *Lancet* 365 (9475): 1961–1970. https://doi.org/10.1016/S0140-6736(05)66665-2.

Alexopoulos, G., K. Buckwalter, J. Olin, R. Martinez, C. Wainscott, K. Krishnan, and R. Ranga. 2002. "Comorbidity of Late Life depression: An Opportunity for Research on Mechanisms and Treatment." *Biological Psychiatry* 52 (6): 543–558. https://doi.org/10.1016/S0006-3223(02)01468-3.

American Psychiatric Association. 2013. *Diagnostic and Statistical Manual of Mental Disorders*, 5. Arlington, VA: American Psychiatric Association.

Apesoa-Varano, E. C., J. C. Barker, and L. Hinton. 2015. "Shards of Sorrow: Older Men's Accounts of Their Depression Experience." *Social Science and Medicine* 124: 1–8. https://doi.org/10.1016/j.socscimed.2014.10.054.

Apesoa-Varano, E. C., L. Hinton, J. C. Barker, and J. Unützer. 2010. "Clinician Approaches and Strategies for Engaging Older Men in Depression Care." *American Journal of Geriatric Psychiatry* 18 (7): 586–595. https://doi.org/10.1097/JGP.0b013e3181d145ea.

Armengol, J. M. 2018. "Aging as Emasculation? Rethinking Aging Masculinities in Contemporary US Fiction." *Critique: Studies in Contemporary Fiction* 59 (3): 355–367. https://doi.org/10.1080/00111619.2017.1386157.

Bohlmeijer, E. T., G. J. Westerhof, W. Randall, T. Tromp, and G. Kenyon. 2011. "Narrative Foreclosure in Later Life: Preliminary Considerations for a New Sensitizing Concept." *Journal of Aging Studies* 25 (4): 364–370. https://doi.org/10.1016/j.jaging.2011.01.003.

Brinker, J. K. 2013. "Rumination and Reminiscence in Older Adults: Implications for Clinical Practice." *European Journal of Ageing* 10 (3): 223–227. https://doi.org/10.1007/s10433-013-0271-y.

Burns, R. A., M. A. Luszcz, K. M. Kiely, P. Butterworth, C. Browning, P. Mitchell, and K. J. Anstey. 2013. "Gender Differences in the Trajectories of Late-Life Depressive Symptomology and Probable Depression in the Years Prior to Death." *International Psychogeriatrics* 25 (11): 1765–1773. https://doi.org/10.1017/S1041610213001099.

Butler, R. N. 1980. "The Life Review: An Unrecognized Bonanza." *The International Journal of Aging and Human Development* 12 (1): 35–38. https://doi.org/10.2190/wc4t-v05j-40g5-3m7e.

Byles, J. E., K. Vo, P. M. Forder, L. Thomas, E. Banks, B. Rodgers, and A. Bauman. 2016. "Gender, Mental Health, Physical Health and Retirement: A Prospective Study of 21,608 Australians Aged 55–69 Years." *Maturitas* 87: 40–48. https://doi.org/10.1016/j.maturitas.2016.02.011.

Cantu, A. G., and K. J. Fleuriet. 2017. "'Making the Ordinary More Extraordinary': Exploring Creativity as a Health Promotion Practice among Older Adults in a Community-Based Professionally Taught Arts Program." *Journal of Holistic Nursing* 36: 123–133. https://doi.org/10.1177/0898010117697863.

Carmel, S., H. Tovel, V. H. Raveis, and N. O'Rourke. 2018. "Is a Decline in Will to Live a Consequence or Predictor of Depression in Late Life?" *Journal of the American Geriatrics Society* 66 (7): 1290–1295. https://doi.org/10.1111/jgs.15394.

Casey, D. A. 2018. "Depression in Older Adults: A Treatable Medical Condition." *Physician Assistant Clinics* 3 (4): 531–542. https://doi.org/10.1016/j.cpha.2018.05.009.

Charon, R. 2006. *Narrative Medicine: Honoring the Stories of Illness.* New York, NY: Oxford University Press.

Courtin, E., and M. Knapp. 2017. "Social Isolation, Loneliness and Health in Old Age: A Scoping Review." *Health and Social Care in the Community* 25 (3): 799–812. https://doi.org/10.1111/hsc.12311.

da Costa Lane Valiengo, L., F. Stella, and O. Forlenza. 2016. "Mood Disorders in the Elderly: Prevalence, Functional Impact, and Management Challenges." *Neuropsychiatric Disease and Treatment* 12: 2105–2114. https://doi.org/10.2147/NDT.S94643.

Davison, T. E., M. P. McCabe, D. Mellor, G. Karantzas, and K. George. 2009. "Knowledge of Late-Life Depression: An Empirical Investigation of Aged Care Staff." *Aging and Mental Health* 13 (4): 577–586. https://doi.org/10.1080/13607860902774428.

Defossez, E. 2018. "Unending Narrative, One-Sided Empathy, and Problematic Contexts of Interaction in David Foster Wallace's 'The Depressed Person'." *Journal of Medical Humanities* 39: 15–27. https://doi.org/10.1007/s10912-017-9478-9.

Demjén, Z. 2014. "Drowning in Negativism, Self-Hate, Doubt, Madness: Linguistic Insights into Sylvia Plath's Experience of Depression." *Communication & Medicine* 11 (1): 41–54. https://doi.org/10.1558/cam.v11i1.18478.

Dezutter, J., U. Wiesmann, S. Apers, and K. Luyckx. 2013. "Sense of Coherence, Depressive Feelings and Life Satisfaction in Older Persons: A Closer Look at the Role of Integrity and Despair." *Aging and Mental Health* 17 (7): 839–843. https://doi.org/10.1080/13607863.2013.792780.

Erikson, E. 1982. *The Life Cycle Completed: A Review*. New York, NY: Norton.

Flood, M., and K. D. Phillips. 2007. "Creativity in Older Adults: A Plethora of Possibilities." *Issues in Mental Health Nursing* 28 (4): 389–411. https://doi.org/10.1080/01612840701252956.

Haber, D. 2006. "Life Review: Implementation, Theory, Research, and Therapy." *International Journal of Aging and Human Development* 63 (2): 153–171. https://doi.org/10.2190/da9g-rhk5-n9jp-t6cc.

Hansen, M., D. J. Smith, and G. Carruthers. 2018. "Mood Disorder in the Personal Correspondence of Robert Burns: Testing a Novel Interdisciplinary Approach." *Journal of the Royal College of Physicians Edinburgh* 48 (2): 165–174. https://doi.org/10.4997/JRCPE.2018.212.

Holvast, F., B. Massoudi, R. Voshaar, and P. Verhaak. 2017. "Non-Pharmacological Treatment for Depressed Older Patients in Primary Care: A Systematic Review and Meta-Analysis." *PLoS ONE* 12 (9): 1–20. https://doi.org/10.1371/journal.pone.0184666.

Hsieh, H., and J. Wang. 2003. "Effect of Reminiscence Therapy on Depression in Older Adults: A Systematic Review." *International Journal of Nursing Studies* 40 (4): 335–345.

Kaufman, J. C. 2001. "The Sylvia Plath Effect: Mental Illness in Eminent Creative Writers." *Journal of Creative Behavior* 35 (1): 37–50. https://doi.org/10.1002/j.2162-6057.2001.tb01220.x.

Kaufman, J. C., and J. D. Sexton. 2006. "Why Doesn't the Writing Cure Help Poets?" *Review of General Psychology* 10 (3): 268–282. https://doi.org/10.1037/1089-2680.10.3.268.

Keller-Cohen, D. 2016. "On Trial: Metaphor in Telling the Life Story." *Narrative Inquiry* 13: 1–40. https://doi.org/10.1075/ni.13.1.01kel.

King, K. D. 2018. "Bringing Creative Writing Instruction into Reminiscence Group Treatment." *Clinical Gerontologist* 41 (5): 438–444. https://doi.org/10.1080/07317115.2017.1405858.

Lewis, B. 2011. *Narrative Psychiatry: How Stories Can Shape Clinical Practice*. Baltimore, MD: Johns Hopkins University Press.

Lewis, R., R. M. Lamdan, D. Wald, and M. Curtis. 2006. "Gender Bias in the Diagnosis of a Geriatric Standardized Patient: A Potential Confounding Variable." *Academic Psychiatry* 30: 392–396. https://doi.org/10.1142/9789813206922_0024.

Lo Gerfo, M. 1980. "Three Ways of Reminiscence in Theory and Practice." *The International Journal of Aging and Human Development* 12 (1): 39–48. https://doi.org/10.2190/cbkg-xu3m-v3jj-la0y.

Lyness, K., and V. Thomas. 1995. "Fitting a Square Peg in a Square Hole: Using Metaphor in Narrative Therapy." *Contemporary Family Therapy* 17 (1): 127–142. https://doi.org/10.1007/BF02249309.

MacCabe, J. H., A. Sariaslan, C. Almqvist, P. Lichtenstein, H. Larsson, and S. Kyaga. 2018. "Artistic Creativity and Risk for Schizophrenia, Bipolar Disorder and Unipolar Depression: A Swedish Population-Based Case-Control Study and Sib-Pair Analysis." *British Journal of Psychiatry* 212 (6): 370–376. https://doi.org/10.1192/bjp.2018.23.

McKie, A., and J. P. Gass. 2001. "Understanding Mental Health through Reading Selected Literature Sources: An Evaluation." *Nurse Education Today* 21: 201–208. https://doi.org/10.1054/nedt.2000.0538.

Metcalf, J. 2018a. *The Canadian Short Story*. Windsor: Biblioasis.

Metcalf, J. 2018b. "The Years in Exile." In *Finding again the World*, 153–174. Windsor: Biblioasis.

Niu, G. C., and P. A. Arean. 2015. "Refining Evidence-Based Treatments for Late-Life Depression." *GeroPsych* 28 (2): 67–76. https://doi.org/10.1024/1662-9647/a000127.

Noice, T., H. Noice, and A. F. Kramer. 2014. "Participatory Arts for Older Adults: A Review of Benefits and Challenges." *Gerontologist* 54 (5): 741–753. https://doi.org/10.1093/geront/gnt138.

Oró-Piqueras, M. 2013. "Narrating Ageing: Deconstructing Negative Conceptions of Old Age in Four Contemporary English Novels." *Journal of Aging Studies* 27 (1): 47–51. https://doi.org/10.1016/j.jaging.2012.10.001.

Polenick, C. A., and S. R. Flora. 2013. "Behavioral Activation for Depression in Older Adults: Theoretical and Practical Considerations." *Behavior Analyst* 36 (1): 35–55. https://doi.org/10.1080/ 136078604100001725054.

Pourjalali, S., E. M. Skrzynecky, and J. C. Kaufman. 2009. "The Creative Writer, Dysphoric Rumination, and Locus of Control." In *The Psychology of Creative Writing*, edited by S. B. Kaufman and J. C. Kaufman, 23–40. Cambridge: Cambridge University Press.

Price, E. C., J. J. Gregg, M. D. Smith, and A. Fiske. 2018. "Masculine Traits and Depressive Symptoms in Older and Younger Men and Women." *American Journal of Men's Health* 12 (1): 19–29. https://doi.org/10.1177/1557988315619676.

Ritchie, C. S., D. L. Roth, and R. M. Allman. 2011. "Living with an Aging Parent: 'It Was a Beautiful Invitation'." *Journal of the American Medical Association* 306 (7): 746–753. https://doi.org/10.1001/jama.2011.1163.

Schmutte, T., M. O'Connell, M. Weiland, S. Lawless, and L. Davidson. 2009. "Stemming the Tide of Suicide." *American Journal of Men's Health* 3 (3): 189–200. https://doi.org/10.1177/1557988308316555.

Segel-Karpas, D., L. Ayalon, and M. E. Lachman. 2018. "Retirement and Depressive Symptoms: A 10-Year Cross-Lagged Analysis." *Psychiatry Research* 269: 565–570. https://doi.org/10.1016/j.psychres.2018.08.081.

Sexton, J. D., and J. W. Pennebaker. 2009. "The Healing Powers of Expressive Writing." In *The Psychology of Creative Writing*, edited by S. B. Kaufman and J. C. Kaufman, 264–274. Cambridge: Cambridge University Press.

Tolan, F. 2017. "Aging and Subjectivity in Margaret Atwood's Fiction." *Comtemporary Women's Writing* 11: 336–353. https://doi.org/10.1093/cwwrit/vpx018.

Tucker, W. M. 1994. "Teaching Psychiatry through Literature: The Short Story as Case History." *Academic Psychiatry* 18: 211–219. https://doi.org/10.1007/BF03341409.

Vasiliu, O., and D. Vasile. 2016. "Risk Factors and Quality of Life in Late-Life Depressive Disorders." *Romanian Journal of Military Medicine* 119: 24–28. https://doi.org/10.1016/j.ypmed.2016.08.014.

Westerhof, G. J., E. T. Bohlmeijer, and D. P. McAdams. 2017. "The Relation of Ego Integrity and Despair to Personality Traits and Mental Health." *Journals of Gerontology—Series B Psychological Sciences and Social Sciences* 72 (3): 400–407. https://doi.org/10.1093/geronb/gbv062.

Wright, J. K. 2018. "The Warm Bathwater of Working Life Slowly Ebbing Away: Retirement Stories and Writing for Therapeutic Purposes." *British Journal of Guidance and Counselling* 46 (3): 293–303. https://doi.org/10.1080/03069885.2018.1431608.

12 *This Aisle Has More Than Two Sides: Insights into Depression, Provided by Medical Doctors*

Angelika Potempa
The University of Texas Rio Grande Valley

Introduction

Memoirs of medical doctors are quite popular; some have even made it on bestseller lists—"Why are memoirs so popular?" (Reisner n.d.; Carr 2014) This is due to various factors, such as, the high social and moral prestige that the medical profession has enjoyed since the 1950s and 1960s (Starr 1982), the readers' interest in intimate and emotionally engaging stories of how illnesses and losses affect people's lives, the accomplishments, failures, and challenges that the healers faced in their professional and private lives and the lessons they learned (Zinsser 1987; Barrington 1997), the fact that the medical profession has traditionally belonged to the occupations with very particular fiduciary rules and been very protective of its social, moral, and professional prestige (Gawande 2007; Ruggieri 2012) as well as the storytellers' desire to validate and "detoxify" their personal lives via writing and to educate their audiences (Broyard 1992, 20–21, 52–55; Nuland 2008, 84–87). That is, the more or less fictitious accounts of medical doctors reflect and partake in the discourses that shape the general public's attitudes towards the roles of medicine, science, and technologies in our lives as well as with regard to what it means to live a meaningful and enjoyable life in the face of suffering, disability, and death.

One of the health challenges in the public eye is depression, a wide-spread condition with a fuzzy definition, and lots of stigmas attached. More than six million Americans are taking antidepressants or other psychiatric drugs (Iliades 2014; Fox 2016). Reports of the Center for Disease Control and Prevention (CDC) (2020), for instance, state that despite a shift to the better, people are still afraid to admit suffering from depression in order to not been seen in a less sympathetic light (see also Lu 2010). More so, they do not want to be labeled unstable and erratic, and, because of that, a potential danger to others. The debates on the recent flurry of mass shootings show that these fears do not come out of thin air. Because some of the shooters suffered mental health problems, among them depression, quite many people jumped to the unsubstantiated conclusion that it is the mental health problems that are the primary cause of the shootings (Matthews 2018; Silver et al. 2018). To the medical professional, depression represents a challenge, as well. After all, it is not just the mental health specialist who sees depressed patients; more than 50% of physician office visits are with non-specialized hospitalists and primary care physicians (Center for Disease Control and Prevention 2017). According to estimations, up to one in four primary care patients suffer from depression, yet only 31% of these patients are diagnosed (American Psychological Association 2018). Moreover, one can expect both the private and professional lives of many doctors and/or their colleagues, friends, and families to be impacted, too—be it as observers or sufferers. Data shows that the substantial professional responsibility and heavy emotional burden on medical professionals lead to high-stress levels, which then cause high turnover rates and/or numbers of *wounded healers* (Hilfiker 1998), that is, sufferers from burnout, depression, PTSD, and alcoholism (Peckham 2015; American Medical Association [AMA] 2016; American Foundation for Suicide Prevention [AFSP] 2018).

With this in mind, one would expect the difficulties of diagnosing, treating, and managing depression to be thematized in the doctors' memoirs in one or another form, even if the topic itself is much less sensational as complicated surgeries or experimental treatments. Whether and how these issues were raised and what kinds of value judgments, epistemological positions, and understanding of illness and the mission of the medical profession might have informed the tales or the lack thereof is at the heart of this chapter. Of interest are how scientific information and "empathetic witnessing" mixed (Broyard 1992, 44), whether and how the writers' attitudes towards depression changed in lieu of the scientific, technological, and pharmaceutical advancements and socio-economic and cultural shifts in society, and whether the readers have been invited to explore new avenues of thought about depression and how depression fits into what is called a successful and meaningful professional and private life.

Because of the vast number of medical memoirs that have been published, especially during the last 10 to 15 years, this investigation cannot by any means be exhausting. It will begin with recollections of the 1950s to

1970s to then move from the 1980s and 1990s to the present. Both the voices of the non-specialist and the specialist for mental illnesses will be heard, among them those whose tales of *doctoring in the presence of depression* also touch upon doctoring *under the influence*, be it as a healer, friend, relative, or sufferer.

Talking or Not and What to Admit

From the Dawn of the Golden Age of Medicine (Burnham 1982) in the 1950s and 1960s to the 1980s

Those who looked back at the 1950s and 1960s invited their readers to partake in the spirit of optimism that accompanied the new era of *scientific medicine*. New medical technologies, research centers, medications, and a slate of new state-of-the-art local hospitals run by well-educated professionals changed the way doctoring was done in rural America as well as in the big cities. Recollections of the 1970s, still the time of *country doctors*, expressed the same high level of trust in science and technology (Starzl 1992; Hellerstein 1994, 168–196; Mitchell 1994; Larimore 2002; Nuland 2008). It seemed that almost anything could be *fixed*: heart disease, cancer, stroke, infectious diseases, and even mental illness (Stevens 1996; Vonnegut 2011, 74, 82). The *repair* of the mentally ill or depressives, though, was almost a non-issue, despite the country doctors' active interest in the lives of their patients and community matters.

How to explain the silence? A primary reason seems to be the writers' focus on new diagnostic tools, treatments, changing living conditions, and community life. That the medical definition of depression and the division of labor within healthcare delivery were different at the time could have played a role, too. Targeting better measurability, the multi-symptom diagnosis of *major depressive disorder* was finally incorporated in the *Diagnostic and Statistical Manual of Mental Disorders* (DSM-3), in 1980. Before that, depression was more associated with hospitalized patients whose care was in the hands of a psychiatrist, the medical mental health specialist. Psychologists and therapists treated others via talking cures. The breadbasket of symptoms without clear etiology (Lown 1999, 313–328) that are now ascribed to depression comprised terms, such as nerves, stress, nervous breakdown, and psychosomatic anxiety, appearing either as a reaction to exogenous factors or resulting from the patient's biological condition. Diagnostic summaries before 1980 show that large numbers of patients received psychoneurosis or just anxiety diagnoses (Horwitz 2010) or, in the 1970s and 1980s, were fit into other *templates*, for example, schizophrenia instead of manic depression or bipolar (Vonnegut

2011). However, patients with these diagnoses were not or only rarely mentioned. The same is true for mental breakdowns and suicides. One of the few examples occurs in Mitchell's stories (1994, 293–297).

Interestingly, though, the accounts reflect the then wide-spread conviction that feeling down and *stressed out* is a weakness or a luxury that working people plainly cannot afford and, therefore, have to fight and get over *it* by an act of sheer willpower. Both Mitchell (1994) and Larimore (2002), for instance, remembered that in the 1960s, '70s, and '80s doctors were only called in cases of serious accidents or when a condition was perceived as life-threatening. For the *rest*, people assumed that *do it yourself* cures such as home remedies, ointments, liniments, or the support of family or neighbors would do. That is, the doctor's help was sought for physical complaints; family doctors had to diagnose and treat physical ills. This does not mean that the doctors were unaware of the psychological problems along with the physical complaints that quite a number of their patients had. Their remedy was excellent listening skills and a caring attitude.

Consequently, the relative silence about depression cannot be explained without recourse to other factors, such as, the division of labor within the medical profession, underestimation and difficulties to correctly diagnose psychological complaints, the stigma and prejudice against those who were thought to have a mental illness as well as the doctors' desire to do no harm and honor the privacy of their patients. The doctors always understood themselves as the "custodians" of their patients' tale (Gask 2015, 10). Privacy issues and the intent to protect the profession played a role in the memoirs of Lerner, Starzl, and the psychiatrist Hellerstein. They wondered whether their fathers or other family members, often doctors themselves, might have suffered from depression, often as part of burnout syndrome. At the time, the issue was not even broached in the family; it belonged to the things that were private and did not fit into the official picture of the profession. The mere suspicion of having a thought or affective disorder that might cloud correct thinking could have had a damaging influence on the patient-doctor relationship. Do not patients expect doctors to be self-assured, have things under control, and precisely know what they are doing? Moreover, vice versa, do not medical professionals have to portray themselves that way in order to gain trust and collaboration? Jamison (1996b), Vonnegut (2011), and Gask (2015) later addressed these questions in more detail. When discussing their and other clinicians' fears concerning making their psychiatric problems known to others, the still wide-spread prejudices and the fears of losing their license or hospital privileges played a big part.

The desire to protect the prestige of the profession and a strong belief in the possibilities of technological progress in the *applied science* medicine shine also through in the accounts of both the surgeon and bio-ethicist Nuland (2008) and the psychiatrist Hellerstein (1994). Both referred to a dark chapter in the history of American medicine, during which the "enthusiastic use of dubious treatments" in psychiatry injured many patients. Hellerstein mentioned—without further commentary—lobotomy and insulin shock, which, because of the success of new medications for psychosis and depression, had become obsolete when he joined the profession (Hellerstein 1994, 248–249). Nuland (2008, 68–74) discussed in much more detail "doctoring in the presence of depression" in order to help rehabilitate ECT (Electroconvulsive or Electroshock Therapy). Nowadays, because of newly available technologies, ECT can be provided without the often-horrible side effects that it once elicited in depressed or psychotic patients. Nuland acknowledged to still be haunted by the harms done to patients, who were exposed to this treatment, although with good intentions in mind: medicine had to try to help, in this case, help people who, during the worst of their illness, are fully absorbed in fighting their demons and do not have any strength left for the world—no hope, no future, "just a forlorn feeling." (2008, 123–144) Nuland wanted the reader to understand the complicated balancing act between the desire to at least try to help and the willingness to take harm into account, hoping that things might go alright. What he did not mention, though, is how widely during the 1950s and 1960s ECT and, also, lobotomies were used on insane asylum patients, the majority of whom were women (Dittrich 2016, 63–74, 192–200, 365–371). Getting committed to one of these asylums and/or treated with such therapies at the time was strongly influenced by the moral and social norms of proper behavior of women. Often, their psychiatrists had admitted them because of upset and irritated behaviors; husbands and families had complained about unbecoming demeanor and that the women did not meet their expectations concerning their marriages (Solomon 2001, 163–165, 176–177; Sweet 2012). Once in the institution, the manageability of significant numbers of patients also played a role. Shock therapy helped to make patients more obedient and (in the case of psychotic behaviors) more "manageable." (Dittrich 2016, 377) In *God's Motel*, psychiatrist and pathologist Victoria Sweet shared parts of the story of what one of these patients suffered, then already an old woman of whom just "a shell" was left (2012, 70–72).

From the 1990s on: Rediscovering that Good Doctoring Is Practicing Medicine and Is an Uncertain Art (Nuland) in the Presence of Depression

In the 1980s and especially the 1990s, the regulatory, economic, and financial environment in which medicine was done drastically changed: a costly specialized and splintered system of corporately managed care had evolved—one of inter-linked government-financed programs, a growing insurance industry, and medical decision-making that curtailed the role of autonomous family physicians and turned hospitals in to businesses. However, the system did not produce excellent health outcomes. In order to remedy the situation, since the 1990s, strong measures have been undertaken to bring down costs and, simultaneously, improve quality and value of care based on better evidence (Brennan et al. 2009). Nevertheless, these measures have not been able to reduce the economic, social, and financial burden for the population (including mental illnesses, Lieberman et al. 2017; Engel 2006). An essential part of the reform movement was the patients' rights movement, which addressed ethical and legal issues, such as the rights to self-determination, and autonomy, to withhold or grant consent, and to keep medical information private. These factors, along with the push for a more open discussion of medical mistakes and tort law reforms and new apology laws that allow admitting mistakes without the fear of getting sued for malpractice, led to changes in the professional culture. The massive increase in depression diagnoses after 1987, when Prozac was marketed as a fix to the chemical brain imbalance that was associated with depression, was another contributing factor (Horwitz 2010). And so were the new social media in the 2000s, which turned the prevalence of depression and the difficulties of living with it into topics of public interest, as social media blogs and vlogs, for instance, show.

The doctors' memoirs, by discussing what it takes to become and stay a good doctor, reflect these changes; they also became much more *confessional.* After Hilfiker had debunked the myth of the physicians' infallibility and started to address the issues of medical mistakes, burnout, and PTSD, which symptoms also include depression, it seemed as if a floodgate had opened: the memoirs talked about the doctors' failures to live up to their own private and professional expectations as well as their efforts to not fail their patients, friends, and families. Now, good doctoring, in the presence of depression, does not only mean to have watched the struggle of one or the other patient or relative with depression symptoms but includes the toll that depression or the symptoms of what is now called bipolar took on their colleagues or themselves. The psychologist Slater (1997), the pediatrician Vonnegut (2011), and the psychiatrists Gask (2015) and Jamison (1996b) provided, for example, first-hand accounts of the difficulties of diagnosing, living, and working with depression. These medical experts shared their astonishment because of having missed the signs of depression or bipolar in others and/or themselves and, also, how they had initially tried to *suck it up* and *get over it.*

Generally speaking, in this time, depression surfaced as a phenomenon that (1) contributes to medical mistakes (e.g. the hospitalist Ofri, cancer, and AIDS doctor Groopman, family doctor Hilfiker, ER doctor Austin, and cardiologist Lown). The general surgeon Ruggieri, for instance, explained how years of stress on the job lead to high depression and burnout rates among surgeons, themselves major contributing factors to surgical errors (2012, 69, 240–241); (2) can be part of the bundle of symptoms of burnout and PTSD and lead to changes in the doctor's living arrangements. Hilfiker, Ofri (2003), Ruggieri, ER doctors Reilly and Austin, psychiatrist Holland, cardiologists Rosenstein and Jauhar, and surgeon Gawande, for instance, diagnosed depression and burnout as a *professional hazard*; (3) belongs to the symptoms of an existential crisis that results from conflicts between the doctors' guiding values and demands to reprioritize the value system (e.g. Hilfiker, Reilly, Austin, Ofri, and Jauhar). That is, depression is not just a side effect of stress, or mere unhappiness, or merely a reaction to multiple causes; it is a dynamic process; (4) can be overcome. It does not always have to be treated, and it does not always respond to treatment (see also 6 and 7); (5) deserves compassion and not demonization or shame; (6) has an ontological reality because of man's being in this world, which is a *mit Sein* (Heidegger), that is, an engaged *Being With*. The *Dasein* of humans is always attuned, and one's mood/attunement is an essential determinant for the ways things matter to us and how we comport ourselves towards future possibilities (Ratcliffe 2013). Depression comes on a scale (from the normal mood to clinical); (7) has a fuzzy bio-psycho-socio etiology and proceeds highly individualized, and, with it, challenges the *hubris* that medical schools often instill in doctors. According to Lown (1999, xiv), for instance, they are too often taught "a reductionist medical model in which human beings are presented as complex biochemical factories," whose malfunctioning regulatory systems will respond to a technical or pharmaceutical "fix." Moreover, since the division between mental and physical health and many processes within the healthcare system are based on that same reductionist model, it (8) cannot be addressed sufficiently by the existing system. Furthermore, it (9) raises a bundle of interconnected psychological, epistemological, moral, and ethical questions that are related to the uncertainties in knowledge, diagnosing and testing, the efficacy, short and long term and side effects of medications as well as to society's understanding of self-determination, well-being, and social involvement.

Before focusing on the experience of an existential crisis and the expressions of a biopsychosocial approach to depression, a brief recourse to the doctors' evaluations of shortcomings of the healthcare system concerning depressed patients is done. Their criticism, although directed at a particular part of the system, also sheds light on the functioning of the whole system.

One of the crucial insights is that corporatist healthcare and the pharmaceutical industry are strongly influenced by the reductionist model of medicine, under which the purpose of medicine is understood as curing and treating of clearly definable diseases. In alignment with it, reimbursement procedures and payment services force the doctors to focus on biological dysfunctions, that is, on diagnosing and treating specific diseases with a clear code (Hilfiker 1998, 47; Reilly 2013, 120–130, 148; Jauhar 2014, chapters 10, 12, 16). This resulted, among others, in a tendency to trivialize the somatization of stress, anxiety, or depression (Reilly 2013, 87–88), as in the past, "it's just in people's heads." Alternatively, some people are simply taken as "difficult" (Tweedy 2015, 145–146) or "hysterical." (Holland 2010, 188–189) This, in turn, adds to the possibilities of making mistakes. As Lown (1999) and Groopman (2007) repeatedly showed, when doctors do not listen carefully enough or do not or cannot, because of time constraints, take the time to get to the *whole* story, they might miss the problems that underlie the chief complaint. The patient's history of stress and/or feeling "low" matters; these phenomena somaticize (Lown 1999, 238–259; Groopman 2007, 276–279).

Conversely, doctors who want to send the patient home with the diagnosis of a pharmaceutically treatable disease can be tempted to somaticize too much and, then, misdiagnose, over-test and over-diagnose for maladies, as, among others, Groopman (2007, 39) and Ofri (2013, 86–93) pointed out.

Even doctors who are aware of the complicated living conditions of their patients and/or the bidirectional relationship between depression and substance use and abuse, and who want to help, are encountering severe problems. Their patients are *failed by the system.* The psychiatrist Tweedy's story of an uninsured drug-addicted teenage mom who, after the loss of her baby, fell into a depression (2015, 51–53) and internist and hospitalist Reilly's case of a manic-depressive homeless person with HEPC (2013, 11) are examples thereof. Cost and availability restrictions prevented both doctors from providing the level of care they felt their ethical obligations required.

Insights into the Ontological Reality of Depression

A recurring motif in tales of many of the doctors is how the evolution of the new corporatist healthcare *industry*, despite its enormous new possibilities to diagnose and treat, threatens to subjugate care to business efficiency. Both their discontent about this situation and the realization that medicine was still marred by "uncertainty, imprecision, and incompleteness" (Mukherjee

2015, 7) contributed to the existential crises and burnouts that many of the authors experienced. The memoirs talked about their or their colleagues' disillusionment with themselves and their ability to treat and diagnose, the fear of making mistakes along with admitting wrongs and getting shamed as well as the emotional fatigue that can come with doctoring. More so, they discussed the long-term effects of being taught to appear self-assured, certain, decisive, and expertly as well as to strive for perfection. Furthermore, is not that what their patients expect? However, how can one be simultaneously a humble and self-assured expert who is aware of his personal limitations and the limitations of the art? How to not lose certainty and confidence in the face of failure and blame? How can one show compassion without being overwhelmed by it and remain *solid as a rock*? Working methodically and precisely requires not to allow personal judgments to interfere. That is, one has to turn oneself into "a robot, blocking out any outside interference," as the surgeon Ruggieri remarks (2012, 32, 168). There is always the danger of complications. Moreover, the emotions, among them the biggest fear of being or doing wrong and the feeling of guilt for having done wrong, persist "deep down" and "percolate." (Austin 2008, 136, 204–209; Ruggieri 2012, 33–35, 204) Being daily confronted with suffering, physical and emotional pain, dying, and death gnaws at the doctors' substance as well.

Things get even more complicated, considering that the doctors' businesses depend on their reputation, which becomes a huge part of who they are and validates their self-worth as a human being (Ruggieri 2012, 44). This behooves doctors to compartmentalize their emotions to keep their flares of anger, disgust, guilt, or other feelings at patients relatively well-controlled, thus limiting outbursts (Austin 2008, 41, 204–209; Ruggeri 2012, 46). In addition to that, the doctors have to deal with value clashes between the patient's and their preferences, as medications, tests, and treatments or apologies are concerned. Wrong words, uttered at the wrong time to patients, can come back, later on, to haunt them, especially where precarious conversations are concerned.

To these stresses come other ones: having to make a living in a supply-and-demand economy, long working hours, being themselves at risk of infections, the fast turnover of evidence-based knowledge and practice recommendations, fear of malpractice litigation, the loss of autonomy due to participating within a bureaucratic system with, sometimes, contradictory rules that do not necessarily serve the patient's health as well as the effects of their jobs on home life. Thus, more value conflicts arise: altruism and care, the drive for a perfect balance of family and professional life, as well as the feeling of making a difference in somebody else's life are challenged by egoism, profit orientation, and time constraints. It is no wonder then that doctoring can take a toll on the physician's body and mind: self-confidence and compassion got "drained out" and self-doubt, fatigue, stress, sadness, the feeling of loss but also frustration and irritability settled in (Austin 2008, 204–209; Ruggieri 2012, 49, 229–254; Jauhar 2014, 170). Moreover, these emotions came to linger and stay, whereas the feelings of being alive, looking forward to new things, and getting excited about them, and of being in control of one's circumstances faded away. What enabled them to leave the state of paralysis and get out of *limbo* were therapies, self-forgiveness, realignment of their priorities, a return to what they had been compassionate about, making appreciation and gratitude for their families and possibilities to help a constant part of their lives, and changes with regard to working and living conditions. They worked out livable compromises that allowed them to refocus on the pursuit of purpose in an imperfect system as flawed and humbled persons with a better understanding of what is in their control.

What the physicians described here were experiences that fit the description of *existential crises.* They were depicted as dynamic bio-psycho-social-moral processes that led to changes not just in energy levels but in the kinds of energies that drive actions. With it, the person's attunedness to reality changes. Alternatively, in Heidegger's terms, the person's mood, which shapes which and how things are entering one's consciousness becomes different (Ratcliffe 2013). That is to say, the way how people open to others (*mit Sein*) shifts. Their sinking into depression also came with the feeling of forfeiture of their future, of being trapped in unpleasant, demotivating circumstances, and general angst of never again regaining the power to exercise control over these circumstances.

The symptoms were similar in Vonnegut's, Jamison's, Gask's, and Slater's stories, although the triggers for their descent into depression were different. For them, it was not primarily the struggle to stay true to themselves and remain caring while *doctoring within the system.* They added a whole array of factors that reached from genetics to hormonal and other balances to concrete fears and experiences of loss. Furthermore, the crises they described were not existential crises that are related to value clashes and the struggle to reorient but existential crises in a more profound sense—a deep suffering that threatened their further existence and that almost totally absorbed their Being With others. They portrayed an existence that felt like they were held down by a *leaden* blanket, both heavy and pain-ridden, where excitement and joy were not just gone but not even recallable or imaginable. If nothing really matters anymore, one is doomed to be in a meaningless, dreadful, and hopeless world. Even their attunedness to time changed, that is, how its flow was perceived; time just disappeared, was gone. What they were left with was loss—loss of meaning and future possibilities and of previous ways of feeling their bodies and caring for them.

But their accounts of deep depression do not exhaust themselves with sympathetic descriptions of their struggles, as important that alone is; they also explain the difficulties of finding treatments that *work* and invite readers to seriously reflect about our ways of thinking about depression and depressives: if depression comes on a scale and together with other ways of being attuned to one's world, what is the *normal* attunedness of a *normal* person? Do we experience a dynamic of different moods, all of them at our disposal (e.g. angst, joyfulness, contentment, hatred, caring, grieve, and boredom), in which certain kinds can dominate by *draining out* others for different periods? Are moods ever-present potentialities that engulf the whole body, not just one's ways of thinking and reacting to others, as Ratcliffe (2013) assumed? Is depression, which seems to be linked to angst, concrete fears, despair, and the feeling of loss and purpose, a normal reaction linked to loss of something or someone that was cared about?—If so, could it be grounded in a feeling of a loss of orientation points, triggered by a *concoction* of interior and exterior influences and, like pain, signaling the need to modify future behavior?—Would not a regrouping take time, a standstill, to do work on opening up new possibilities? Is depression linked to the same processes that keep our curiosity and explorative behavior in check, as is the case with anxiety and concrete fears? Could deep depression then also be considered a paradoxical form of caring, a caring that has turned in-itself and, with it, expunged itself and leaves people with an *inner climate* of loss?

Another very different but no less intriguing train of thought can be found in these writings. They raised the question of whether depression could also be seen as *a certain kind of gift* that allows obtaining insights into the complexities of people's *inner life* that might be closed off to others. As Hilfiker put it, his depression may have made him be a better listener and "feel more deeply things that others might only be vaguely aware of." (1998, Postscript) Jamison's *Touched with Fire* (1996a) went even further and discussed links between manic depression and creativity.

Other queries in these memoirs contributed to the critical public discourses on our understanding of illness and the reasonability and acceptability of treatments. Hellerstein, Nuland, Hilfiker, Gask, Jamison, Ofri, and Vonnegut, for instance, defended the new hybrid model of depression that takes complex interactions of biological, psychological, and social factors in a patient's course of life into consideration and rehabilitates the view that depression is an integral part of a person. Consequently, they defended psychoanalysis and psychotherapy against accusations of *fraud*, useless and expensive placebos, and demanded comprehensive assessment and treatment. In the old bio-psychological model, which reduces the cluster of depression symptoms to a localizable, and with it, treatable physio-pathology, medication is expected to restore a lost chemical balance and allow *proper functioning*. The problems with regard to the restoration of *proper functioning*, however, are that there are no clear answers to what the *correct balance* would be, what *proper functioning* means, and what the *proper* cause of the symptoms is, because of the multiplicity of interacting social, biological, and psychological factors (Popoveniuc 2014). Therefore, any expectation of a single *proper* diagnostic is unrealistic. All this is linked to the fact that what we consider as *normal* comes on a scale and is dependent on moral, religious, and socio-political and also highly personal judgments.

Moreover, in the case of mental illnesses, the subject of medical trials or just the process of finding the *right* medication is itself changing with the interference, for example, the memory of how one felt and feels changes. How can how one feels as *Self* be objectified? Are there ways one should feel, and how would that be? What side effects are *acceptable*? Does society have a right to make someone *functioning* by forcing medications on them, even if that causes these individuals to feel alienated from themselves, numbed, and/or experience other unpleasant side effects? How much participation in *social life* is good, necessary, and rationally expectable?

Furthermore, connected to these questions, the readers were also presented with concerns about possible moral conflicts that both doctor and patient have to face when discussing symptomatology and treatment options. This concerns, for instance, the questions of what it means for a doctor not to be paternalistic and honor a patient's autonomy and when the doctor's or another decision-maker's opinion should take precedence. What does informed consent mean when dealing with all the uncertainties mentioned above? What should patients know about their doctors and their ability to *doctor*? Vice versa, what do doctors need to know from their patients in order to diagnose and develop workable long-term treatment plans and for a trustful relationship to emerge?

To conclude, by honestly and sincerely sharing their thoughts on these and other issues, including their uncertainties, the memoir writers did not only allow their readers to peek into their personal and private lives but left them with lots of food for thought—something, good memoirs should do. With it, they did not only hit the demands of the market place but tremendously enriched the public discourse. This became especially true with the 1990s and following years when the focus shifted to also include the discussions of premature and/or exaggerated hopes concerning the *soft science* medicine and the infallibility of doctors. Now, the doctors took it upon themselves to actively address existing prejudices linked to mental health issues and without the sarcasm that shaped *The House of God* (Shem 1978), for instance. They did this by sharing their personal queries with doctoring in the presence of depression and characterized depression as a normal part of life and a part of our attunedness to our world that can also spiral into a severe illness. Depression can become part of an existential crises that encompasses people's value systems and requires its realignment; it can also lead deeper into an all-encompassing and paralyzing condition, with the feeling of an excessive loss of meaning. Fighting both kinds of existential crises is rather heroic, and shame is entirely inappropriate. Moreover, as the doctors stressed, for the fight, both therapy and medication, although not always working, are important, in addition to a good support system. So, despite not being able to provide *the* remedy for severe clinical depression, they do not leave their readers without hope.

References

AMA. 2016. "Medical Specialties with the Highest Burnout Rates." *AMA Wire*. Accessed May 2, 2019. https://wire.ama-assn.org/life-career/medical-specialties-highest-burnout-rates.

American Foundation for Suicide Prevention. 2018. "Healthcare Professional Burnout, Depression and Suicide Prevention." *American Foundation for Suicide Prevention*. Accessed May 2, 2019. https://afsp.org/our-work/education/healthcare-professional-burnout-depression-suicide-prevention/.

American Psychological Association. 2018. "Data on Behavioral Health in the United States." *American Psychological Association*. Accessed May 2, 2019. http://www.apa.org/helpcenter/data-behavioral-health.aspx.

Austin, P. 2008. *Something for the Pain: Compassion and Burnout in the ER*. New York, NY/London: W. W. Norton & Company.

Barrington, J. 1997. *Writing the Memoir: From Truth to Art*. Portland, OR: The Eighth Mountain Press.

Broyard, A. 1992. *Intoxicated by My Illness and Other Writings*. New York, NY: Fawcett Columbine.

Brennan, N., N. Cafarella, S. L. Kocot, A. McKethan, M. Morrison, N. Nguyen, M. Shepard, and R. D. Williams II. 2009. "Improving Quality and Value in the U.S. Health Care Systems. Executive Report." *Brookings*. August 21, 2009. https://www.brookings.edu/research/improving-quality-and-value-in-the-u-s-health-care-system/.

Carr, E. A. 2014. "Modern Memoir: Popular Confession and How It Sells 'A Million Little Pieces'." *Inquiries Journal* 6 (11): 1–4.

Center for Disease Control and Prevention. 2017. "Ambulatory Care Use and Physician Office Visits. Fast Stats." *CDC. National Center for Health Statistics.* Accessed May 2, 2019. https://www.cdc.gov/nchs/fastats/physician-visits.htm.

Center for Disease Control and Prevention. 2020. "Attitudes Towards Mental Illness—35 States, District of Columbia, and Puerto Rico, 2007." *MMWR* 59 (20): 619–625.

Dittrich, L. 2016. *Patient H.M.: A Story of Memory, Madness, and Family Secrets.* New York, NY: Random House.

Engel, J. 2006. *Poor People, Medicine, Medicaid, and American Charity Since 1965.* Durham, NC: Duke University Press.

Fox, M. 2016. "One in Six Americans Take Antidepressants, Other Psychiatric Drugs: Study." *NBC Health News*, December 12, 2016. https://www.nbcnews.com/health/health-news/one-6-americans-take-antidepressants-other-psychiatric-drugs-n695141.

Gask, L. 2015. *The Other Side of Silence. A Psychiatrist's Memoir of Depression.* Chichester: Summersdale Publishers Ltd.

Gawande, A. 2002. *Complications: A Surgeon's Notes on an Imperfect Science.* New York, NY: Picador. Henry Holt and Company.

Gawande, A. 2007. *Better: A Surgeon's Notes on Performance.* New York, NY: Picador. Henry Holt and Company.

Groopman, J. 2007. *How Doctors Think.* Boston, MA/New York, NY: A Mariner Book, Houghton Mifflin Company.

Hellerstein, D. 1994. *A Family of Doctors.* New York, NY: Ivy Books.

Hilfiker, D. 1998. *Healing the Wounds: A Physician Looks at His Work.* Omaha, NA: Creighton University Press.

Holland, J. 2010. *Weekends at Bellevue.* New York, NY: Bantam Books.

Horwitz, A. V. 2010. "How an Age of Anxiety Became an Age of Depression." *The Milbank Quarterly* 88 (1): 112–138. https://doi.org/10.1111/j.1468-0009.2010.00591.x.

Iliades, C. 2014. "Facts about Depression: Who's at Risk?" *Everyday Health*, April 5, 2014. https://www.everydayhealth.com/depression/facts-about-depression-whos-at-risk.aspx.

Jamison. K. R. 1996a. *Touched with Fire. Manic-Depressive Illness and the Artistic Temperament.* New York, NY: Free Press.

Jamison, K. R. 1996b. *An Unquiet Mind.* New York, NY: Vintage Books.

Jauhar, S. 2014. *Doctored: The Disillusionment of an American Physician.* New York, NY: Farrar, Straus & Giroux.

Larimore, W. 2002. *Bryson City Tales: Stories of a Doctor's First Year of Practice in the Smokey Mountains.* Grand Rapids, MI: Zondervan.

Lerner, B. H. 2014. *The Good Doctor: A Father, a Son, and the Evolution of Medical Ethics.* Boston, MA: Beacon Press.

Lieberman, J. A., M. L. Goldman, M. Olfson, H. A. Pincus, and L. I. Sederer. 2017. "America: An Opportunity for Comprehensive Reform." *Modern Medicine Network*

34 (4). April 17, 2017. https://www.psychiatrictimes.com/cultural-psychiatry/improving-mental-health-care-america-opportunity-comprehensive-reform.

Lown, B. 1999. *The Lost Art of Healing: Practicing Compassion in Medicine.* New York, NY: Ballentine Books.

Lu, S. 2010. "Destigmatizing Mental Illness Needs a National Push, Report Says." *APA. Monitor on Psychology* 47 (7): 10.

Matthews, D. 2018. "Stop Blaming Mental Illness for Mass Shootings." *Vox*, March 14, 2018. https://www.vox.com/policy-and-politics/2017/11/9/16618472/mental-illness-gun-homicide-mass-shootings.

Mitchell, G. D. 1994. *Dr. George: An Account of the Life of a Country Doctor.* Carbondale, Edwardsville, IL: Southern Illinois University Press.

Mukherjee, S. 2015. *The Laws of Medicine.* New York, NY/London: TED Books. Simon & Schuster.

Nuland, S. B. 2008. *The Uncertain Art: Thoughts on a Life in Medicine.* New York, NY: Random House.

Ofri, D. 2003. *Singular Intimacies: Becoming a Doctor at Bellevue.* New York, NY: Penguin Books.

Ofri, D. 2013. *What Doctors Feel: How Emotions Affect the Practice of Medicine.* Boston, MA: Beacon Press.

Peckham, C. 2015. "Physician Burnout: It Just Keeps Getting Worse." *Medscape. Cme.* Accessed May 2, 2019. https://www.medscape.com/viewarticle/838437.

Popoveniuc, B. 2014. "The Philosophy of Depression." *Outlook on Communication Journal* 4 (1): 22–31.

Ratcliffe, M. 2013. "Why Mood Matters." In *Cambridge Companion to Being and Time*, edited by M. Wrathall, 157–176. Cambridge: Cambridge University Press.

Reilly, B. 2013. *One Doctor: Close Calls, Cold Cases, and the Mysteries of Medicine.* New York, NY: Atria Books.

Rosalind, R. n.d. "Why are Memoirs So Popular?" *A Reader's Place.* Accessed May 2, 2019. https://areadersplace.net/memoir/popular/.

Rosenfeld, I. 2010. *Doctor of the Heart. My Life in Medicine.* New Rochelle, NY: Mary Ann Liebert Incorporation Publishers.

Ruggieri, P. A. 2012. *Confessions of a Surgeon: The Good, the Bad, and the Complicated … Life behind the O.R. Doors.* New York, NY: Berkeley Books.

Shem, S. 1978. *The House of God.* New York, NY: Dell Publishing.

Silver, J., A. Simons, and S. Crauns. 2018. *A Study of Pre-Attack Behaviors of Active Shooters in the United States between 2000–2013.* Washington D.C.: Federal Bureau of Investigation, U.S. Department of Justice.

Slater, L. 1997. *Welcome to My Country.* New York, NY: Anchor Books.

Solomon, A. 2001. *The Noonday Demon. An Atlas of Depression.* New York, NY/London: Scribner.

Starr, P. 1982. *The Social History of American Medicine.* New York, NY: Basic Books.

Starzl, T. E. 1992. *The Puzzle People: Memoirs of a Transplant Surgeon*. London: University of Pittsburg Press.

Stevens, R. A. 1996. "Health Care in the Early 1960s." *Healthcare Financing Review* 18 (2): 11–21.

Sweet, V. 2012. *God's Motel. A Doctor, a Hospital, and a Pilgrimage to the Heart of Medicine*. New York, NY: Riverhead Books.

Tweedy, D. 2015. *Black Man in a White Coat. A Doctor's Reflection on Race and Medicine*. New York, NY: Picador.

Vonnegut, M. 2011. *Just Like Someone without Mental Illness Only More So. A Memoir*. New York, NY: Bantam Books.

Zinsser, W. 1987. *Inventing the Truth: The Art and Craft of Memoirs*. Boston, MA: Houghton Mifflin Company.

13 Metaphors of Depression in American Short Fiction

Ioana Unk
Independent Scholar, California

Depression and Metaphor

Although the diagnostic manuals for mental illnesses provide numerous definitions and descriptions of symptoms, depression remains a personal experience, that is most likely to be depicted by depressed persons with less technical wording.

> A sequence of metaphors—vines, trees, cliffs, etc.—is the only way to talk about the experience. It's not an easy diagnostics because it depends on metaphors, and the metaphors one patient chooses are different from those selected by another patient. (Solomon 2015, 29)

We contend that an investigation of the use of conventional metaphors, as well as of the occurrence of new imaginative and creative metaphors, establishes a new understanding of depression, and, also, raises questions regarding a possible shift in perspective.

While the connection between emotions and meanings may not always be in sync, a constant reevaluation of the linguistic tools that we use to express how we feel may lead to new expressions, that is, new metaphors. "Old stories may in turn come to be understood in new ways and new metaphor themes may emerge to represent this different way of seeing and experiencing an aspect of self." (Angus and Korman 2002, 154)

The Conceptual Metaphor Theory devised by Lakoff and Johnson (1980) revolutionized the classic understanding of metaphor, as defined by the comparison theory, and extended its usage from the realm of language to that of thought and action. Metaphor is no longer perceived as a mere poetic and linguistic device, but as a reflection of the conceptual system that is, in its turn, metaphorical in nature, and that comprises all concepts that drive our everyday functioning and the way we perceive the world around us. Following this line of thought, we may conclude that, if our conceptual system is metaphorically structured, then the same kind of structure, that is, metaphorical, is characteristic of our thinking process, language, and action. Considering this close connection between metaphorical linguistic expressions and metaphorical concepts, *the metaphors we live by* support the deciphering of the metaphorical nature of our activities. The two theorists emphasized the experiential basis of metaphors (metaphors are grounded in the human experience) and also the culture-embedded feature of metaphors (metaphors are specific to a culture), as "the most fundamental values in a culture will be coherent with the metaphorical structure of the most fundamental concepts in the culture." (Lakoff and Johnson 1980, 22) The values of the subculture one determine One's preference for certain metaphors adheres to, and by one's values. While acknowledging the universality of metaphor, as "linguistic, conceptual, neural, bodily, and social" construct, Kövecses (2007, 15) distinguishes two dimensions along which metaphors vary: "the cross-cultural and the within-culture dimension." (2007, 18) In the case of the latter, the variation is determined by social categories (women-men, young-old, etcetera), geographical regions, style, subcultures, and individual preferences.

Lakoff and Johnson opt for a simplified definition of metaphor: "*The essence of metaphor is understanding and experiencing one kind of thing in terms of another.*" (1980, 5) Thus, the prerequisite for a metaphor is the existence of certain similarities between two objects or situations, but in several cases, such similarities can be based on conventional metaphors—that is, metaphors that "partly define what we find real." (1980, 153) The essential condition for these similarities to be relevant is that they be experiential (i.e. grounded in our experience), and not objective.

A few more aspects of the metaphor discussed by Lakoff and Johnson are worth mentioning concerning depression. Metaphors entail parts that underline and explain certain aspects of our experience and, in particular instances, metaphors can be the only way to express human experience. Metaphors also have the power to "create realities for us," (1980, 156) to redefine reality through their entailments that are focused on some aspects of our experience, while ignoring others. Looking at a situation through the conceptual lens of a metaphor leads to inferences that are coherent with the facets highlighted by the metaphor entailments and, subsequently, to actions that are coherent with the metaphor itself. As such, metaphors can be "a guide for future action" (1980, 156) and "self-fulfilling prophecies." (1980, 156) Their use is often instinctive; they work as automatic mechanisms whenever we face conceptual and linguistic uncertainties (Stott et al. 2010).

Discussing the complicated relationship between memory and metaphor, Ozick notices that the metaphor also has interpretative functions, memory being the object of its interpretation. Its close connection with language, which results from this transformation mission—transforming the unfamiliar experience of the others into common knowledge—makes the metaphor appear as something concrete, as a "shocking extension of the unknown into our most intimate, most feeling, most private selves." (1991, 282) In this sense, the metaphor is a gateway to the innermost experience of others, even if such an experience is foreign to us.

Metaphors and science suggest two different kinds of understanding that are most valuable to mankind: metaphors establish an existential understanding of human experiences, which is essentially a personal type of knowledge, while scientific knowledge is mainly shareable and enhances the first type of experience (Pribram 1990, 80).

The Metaphors of Depression in Psychology

Some theorists understand the term depression *per se* as metaphorical: it comes from the Latin word *deprimere*, meaning "to press down" and it "implies a feeling of being weighed or pressed down." (Angus and Korman 2002, 151) The high incidence of its diagnosis made it the "common cold of psychiatric ills." (Kline, qtd. in McMullen and Conway 2002, 179) The practitioners of cognitive-behavioral therapy sometimes refer to depression as a "broken leg," (Stott et al. 2010, 1) suggesting a hopeful, even if long-term recovery.

In the section dedicated to detailing the diagnostic features for major depressive disorder, the *Diagnostic and Statistical Manual of Mental Disorders* (DSM-5) makes use of a couple of metaphors, to help practitioners recognize the criterion symptoms in patients: The phrase "down in the dumps" is used to describe the mood in a major depressive episode, while the lack of feelings may be expressed as "feeling 'blah'." (American Psychiatric Association 2013, 163)

In his detailed account of the history of depression and melancholia, Jackson identifies two most recurrent metaphors for depression, both with ancient roots: "being in a state of darkness" and "being weighed down" (1986, 396), and a third, more recent phrase: "being slowed down." (1986, 398) The metaphorical use of the theme of darkness started with Galen, who employed this notion as a means to illustrate what the fear associated with melancholia might feel like. The darkening sensation thought to be caused by black bile. This metaphor can also be read in Alexander of Tralles, Ishaq ibn Imran, Avicenna, Constantinus Africanus, and Burton. The theme of feeling "weighted down" (1986, 397) is mentioned in Homer's *Odyssey*, Ishaq's writings, Alexander of Tralles, depicting a sensation of bodily heaviness that was characteristic of people suffering from melancholia. In the 17th and 18th centuries, the use of these metaphors was extended to depression, as well. The newer metaphor "being slowed down" (1986, 398) was first used in the 17th century, being inspired by hydrodynamics (the flow of fluids can be slowed down or speeded up). Similarly, slowing down the circulation of the blood resulted in such phenomena as "slowing of thought," "mental sluggishness," "retardation of the mental stream." (1986, 398)

Analyzing the phrasing used to express their emotions, moods and affects by 21 clients in audiotaped therapy sessions, McMullen and Conway identified four of the most frequent metaphors: *Depression is darkness*, referring to depression perceived as "cloudy, rainy weather," (2002, 170) *Depression is weight*, describing a sensation of heaviness characteristic of the whole body, not just the mind, *Depression is captor*, expressing a "sense of restriction," (2002, 171) a particular confinement, and *Depression is descent*, as an expression of "being *down* or *low*." (2002, 171) The authors draw attention to the fact that the metaphor *Depression is descent* is the most dominant one to describe depression, and that it leads to a series of metaphorical entailments: "depression is conceptualized as a downward progression that, once begun, is difficult, if not impossible, to stop," (2002, 172) extending its significance to the level of a cultural metaphor, symptomatic of a conventionalized understanding of this mental illness as undesirable and negative. These exclusively negative connotations may accentuate the negative experiences of the depressed person.

Analyzing the variation in metaphor, Kövecses refers to the metaphors employed by certain subcultures, that is, subgroups, and exemplifies this distinction with the metaphor *Depression is captor* (2007, 23) that seems to be used exclusively by the people suffering from depression, as opposed to such metaphors as *Depression is darkness*, *Depression is heavy*, *Depression is descent/down* (2007, 23) that may also be found in the language of *non-depressed* people. This unconscious preference for a distinctive metaphor is a unique way of expressing certain feelings that differentiates this subgroup, that is, the depressed people from the others (2007, 31).

As it results from the cognitive-behavioral psychotherapeutic practice, most of the metaphors assigned to depression are based on the vertical perception of mood, where happiness takes the top place, and sadness and melancholia take the bottom place; therefore depression is associated with concepts such as "sinking," "low," "rock bottom," (Stott et al. 2010, 105) etcetera.

The idea of "sinking" also suggests a certain "passivity, lack of control, and hopelessness." (2010, 105) When a mood is described in terms of color, language gives birth to metaphors that describe depression as "black," "dark," "wearing dark glasses," (2010, 114) etcetera. Depressed people can experience the same burden of depression as a weight that can hardly be lifted, or as a trap: "being in the grip of depression," "not being able to shake off their mood." (2010, 105) The feelings of isolation and withdrawal that often overcome depressed people have been expressed as being "cut off," (2010, 111) which renders the distance between them and the rest of humanity, leaving them to feel like they cannot "escape this pattern." (2010, 112) Another specific symptom of depression that is often uttered in the psychotherapeutic sessions is the propensity for rumination, conveyed as inclination to "chew over" (2010, 119) present or past events, often referred to as "ghosts from the past." (2010, 124)

The phrases "over the edge" and "into the abyss" (Solomon 2015, 27) are used by depressed persons to describe the transition from pain to madness, relating to the metaphors *Depression is abnormality* and *Depression is descent.*

The psychoanalytic tradition associates depression with the sorrow brought about by the loss of an object, the guild over losing it, the anxiety caused by the loss of well-being, the identification with the lost object, that affects one's self-esteem and a lack of interest for the external world (Weiner Bakur and White Taggart 1982, 491). This narcissistic identification with the lost object leads to feelings of self-loss and loss of self-esteem and suggests a new metaphor for depression, that is, *depression as a search for the lost self.* The psychodynamic practice established that patients suffering from depression described it as a "journey back from abyss," (Valerio 2015, 53) a sensation of being "trapped" (2015, 54) or "cornered," (2015, 55) a feeling of "drifting away," (McCarthy 2015, 95) while the recovery is seen as a "coming back to life." (2015, 53) Patients describe the general tendency toward rumination as "digging deep" (Previdi 2015, 69) inside one's head.

Metaphors of Depression in Short Stories

The usefulness of art in general, and literature in particular for the understanding of certain mental disorders has been explained by Stott et al. (2010, 3): "poems, scenes from books, plays and films, works of art, and news stories have the capacity to transform meaning by sharing a conceptual similarity to our client's experiences, yet superficially involving very different subject matter." This similarity leads to a connection that the psychotherapy client may develop with a fictional character and, while this connection is strong enough to allow the message to be understood, it also creates distance from oneself (2010, 7–8). As far as the reader is concerned, this connection stimulates, besides a new perspective on the phenomenon, the creation of new meaning, in the sense of discovery of new facets of the same phenomenon, especially with creative metaphors. According to the same authors, the metaphor elicits a more rapid "conceptual travel" (2010, 8) to the narrative world, as "often the metaphors are more elaborate visual descriptions that can resemble short stories and parables." (2010, 3)

There is a structural and functional resemblance between psychological investigation and short stories. Psychology never claims to grasp everything of humans and to explain the functioning of the human psyche as a result of an exhaustive investigation; on the contrary, it sets out to identify significant episodes in a person's life and to draw coherent inferences from them. Short stories are also bound to brevity and concision, due to their structure, and to relevance, due to the impact they have to make on the reader in a short amount of time. "Stories are small gems, perfectly cut to expose every facet of an idea, which is, in turn, illuminated by ten thousand tiny shafts of light." (Mosley 2003, xiii) To capture the human essence is what both psychology and short stories strive to achieve:

> Stories, after all, are short, just like our human moments … To me this form captures better than any other what it is to be human—the brevity of our moments, the cruel irrevocability when those times places and people we hold the most dear slip through our fingers. (Díaz 2016, xiii-xiv)

Based on this similarity, I have investigated descriptors of depression in American short stories, to see to what extent the metaphors used in short fiction relate to the ones employed in psychotherapy, and I have identified the following themes.

Depression Is Descent

This is one of the most common metaphors used for depression, and it originates in what Lakoff and Johnson called "orientational metaphors," (1980, 14) a class of metaphors mimicking the spatial orientation of the human body (up-down, front-back, etcetera). These suggestive metaphors are paired in dichotomic generic couples: "Happy is up; sad is down," "Health and life are up; sickness and death are down," resulting in such metaphors as "He's really low these days. I fell into depression. My spirits sank," (1980, 15) that are inspired by the dropping posture of the human body when overcoming feelings of sadness and depression.

Similarly, this metaphor was favored by writers of short fiction, to suggest an undesirable negative state: "A low mood *was creeping* up on him" (Antrim 2011); "The motel had declined steadily in the few months that Loomis had been staying there, like a moderately stable person *drifting and sinking into the lassitude of depression*" (Watson 2009, 4); "most of the time he felt as if *he were drowning* and couldn't find the bottom or the surface of this murky body of water he had fallen, or dived, into" (Watson 2009, 7); "the depressed person always apologized for *dragging them down*" (Wallace 1998, 57); "she *slipped into this depression*" (Evarts 1949, 69); "he found that his mind was frantic. This was his disorder. *This was his descent*" (Antrim 2008); and "Then *his thinking disintegrated* into bitter resignation. Everything he touched was *ruined*. The flowers were almost *destroyed*." (Antrim 2008)

Depression Is Darkness and Depression Is Evil

Another metaphor that derives from the theme *depression is descent* is based on the association between negative attitudes and affects that characterize depression, and "cloudy weather." (McMullen and Conway 2002, 179) When these moods are out of one's personal control, they are attributed to evil forces, underlining the feeling of helplessness when facing such pervasive negativity. This type of metaphorical thinking is specific mostly to personal accounts of depression: "if her life depended on describing the sun but she [the depressed person] were allowed to describe *only shadows on the ground*" (Wallace 1998, 62); "But the night folded again into the quiet of its soft enclosure. It was moonless and *the great dark pressed in. She reached out for him in the dark*" (Barry 2016, 89); "Sometimes you just have *to shake the devil off you*, whatever the devil is" (Danticat 2017, 57); "his *death-trip history*, considered alongside the 'conspicuous' spending on coats, ties, shirts, and shoes, represented, at the least, she thought, a mixed-state depression" (Antrim 2008); and "nonetheless [he] had a notion that he might soon be *coming out of the Dread*, as he called it." (Antrim 2011)

Depression Is Abnormality and Mind Is a Broken Machine

Depression is associated with the lack of normality, the unpleasant and disturbing dissimilarity of human experience, or even with the weird abnormality: "I don't want you to get it into your head that *being depressed is all beer and skittles*" (Evarts 1949, 75); "if she begins *acting funny*, don't be surprised if I just make some excuse and leave quietly" (1949, 70); and "She's *out of her head*, but completely." (1949, 69)

I would include in the same category the metaphors that rely on the traditional metaphor "Mind is a machine," (Hoffman et al. 1990, 181) that is to be found in the mechanistic view on mind and mental life, and used by Descartes, Leibnitz, La Mettrie, and Hobbes, as a descriptor of mental life. Lakoff and Johnson also discuss the ontological metaphor "The mind is an entity," with its variations, "The mind is a machine" (1980, 27) and "The mind is a brittle object." (1980, 28) Following this tradition, we have the metaphor *Mind is a broken machine*: "a young man who was incurably *deranged in his mind*" (Nabokov 1948); "before she got *sidetracked*." (Evarts 1949, 69)

Depression Is Weight/Heavy

The metaphor *Depression is weight/heavy* is based on a conceptual metaphor frequently used in the cognitive paradigm to describe emotions, that is "Emotion is a force" (Kövecses 2002, 112), that, in this particular case, presses down on the person experiencing it: "Billy could sense *the weight of low pressure bearing down*" (Antrim 2014); "But that evening his body was compressing: *the weight of the air was on him*, flattening his libido and his trust in humankind" (Antrim 2008);

> After Julia left, in his worsening he'd walked and moved as if *crushed by some stronger form of gravity. The air had pressed him down*, and he could not get out from under it. Some days, he'd curled in a ball on the floor and promised himself that soon, soon, soon—it would be his gift to himself—he'd walk up to the barn and lie down with the rifle ... He remembered how *the misery had bowed him over*: he'd gone everywhere, in those days, *with his head down*, barrelling rigidly forward, compounding with pain by moving at all; but when he touched himself to find where the pain was coming from he couldn't find the spot. (Antrim 2014)
>
> The roar of the air-conditioner and the cold *pressing down* were the only things that kept his soul from slipping out of his body. The few times he got up to go to the bathroom, he thought the quiet outside the guest room would *pound him into the ground*. The warm air was *too heavy* to push out of his way. (Earley 2018, 60)
>
> [H]e'd had the strong sensation that the air through which he moved was gathering around him and becoming—really, no word was sufficient to name it—substantive. *Its weight pressed in on him*. This hurt, it hurt terribly, yet when he tried to locate the source of the pain he could not: it came, as he knew, only from himself. On the mattress, shattered and sobbing over, say, Kate and their messed-up love, *he'd lain crushed*, as if by atmospheres. (Antrim 2008)

Depression Is Captor

This metaphor conveys the feeling of entrapment, the lack of control of one's personal life: "*I'm stuck* on this rock" (Antrim 2014); "He was forty-four years old, *trapped in his body*. Arms, legs, torso" (DeLillo 2017, 59); "What he had really wanted to do was to *tear a hole in his world and escape*" (Nabokov 1948); "to the bottomless, chronic adult despair she suffered every day and felt *hopelessly trapped in*" (Wallace 1998, 57); and "John began to sense the world unravelling behind him, the *tightly braided strands of his life* snapping free with sharp cracks." (Earley 2018, 57)

Depression Is Unutterable

This metaphor stands in opposition to the theme *understanding is seeing*, used by John Locke, to explain the novelty and creativity of mental processes and operations (Hoffman et al. 1990, 179), and, as such, its logic is based on a reversed mechanism: not understanding one's own feelings or not being able to express them in a coherent manner, means not seeing things clearly, which condemns depression to a gray area of incertitude: "It was a feeling, *hard to shape into words*" (Antrim 2011);

> *not being able to share the way it felt*, what it actually felt like for the depressed person to be *literally unable to share it*, as for example if her life depended on describing the sun but she were allowed to describe only shadows on the ground. (Wallace 1998, 62)

Other examples include: "He said, 'Has he taken care with you, since I've been gone?' 'Gone?' she said. '*I don't know how else to put it*'" (Antrim 2008); as well as

> he'd had the strong sensation that the air through which he moved was gathering around him and becoming—really, *no word was sufficient to name it*—substantive. Its weight pressed in on him. This hurt, it hurt terribly, yet *when he tried to locate the source of the pain he could not*: it came, as he knew, only from himself. On the mattress, shattered and sobbing over, say, Kate and their messed-up love, he'd lain crushed, as if by atmospheres. (Antrim 2008)

Depression Is Isolation and Depression Is a Burden

This category of metaphors combines feelings of inadequacy, confusion and loss that a depressed person may experience, with the impression of emotional clinginess that the behavior of such a person may suggest, also alluding to her needs: "They'd been *lost in these woods* before" (Antrim 2011); "Loomis felt no affinity for any of them. There wasn't a single person in the entire place with whom he *felt a thing in common*—other than being, somehow, human" (Watson 2009); "and indeed he had been *drifting in his grief*" (2009); " 'you are a ghost. *Walking between two worlds*'" (2009); "had verbally detached *the depressed person's needy fingers* from her pantcuff" (Wallace 1998, 58); "was waiting to come in and *cling* pathetically *to the hem of the therapist's pelisse*" (1998, 62); "The depressed person said that she was all too excruciating aware of what a *joyless burden she was*" (1998, 58); and "When he walked on the beach, *he barely left footprints.*" (Earley 2018, 56)

Metaphors for the Cure and Effects of Medication

An interesting category of metaphors is the one delineating the effects of certain medication and treatments, describing the dependence they sometimes create, and also the distortion of mood and thought process:

> Richard's pills were in his bag, consolidated in one container. He could easily identify them by shape and color, the pills for depression and insomnia. *Offering nudges in his mood like the touch of a dance partner. A subtle but real pressure.* He felt for the pill tube through the bag's front pocket—there it was—and he was reassured, *lightened* … The white wine *tasted like granite.* (Cline 2017, 59)
>
> The problem was his thought process: the lithium he was taking in small doses *brought a slower speed to reality.* It was the lithium or the antidepressant cocktail or all of it in concert. At times, when he spoke, he felt as if a kind of *mental wind were blowing his thoughts back to him*, forcing him to self-consciously order his syntax as he pushed words out … it was the medication, *warping his mind and delaying his reaction.* (Antrim 2008)
>
> At the booth, he counted out pills, his anti-depressants and her anti-anxieties—he carried and dispensed for her more often than not, ever since her suicide attempt—and he asked her, 'How many do you think *will do the trick*? One? Two? Do you need two? Honey, can you talk?' (Antrim 2011)

Creative Metaphors

The beauty of fiction is that it has the power to surprise its readers. This is also true for the creative metaphors employed by writers to render the complex facets of mental illness. "New metaphors have the power to create a new reality." (Lakoff and Johnson 1980, 145) The authors draw attention to the fact that the new metaphors may enter our conceptual system, determining a change in our perceptions. "Much of cultural change arises from the introduction of new metaphorical concepts and the loss of old ones." (1980, 145) When considering how these innovative metaphors operate, a few words of caution are in place. As El Refaie noted: "In order to be considered truly creative, however, the new metaphor must accord with our basic embodied experiences and be well suited to the medium and context of communication." (2014, 152) The creative process of generating new metaphors may involve formulating new connections between two areas of experience or reinterpreting common, conventional metaphors, but the main prerequisite for the success of this process is the degree of appropriateness, that is, how they conform to a personal and cultural context.

The metaphor *Depression is an itch*, to be found in two short stories, "The Itch" by Don DeLillo (2017) and "The Emerald Light in the Air" by Donald Antrim (2014) complies with the prerequisite for compatibility, as it is based on the conventional conceptual metaphor *Mind is body*, but the mapping is innovative. If the human mind is compared to the human body and acquires the qualities and flaws of the human body, the symptoms of mental diseases can have visible physical manifestations: "he'd felt the burning. He'd felt it in his temple. It was, somehow, he knew, both imaginary and real, a beckoning, *an itch*, a need for a bullet" (Antrim 2014); "He is funnelled into himself, no past or future, *the living itch*, man-shaped, Robert T. Waldron, thinking incoherently, a body in a bedsheet." (DeLillo 2017, 65)

The issue of creative metaphors raises new questions as to their *modus operandi* and the relationship between metaphor, image, and text. Since metaphor is a component of thought and thought processing, and it is not a mere linguistic device, its essence is visual, as the metaphor itself is said to be centered around a visual image (Stott et al. 2010, 14). The metaphor defines our psychological existence as human beings; it embodies our ontological structure, that is, acts as a mirror in which we discover the "images in our reflection about experiences of what it means to be in the world as a human being." (Olson 2019, 95) Moreover, this reflection "deepens and re-figures reality." (Romanyshyn, qtd. in Olson 2019, 95) Therefore, metaphor deepens the reflected reality by "refiguring the context in which it appears." (qtd. in Olson 2019, 95) If we agree that deepening means always contextual re-figuring, and that the metaphor acts as a mirror, we have to underline the fact that some extensive creative metaphors operate visually, as they continually refigure the context. This draws them very closely to the concept of image metaphors.

Coëgnarts and Kravanja discuss the category of image metaphors, defined as "short-lived metaphors which involve not the mapping of conceptual *domains*, but rather the mapping of *images*," (2012, 99) that differ from the usual conceptual metaphors in the fact that both target and source domain refer to concrete things and create a strong imagery. Such rich imagery has an obvious downside: the specificity of the suggested images limits their application. Nonetheless, the image metaphors are conceptual, but they are also imagistic in function. The image metaphors may have a linguistic expression, but words "are prompts for us to map from one conventional image to another," (Lakoff 1993, 229) and, what is most important, this kind of mapping also entails "our evaluation of the source domain onto the target," (Lakoff 1993, 245) that is, our knowledge about a particular experience.

The use of the creative metaphor *Depression is an itch* might suggest that we are dealing with an image metaphor, but more careful consideration of its prerequisites indicates that this metaphor does not qualify as an image metaphor. Despite the strong imagery—depression as itch—only one of the domains, namely the source domain—the itch—depicts a concrete object, while the target domain—depression—is an abstract term (depression requires a more detailed definition and does not prompt a single mental concept). The strong image that this metaphor creates suggests that this type of metaphors operates visually, even if they cannot be constructed as image metaphors *per se*.

The itch as a metaphor of depression maps the specific features associated with the source domain—the itch—onto the target domain—depression—but also our negative evaluation of the two experiences.

As I mentioned before, "The Itch" (2017) is centered around one of the traditional metaphors used for understanding the functioning of the human brain, that is, *Mind is body*. Therefore, depression is depicted as a chronic ailment of the skin, as long-term suffering that disrupts all aspects of the character's life. His battle with *the itch* is described as a journey, leading to the use of the metaphor *Depression is a journey* (derived from the conventional metaphor *Life is a journey*). The onset of depression is delineated: "After the divorce he felt an odd numbness, mental and physical." (DeLillo 2017, 59) Shortly after this episode, the suffering caused by depression acquires a physical component: "Scalp developed something that a doctor gave a name to, but it itched only rarely, then not at all, so the name didn't matter." (2017, 59) The character looks for an explanation: "He began to think of the itch as sense data from the exterior, caused by some outlying substance, unanalyzable, the air in the room or on the street or in the atmosphere itself, a corruption of the planetary environment." (2017, 59) He soon comes to the realization that the itch is a chronic condition that he identifies with, at least partly: "When itching stops now and then, five minutes, six minutes, you are a little bereft," (2017, 63–64) "You are nobody without the itch" (2017, 64), and that the cure has to come from within: "Do not let others scratch your itch. It will not succeed," she said, "You yourself must scratch." (2017, 63) "His plan was to avoid details and simply say that the itch was a livable condition but not likely to be alleviated anytime soon." (2017, 64)

In the story "Backpack," (2018) depression is depicted with the metaphors *Depression is a journey*, *Depression is abnormality*, and *Depression is a burden*. The character oscillates between two states: an apparent normality, described as a state of full inflation, when depression is kept at bay, and episodes of depression, when deflation starts: "She showed John a photo of him in his classroom at Orange Academy, his feet crossed on his desk, his hands behind his head, a big grin on his face. Chairman of the History Department. *Fully inflated*" (Earley 2018, 61); "John *developed a slow air leak*. He *could not stay properly inflated*. He could not be patched. He wandered around late at night starring at his phone. He bought a *backpack*." (2018, 57)

This duality of the states of mind is beautifully reflected by the character and his persona: John, the successful academic who can mask his depression, and Jimmy Ray Gallup, the rugged ship's mechanic traveling to Lake Superior to commit suicide amid depression. When deflection reaches the lowest point, depression is high, and the character faces many commutes from one state of mind to the other. The character's journey through a life with depression invokes the metaphor *Depression is a journey*, which is based on the conventional metaphor *Life is a journey*. The backpack itself stands for the character's depressive moods: it is something that he carries with him during the whole journey; it contains his identity. The backpack, as any piece of luggage, is a traditional symbol of the traveler; it stands for his identity and the heritage that he brings from his world into the world he travels to. In the case of Earley's story, depression symbolized by the backpack is not something that can be shaken off easily. The suggestive image of the backpack, as excessive baggage, alludes to the writer's use of a creative metaphor—*Depression is a backpack*—that originates from a conventional metaphor—*Depression is a burden*. The imagery is innovative, and even if the metaphor does not qualify as a pictorial metaphor, it operates visually.

A psychoanalytic take on the short story might suggest the use of the metaphor *Depression is a search for the lost self*, in the sense that John becomes Ray, takes on a journey, at the end of which he becomes John again, on the verge of his imminent return home.

Regardless of their nature and the way they operate, the metaphors of depression provide a useful tool for a better understanding of this mental disease, for readers, psychotherapists, and the people suffering from depression. By all accounts, metaphors are condensed vehicles carrying a vast cumulus of human knowledge and opening the way toward an emphatic interdisciplinary approach. As Ozick pleads:

> Through metaphorical concentration, doctors can imagine what it is to be their patients. Those who have no pain can imagine those who suffer. Those at the center can imagine what it is to be outside. The strong can imagine the weak. Illuminated lives can imagine the dark. Poets in the twilight can imagine the borders of stellar fire. We strangers can imagine the familiar hearts of strangers. (1991, 283)

This study investigated the conventional and creative metaphors used to describe depression in American short stories, their origins, and their meeting point in different psychotherapy paradigms. A new category of metaphors—those describing the effects of the medication used for depression—has been identified, suggesting a further interest in the metaphors employed by clinical psychologists to initiate the healing process and in the way metaphors used in fiction might be assimilated into psychotherapy.

References

American Psychiatric Association. 2013. *Diagnostic and Statistical Manual of Mental Disorders*, 5. Washington, D.C.: American Psychiatric Publishing.

Angus, L., and Y. Korman. 2002. "Conflict, Coherence, and Change in Brief Psychotherapy. A Metaphor Theme Analysis." In *The Verbal Communication of Emotions. Interdisciplinary Perspectives*, edited by S. R. Fussell, 151–165. New York, NY: Psychology Press.

Antrim, D. 2008. "Another Manhattan." *The New Yorker*, December 22, 2008. https://www.newyorker.com/magazine/2008/12/22/another-manhattan.

Antrim, D. 2011. "He Knew." *The New Yorker*, May 9, 2011. https://www.newyorker.com/magazine/2011/05/09/he-knew.

Antrim, D. 2014. "The Emerald Lights in the Air." *The New Yorker*, January 26, 2014. https://www.newyorker.com/magazine/2014/02/03/the-emerald-light-in-the-air.

Barry, K. 2016. "Deer Season." *The New Yorker*, October 10, 2016. https://www.newyorker.com/magazine/2016/10/10/deer-season.

Cline, E. 2017. "Northeast Regional." *The New Yorker*, April 3, 2017. https://www.newyorker.com/magazine/2017/04/10/northeast-regional.

Coëgnarts, M., and P. Kravanja. 2012. "From Thought to Modality: A Theoretical Framework for Analysing Structural-Conceptual Metaphors and Image Metaphors in Film." *Image & Narrative* 13 (1): 96–113.

Danticat, E. 2017. "Sunrise, Sunset." *The New Yorker*, September 18, 2017. https://www.newyorker.com/magazine/2017/09/18/sunrise-sunset.

DeLillo, D. 2017. "The Itch." *The New Yorker*, July 31, 2017. https://www.newyorker.com/magazine/2017/08/07/the-itch-don-delillo.

Díaz, J. 2016. "Introduction." In *The Best American Short Stories 2016*, edited by J. Díaz and H. Pitlor, xii–xx. Boston, MA: Houghton Mifflin Harcourt Publishing Company.

Earley, T. 2018. "Backpack." *The New Yorker*, November 5, 2018. https://www.newyorker.com/magazine/2018/11/05/backpack.

El Refaie, E. 2014. "Looking on the Dark and Bright Side: Creative Metaphors of Depression in Two Graphic Memoirs." *a/b: Auto/Biography Studies* 29 (1): 149–174. https://doi.org/10.1080/08989575.2014. 921989.

Evarts, E. 1949. "Just Depressed." *The New Yorker*, May 7, 1949. https://www.newyorker.com/magazine/1949/05/07/just-depressed.

Hoffman, R. R., E. L. Cochran, and J. M. Nead. 1990. "Cognitive Metaphors in Experimental Psychology." In *Metaphors in the History of Psychology*, edited by D. E. Leary, 173–229. New York, NY: Cambridge University Press.

Jackson, S. W. 1986. *Melancholia and Depression. From Hippocratic Times to Modern Times.* New Haven, CT: Yale University Press.

Kövecses, Z. 2002. "Emotion Concepts: Social Constructionism and Cognitive Linguistics." In *The Verbal Communication of Emotions. Interdisciplinary Perspectives*, edited by S. R. Fussell, 109–124. New York, NY: Psychology Press.

Kövecses, Z. 2007. "Variation in Metaphor." *Ilha do Desterro: A Journal of English Language, Literatures in English and Cultural Studies* 53: 13–39. https://doi.org/10.5007/%25x.

Lakoff, G. 1993. "The Contemporary Theory of Metaphor." In *Metaphor and Thought*, edited by A. Ortony, 202–251. New York, NY: Cambridge University Press.

Lakoff, G., and M. Johnson. 1980. *Metaphors We Live By.* Chicago, IL: The University of Chicago Press.

McCarthy, K. 2015. "Drifting Away. A Case of Depression and Obsessionality." In *Practicing Psychodynamic Therapy. A Casebook*, edited by R. F. Summers and J. P. Barber, 83–100. New York, NY: The Guilford Press.

McMullen, L. M., and J. B. Conway. 2002. "Conventional Metaphors for Depression." In *The Verbal Communication of Emotions. Interdisciplinary Perspectives*, edited by S. R. Fussell, 167–181. New York, NY: Psychology Press.

Mosley, W. 2003. "Introduction: Americans Dreaming." In *The Best American Short Stories 2003*, edited by W. Mosley and K. Kenison, xii–xv. Boston, MA: Houghton Mifflin Company.

Nabokov, V. 1948. "Symbols and Signs." *The New Yorker*, May 15, 1948. https://www.newyorker.com/magazine/1948/05/15/symbols-and-signs.

Olson, R. 2019. "Archetypal Poetics: A Note on Hillman, Romanyshyn, and the Meaning of Text in Jungian Psychology." *The Humanistic Psychologist* 47 (1): 92–103. http://dx.doi.org/10.1037//hum0000114.

Ozick, C. 1991. "Metaphor and Memory." In *Metaphor and Memory*, 265–283. New York, NY: Vintage Books.

Previdi, B. 2015. "The Lonely Freshman. A Case of Depression." In *Practicing Psychodynamic Therapy. A Casebook*, edited by R. F. Summers and J. P. Barber, 68–82. New York, NY: The Guilford Press.

Pribram, K. H. 1990. "From Metaphors to Models: The Use of Analogy in Neuropsychology." In *Metaphors in the History of Psychology*, edited by D. E. Leary, 79–103. New York, NY: Cambridge University Press.

Solomon, A. 2015. *The Noonday Demon. An Atlas of Depression.* New York, NY: Scribner.

Stott, R., W. Mansell, P. Salkovskis, A. Lavender, and S. Cartwright-Hatton. 2010. *The Oxford Guide to Metaphors in CBT. Building Cognitive Bridges.* New York, NY: Oxford University Press.

Valerio, H. 2015. "Permission to Take a Breath: A Case of Depression." In *Practicing Psychodynamic Therapy. A Casebook*, edited by R. F. Summers and J. P. Barber, 52–67. New York, NY: The Guilford Press.

Wallace, D. F. 1998. "The Depressed Person." *Harper's Magazine*, January, 1998. https://harpers.org/wp-content/uploads/HarpersMagazine-1998-01-0059425.pdf.

Watson, B. 2009. "Visitation." *The New Yorker*, March 30, 2009. https://www.newyorker.com/magazine/2009/04/06/visitation-3.

Weiner Bakur, M., and M. White Taggart. 1982. "Depression as the Search for the Lost Self." *Psychotherapy: Theory, Research and Practice* 19 (4): 491–499.

Index

N

O

P

R

S

T

U

V

W